Transcultural Research – Heidelberg Studies on Asia and Europe in a Global Context

Series Editors:

Madeleine Herren
Axel Michaels
Rudolf G. Wagner

For further volumes:
http://www.springer.com/series/8753

Markus Pohlmann • Jonghoe Yang •
Jong-Hee Lee
Editors

Citizenship and Migration in the Era of Globalization

The Flow of Migrants and the Perception of Citizenship in Asia and Europe

 Springer

Editors

Markus Pohlmann
Inst. f. Soziologie
Univ. Heidelberg
Heidelberg, Germany

Jonghoe Yang
Department of Sociology
Sungkjunkwan University
Seoul, Korea

Jong-Hee Lee
National Election Broadcasting
Debate Commission
Seoul, South Korea

ISSN 2191-656X ISSN 2191-6578 (electronic)
ISBN 978-3-642-19738-3 ISBN 978-3-642-19739-0 (eBook)
DOI 10.1007/978-3-642-19739-0
Springer Heidelberg New York Dordrecht London

Library of Congress Control Number: 2012956532

Printed on acid-free paper

Springer is part of Springer Science+Business Media (www.springer.com)

Contents

About the Contributors

Markus Pohlmann is a full professor in Sociology at the University of Heidelberg, Germany. His major fields of research are Sociology of Organization, Sociology of Management, and Cultural and Regional Studies, especially East Asia, USA, and Germany. He received his diploma in Sociology at the University of Bielefeld and worked as a lecturer at the University of Lüneburg. After his Ph.D., he went to the University of Jena in the eastern part of Germany as an assistant and associate professor. He stayed several years abroad, doing research in the USA, in South Korea, Taiwan, Singapore, and Hong Kong. His recent publications include *Gesund altern: Individuelle und gesellschaftliche Herausforderungen* (2013), *Soziologie der Organisation: Eine Einführung* (2011), and "Globale ökonomische Eliten? Eine Globalisierungsthese auf dem Prüfstand der Empirie" (*KZfSS* 61(4): 513–534 (2009)).

Jonghoe Yang is emeritus professor of sociology at Sungkyunkwan University, Seoul, Korea. He received his B.A. and M.A. from Seoul National University and Ph.D. in sociology from the State University of New York at Buffalo. He taught and did research at SUNY at Buffalo, Princeton University as a Fulbright Senior Research Scholar, and EHESS in Paris. He was the director of the Institute of Social Sciences and of the Survey Research Center of Sungkyunkwan University. He was president of the Korean Sociological Association in 2005. His major areas of interest are the sociology of culture and the arts, social change and development, environment, and citizenship and globalization. His publications include *The Sociology of Culture and the Arts*; *The Korean Culture Industry System*; *Environmental Problems, Movements and Policies in the Asia-Pacific Region*; *New Social Movements and Civil Society in Korea*; and *Development, Class and Culture: Aspects of Socio-cultural Change in Modern Korea*.

Seungsook Moon is Professor of Sociology and was Chair of the Sociology department (2010–2013) and Director of the Asian Studies Program (2006–2009) at Vassar College. She received her Ph.D. in Sociology from Brandeis University.

She is the author of *Militarized Modernity and Gendered Citizenship in South Korea* (Duke University Press 2005; reprinted in 2007; its Korean edition in 2007 by Alternative Culture Press 2007) and a coeditor and contributor of *Over There*: *Living with the U.S. Military Empire from World War Two to the Present* (Duke University Press, 2010). She has also published numerous articles on political and cultural sociology, including gender and military service, nationalism, civil society and social movements, globalization, collective memories, and Buddhist temple food in contemporary Korea.

Hyun-Chin Lim is Professor of Sociology and Director of Asia Center, Seoul National University, South Korea. He received his B.A. and M.A. in Sociology from Seoul National University and his Ph.D. in Sociology from Harvard University. He was previously the Dean of the College of Social Sciences and served as the President of Korean Sociological Association. His publications include more than 40 books and over 200 scholarly articles on dependency, development, democracy, and civil society in East Asia and Latin America.

His major works are *Globalization and Anti-Globalization: The Development Strategy for 21st Century Korea*, Seoul: Sechang (2011); *Global NGOs: Beyond 'Wild Card' in World Politics* (with Suk-Ki Kong), Seoul: Nanam. (2011); *New Asias: Global Futures of World Regions* (with Wolf Schaefer and Suk-Man Hwang), Seoul: Seoul National University Press (2010); *Social Movements and Progressive Politics in Korea*, Seoul: Seoul National University Press (2009); *Social Policy in North Korea's Transition*, Seoul: Seoul National University Press (2008); *East Meets West: Civilizational Encounters and the Spirit of Capitalism in East Asia*, Leiden and Boston: Brill (2007); and *Politics and Society of Korea in Transition: Knowledge, Power, and Social Movement*, Seoul: Jipmundang (2005).

Suk-Ki Kong is Research Professor of Asia Center at Seoul National University. He studied sociology and received his B.A. and M.A. from the Department of Sociology at Seoul National University and his Ph.D. from the Department of Sociology at Harvard University. He was Senior Research Fellow at the Center of Social Sciences at Seoul National University. His major fields of research are social movements, NGO studies, and political sociology. His recent publications include articles entitled "Measuring National Human Rights: A Reflection on Korean Experiences" (2012), *Human Rights Quarterly* Vol. 34(4): 986–1020 (with Jeong-Woo Koo, and Chinsung Chang); "Politics of Cosmopolitan Citizenship: The Korean Engagement in the Global Justice Movements" (2012), *Citizenship Studies*, Vol. 16(1): 69–84; and "Let's Build A New World Order: Tripartite Dynamics of Inter-State System, World Capitalist Economy, and Global Civil Society" (2011), *Korean Journal of Sociology*, Vol. 45(6): 1–19 (with Hyun-Chin Lim).

Jong-Hee Lee is Chief of the Broadcasting Debate Team of the National Election Broadcasting Debate Commission in Korea and an Adjunct Professor of Korean Civic Education Institute for Democracy. She received her M.A. and Ph.D. in Sociology from the Department of Sociology of Heidelberg in Germany. Her major fields of research are Gender Studies, Global Migration, Sociology of Management, Political Sociology, and Cultural Studies. Her recent publications include articles entitled "*Multicultural Society and Social Integration: Focus on the German Case*" (2012), Journal of Korean-German Association for social science, 22(2), 54–84 (in Korean); *German Unification and Power Elites in the East Germany: Lessons for the Korean Unification* (2011), Seoul: Hanul (with Seung Hyeob Lee, Tae Guk Jeon, et al. (eds.)) (in Korean); "Efforts by the Election Broadcasting Debate Commission to Establish a Culture of Debate" (2011), *Journal of Communication*, 20, 85–128 (in Korean); "Studies on the Candidate's TV Debate Format: Focus on the Mayoral Race in Seoul in the 5th Nationwide Local Elections" (2011), *Korean Journal of Journalism* & *Communication*, 55(1): 7–78 (with Ji-Yang Oh) (in Korean); "Konfuzianische Kultur und geschlechtsspezifische Ungleichheit: Der südkoreanische Arbeitsmarkt als Beispiel (Confucian culture and gender-specific inequality: the Korean labor market as an example)" (2006), in: Gert Albert, Agathe Bienfait, Steffen Sigmund, Mateusz Stachura (eds.), *Aspekte des Weber-Paradigmas (Aspects of Weber's Paradigm)*, 193–217 (in German). She has also published articles on political and cultural sociology, including gender and globalization.

Sung-Nam Cho is currently a Professor at Ewha Womans University, Seoul, Korea. She studied sociology and received her B.A. and M.A. from the Department of Sociology at Ewha Womans University and her Ph.D. from the Department of Sociology in the University of Hawaii, USA. She was the Dean of International Education Institute and the Director of the Research Institute of Social Sciences at Ewha Womans University. She was President of the Korean Federation of Women Professors in 2011. She is currently Vice President of the Medical Peace Foundation, which has built and donated 18 hospitals for people in need around the world, especially in Africa, Latin America, and Southeast Asia. Her major fields of research are Health and Medical Sociology, Population, Aging and Elderly Issues, and Global Migration. Her recent publications include articles entitled *Age-Boom Generation: Preparing for the Ageing Society* (2006) (in Korean); "Globalization and Women in South Korea: Labor Participation and Women's Identity" *Korea Confronts Globalization* London/US/Canada: Routledge (2009): 43–62; "Physicians and the Satisfaction with Medical Services," *Population Studies* (2009) Vol.3, Num. 3: 1–23 (in Korean); "International Marriages in South Korea: The Significance of Nationality and Ethnicity," *Journal of Population Research* (2007):165–182.

Jungwhan Lee is a professor in the Department of Sociology at Cheongju University in Korea. He received his B.A. from Sungkyunkwan University and his M.A. and Ph.D. in sociology from Rutgers University. His research interests are international migration, multiculturalism, social epidemiology, and social stratification. His recent publications include "The Korean Government's Migration Policy on HIV/AIDS: Comparing with Migrant-Receiving and Migrant-Sending Countries in East Asia," *International Area Studies Review*, 2009; "Migrant Workers and HIV Vulnerability in Korea," *International Migration*, 2008; and "Migrant Characteristics of Foreign Workers and Research Trends in Korea," *Korea Journal of Population Studies*, 2007.

Sang-Hui Nam is research fellow in the Institute of Sociology at Heidelberg University. She holds a Ph.D. from the Department of Sociology at Freiburg University. She was research fellow at Yonsei University (Seoul, 2000–2003) and conducted the research project "Innovation and Contention. Protest Waves in South Korea" at the Institute of Asian Studies in the German Institute of Global and Area Studies (Hamburg, 2006–2008). Her major fields of research are cultural studies, social movements, and media. Her recent publications include articles entitled "The Making of a Social Movement" (2009), "The Women's Movement and the Transformation of the Family Law in South Korea" (2010), and "Werte, kollektive Identität und Protest" (2012).

Seokho Kim is an assistant professor in the Department of Sociology at Sungkyunkwan University, Seoul, Korea. He received his Ph.D. in Sociology from the University of Chicago in 2008. His dissertation title was "Voluntary Associations, Social Inequality, and Participatory Democracy from a Comparative Perspective." He has joined the Korean General Social Survey (KGSS) and East Asian Social Survey (EASS) since 2008. His research interests are political sociology, civil society, social networks, migrant workers, and survey methodology. His publications include Personality Traits and Political Participation; The Effects of Political Mobilization on Voter Turnout and Vote Choice in the 2012 National Assembly Election; Voluntary Associations, Social Inequality, and Participatory Democracy in the United States and Korea; Personality Traits and Response Styles; Social Distance between Foreign Workers and Koreans; and National Pride in Comparative Perspective: 1995/1996 and 2003/2004.

Subrata K. Mitra, B.A. (Utkal, Orissa), M.A. (Delhi), M.Phil. (JNU), M.A. and Ph.D. (Rochester) is Professor and Head of the Department of Political Science and Board Member and former Director of the South Asia Institute at the University of Heidelberg, Germany. His has published widely in the fields of Comparative Politics, Rational Choice, Citizenship, Re-use, and South Asian Area Studies. His books include *Citizenship and the Flow of Ideas: Structure, Agency and Power* (Delhi: Samskriti; 2012) (co-editor); *Reuse: The Art and Politics of Integration and Anxiety* (Delhi: Sage; 2012); *Politics in India: Structure, Process, Policy* (London:

Routledge; 2011); and *When Rebels become Stakeholders* (Delhi: Sage; 2009). In addition, he has published articles in the *Annual Review of Political Science, Asian Journal of Political Science, British Journal of Political Science, Contemporary South Asia, Comparative Politics, Comparative Political Studies, Democratization, Economic and Political Weekly, India Review, Journal of Commonwealth and Comparative Politics, Journal of Development Politics, International Social Science Journal, International Political Science Review, Third World Quarterly, and World Politics.*

Chapter 1
Introduction

Markus Pohlmann, Jonghoe Yang, and Jong-Hee Lee

1.1 Introduction

The twentieth century has been proclaimed as the "Age of Mobility" (Papademetriou 2007) as well as an "Age of Migration" (Castles and Miller 2009). People from all over the world and with vastly diverse social backgrounds are said to be moving and migrating increasingly around the globe. With regard to the developed countries, fears and concern are growing among the general public due to the perception of foreigners pouring into their national homelands. As a consequence the legal concept of *citizenship* has recently become one of the key issues for political debates revolving around immigration policies. But citizenship is not merely a concept; it is also an emotional issue. The concomitant change in the migrants' legal status serves as a bureaucratic bottleneck for many other social policy issues, including the citizen's right to vote – issues that are crucial for the architecture of a modern nation state.

M. Pohlmann (✉)
Department of Sociology, Heidelberg University, Bergheimer Str. 58, 69115 Heidelberg, Germany

Im Schulzengarten 20, 69151 Neckargemünd, Germany
e-mail: markus.pohlmann@soziologie.uni-heidelberg.de

J. Yang
Department of Sociology, Sungkyunkwan University, 53 Myungryun-dong, Jongro-gu, Seoul 110-745, Korea

#1104 Lotte Castle Forest, Seocho-gu, Bangbae 4-dong, Seoul 137-836, Korea
e-mail: jhyang@skku.edu

J.-H. Lee
National Election Broadcasting Debate Commission, 23, Nam-bu sun-hwan-ro 272 gil, Gwan-ak-gu, Seoul 151-800, Korea

Silim-ro 58 ga gil 64-3(601), Gwan-ak-gu, Seoul 151-015, Korea
e-mail: doreaner@hanmail.net

M. Pohlmann et al. (eds.), *Citizenship and Migration in the Era of Globalization*, Transcultural Research – Heidelberg Studies on Asia and Europe in a Global Context, DOI 10.1007/978-3-642-19739-0_1, © Springer-Verlag Berlin Heidelberg 2013

In marked contrast, throughout the 1990s globalization was said to have brought about a change in the concept of citizenship, which used to bear on close connections with the nation-state. Soysal (1994) and Jacobson (1997) for instance both predicted a diminishing importance of citizenship and even the advent of a post-national notion of citizenship.

Are these predictions already coming true? Are we about to see the coming of the age of the *transnational citizen*? Before delving into the empirical realm for evidence regarding such far-reaching assumptions, we have to consider first what we are actually talking about by tackling the conceptual issue of citizenship.

From a sociological perspective, there are at least two ways to define citizenship. (1) In a formal way, in which we talk about membership to a political community. Being a citizen is having the formal status of a member, regardless of specific qualifications needed or whatever is expected from the member. "A citizen is", as Walzer (1989) put it, "most simply, a member of a political community, entitled to whatever prerogatives and encumbered with whatever responsibilities are attached to membership" (Ibid: 211). (2) In a less formal and more conventional and emphatic understanding, we focus on the question of *if* and *how* being a citizen requires that the individual shares a specific set of values, and also acknowledges substantial rights and duties. This emphatic notion of citizenship basically builds on the characteristics of a "polis" and how it enables or empowers its citizens. While the non-formal conditions of being a citizen are much discussed, the formal side is somewhat neglected.

In this volume, we draw upon a combination of the formal and the non-formal aspects of citizenship in our analyses. On the one hand we are dealing with citizenship in regard of the formal conditions of how to become a citizen. On the other hand, we are taking into account aspects of its non-formal side, such as the notion of values and attitudes towards the nation-state, by asking how citizenship is perceived and what duties and rights have been acknowledged.

In view of the nation-state, citizenship is constituted by a special kind of membership. Most of the time, the majority of citizens of a nation-state are "born citizens", following the emergence and establishment of a nation-state. Usually, the attribution and acquisition of citizenship is structured upon two principles: *jus soli* (the conferral of citizenship on persons born in the state's territory, viz. on its soil) and *jus sanguinis* (the conferral of citizenship on persons with a citizen parent or parents, viz. by blood). Most nation-states base their citizenship laws on a combination of *jus soli* and *jus sanguinis* (see Gilbertson 2006). Naturalized migrants are very often in the minority among the citizens of a country.

If we direct our special attention to the mechanisms of becoming a member of a nation-state, we are able to distinguish at least three separate rules of membership that are valid in most nation-states:

1. Most of the members are not recruited voluntarily, but naturally by birth or descent.
2. Unlike other forms of membership, for most citizens citizenship is not conferred via a contract, but as a constitutional right.

3. Once the membership of a nation has been established, one will not lose that membership easily. Even if one is acting against the constitutional law and is imprisoned for that reason, one will remain a citizen of that country, though one might lose some of one's citizen's rights.

Thus, in its particular mode of membership, nation-state citizenship is even more inclusive than family membership usually is. Very often, the "divorce rate" in nation-states is lower than in families, because nation-states often have strong restrictions against the expulsion of its members.

At its most basic, the definition of citizenship is "a secular system of contributory rights, involving entitlements and duties, binding people to the nation-state" (Turner 2006: 608) and focuses on the relationship between the individual and the state.

The present volume comprises a collection of selected articles that tackle these aspects by providing empirical evidence concerning (1) the ideas associated with citizenship, (2) the flow of people, and (3) the perceptions of citizens in Korea, East Asia and Europe.

The first part deals with the *flow of ideas*. The idea of citizenship in Korea is examined by Seungsook Moon, who looks at its connotations in different forms of translation and shows how the idea of citizenship has been employed by different political regimes and different political movements in Korea. She shows that the understanding of (the imported concept of) citizenship has been fiercely contested since the nineteenth century in Korea. In various historical phases, political elites and social movements have fought over the definition of social, political and civil rights in a long-lasting process of political transformation. After the democratization process in 1987, citizenship became deeply intertwined in Korea with the ideas and the working of civil society, as Lim, Hyun-Chin and Kong, Suk-Ki subsequently highlight. In the aftermath of democratic transformation, human rights and environmental rights movements gained in importance and transnationalized their structures. Especially ideas connected to human rights were in part an expression of an altered perception of citizenship, often articulated in opposition to the government.

The three chapters in the second part of this volume cover the issue of the *flow of people* between Europe and East Asia and the question of how far actual migration patterns can be characterized as "global" or "transnational". Markus Pohlmann takes one particular assumption behind mainstream globalization literature as a starting point in order to reassess whether there is actually an emerging "global class" of high-level professionals and top-managers. He asks: have the formal open-door policies in East Asia, USA and Europe for highly skilled people led to high naturalization rates as well as to international career and migration patterns? Jong-Hee Lee supplements this analysis of the flow of people by concentrating on the migration and naturalization of low-skilled labor, while comparing South Korea and Germany. In her chapter, Sung-Nam Cho addresses the role of marriage for immigrants in Korea, an important social issue in contemporary Korean society. Her study tries to analyze the current phenomenon of an upsurge in international marriages in Korea, asking what countries and families the immigrants are from and what partners and families they are marrying (into).

The focus of the third part is on the non-formal side of citizenship in South Korea, Germany and the USA, analyzing and comparing *perceptions of citizenship*. What kind of values, duties and rights are connected with citizenship and what do the citizens' expectations entail? Jonghoe Yang argues that research on citizenship has mostly been centered on its legal or institutional aspects and that only few empirical studies both in Korea and worldwide have focused on the experiences of ordinary people. But the understanding, competence, and active participation of ordinary citizens are essential for the working of nation-states. According to his analysis of a set of survey data, Korean people's ideas on citizenship vary widely in accordance with different background factors. As a result, there is a variety of mixed forms of citizenship concepts, reflecting Korea's recent history of turbulent political change. Supplementing the perspective of Jonghoe Yang, the paper of Jungwhan Lee examines the attitudes of Korean workers towards the civil rights of migrant workers. He asks: what do Korean workers think about the question of conferring civil rights on migrant workers? What factors affect the Korean workers' attitudes towards the civil rights of migrant workers? Lee's study gives seminal answers to these questions. The chapter by Sang-Hui Nam aims to illuminate factors which led to the currently changing status of ethnic Chinese in Korean society. Formal citizenship of the ethnic Chinese has been enhanced since the 1990s. Democratization and globalization have put the citizenship issue of the ethnic Han Chinese back on the agenda. But structural patterns to exclude the ethnic Chinese from citizenship manifest themselves repeatedly. On its way to a welfare state, South Korea has provided social rights such as the right to health care, a national pension and unemployment compensation and so on since about the turn of the century. Nam's study shows that so far the ethnic Chinese have not been included. In their closing chapter, Seokho Kim and Jonghoe Yang explore cross-national differences in patterns of citizenship by comparing Korea, Germany and the United States. Due to uncertainty about how and why institutional and attitudinal aspects of citizenship vary among nations, the authors compare Korea, Germany and the United States by analyzing data from the International Social Survey Programme (ISSP) from 2004.

The concluding remarks by Subrata Mitra draw together the results concerning the flow of ideas, the flow of people and the perception of citizenship and discuss them within the broader scope of the Cluster of Excellence regarding "The Flow of Ideas between Europe and Asia" at Heidelberg University.

References

Castles, Stephen, and Mark Miller. 2009. *The Age of Migration. International Population Movements in the Modern World*, 4th ed., Basingstoke, London: Macmillan Press.

Gilbertson, Greta. 2006. *Citizenship in a Globalized World*. Migration Information Service, Washington: Migration Policy Institute.

Jacobson, David. 1997. *Right across Borders: Immigration and the Decline of Citizenship*. Baltimore: The Johns.

Papademetriou, Demetrios G. 2007. *The Age of Mobility. How to Get More Out of Migration in the 21st century.* Migration Policy Institute.

Soysal, Yasemin Nohoglu. 1994. *Limits of Citizenship: Migrant and Postnational Membership in Europe.* Chicago: University of Chicago Press.

Turner, Bryan S. 2006. Citizenship and the Crisis of Multiculturalism. *Citizenship Studies* 10 (5), 607–18.

Walzer, Michael. 1989. *Citizenship.* New York: Cambridge University Press.

Part I

Chapter 2
The Idea and Practices of Citizenship in South Korea

Seungsook Moon

Abstract This essay examines a history of the idea of citizenship and its practices in Korea from the late nineteenth to the early twenty-first centuries. Based on this historical survey, it argues that the prototype of citizenship constructed from the nationalist discourse on building a modern nation is simultaneously collectivist and elitist. This prototype shows that individualistic assumptions implied in the liberal notion of citizenship were selectively modified and reinvented in the Korean context. This prototype became more authoritarian in the discourse of *kungmin*, and was at times challenged by a populist view among some leftist thinkers and activists. But such challenges were usually unsuccessful in the face of power politics during Japanese colonial rule, US Army Military Government rule, and the authoritarian rule imposed by Korean civilian and military regimes. A significant change in this persistent pattern has emerged since the establishment of procedural democracy.

2.1 Introduction

Historically, the idea of citizenship reflects the development of a new type of membership in a nation-state, characterized by legal equality among its members who bear rights and responsibilities. This characteristic stems from the elevated status of citizen in the ancient Greek *polis*, popularized by the modern nation-state; as a prototype, the citizen was a free and property-owning political actor, engaged in running affairs of the state. In the postcolonial era after World War II, citizenship has become a normative component of political modernity, and most nation-states have adopted it with variations in their actual practices. Marshall (1950) devised the

S. Moon (✉)
Department of Sociology, Vassar College, 124 Raymond Avenue, Poughkeepsie, NY 12604, USA

4 Watson Road, Poughkeepsie, NY 12603, USA
e-mail: semoon@vassar.edu

M. Pohlmann et al. (eds.), *Citizenship and Migration in the Era of Globalization*,
Transcultural Research – Heidelberg Studies on Asia and Europe in a Global Context,
DOI 10.1007/978-3-642-19739-0_2, © Springer-Verlag Berlin Heidelberg 2013

classic typology of civil, political and social rights based on the historical development of citizenship in Britain, but applying this typology to other societies requires
careful attention to the historical and social contexts that have shaped the idea and
practices of citizenship in a given society, including citizens' rights and responsibilities, and the balance between them. This chapter explores how the idea of
citizenship as *equal membership in a nation-state* was adopted and has developed,
in conjunction with the ways it has been practiced in Korea, since the turn of the
twentieth century.[1]

This broad definition of citizenship is necessary in order to avoid the automatic
association of citizenship with democracy, which reflects the development of
citizenship mostly in the West.[2] This avoidance means "provincializing" Western
historical experiences of citizenship development as significant yet not necessarily
the normative standard to measure or interpret such development in a non-Western
context as a lack or aberration. This broad definition also helps us navigate
ambiguities in the Korean translation of citizenship (*siminkwŏn*) and citizen
(*simin*) and their usages. In fact, throughout most of the twentieth century, these
words were not commonly used to refer to political membership in Korea. When
simin was occasionally used, it simply referred to urban residents as opposed to
residents of villages, counties, or other administrative units[3]; when *siminkwŏn* was
used, it strictly meant citizen's rights, rather than the complex of conditions and
relationships implied in the political status of being a citizen. It was not until the late
1980s that various types of grassroots organizations reclaimed the term citizen to
redefine people's relationship to the state that they had fought to democratize
(Moon 2005). Although these movements, known as "citizens' movements"
(*siminundong*), popularized terms such as citizen and civil society (*siminsahoe*)
during the democratization of Korea, ordinary Koreans who are not particularly
political do not generally identify with these terms to indicate their own political
status. Instead, many Koreans continue to use *kungmin* (national or state's people),
which has been in currency since the early twentieth century.[4] Others altogether
avoid this politically tainted term, which has been overused by authoritarian
regimes, in favor of the politically neutral term *chumin* (resident).[5]

In the first section of this chapter, I will discuss how the idea of citizenship was
introduced into Korea at the turn of the twentieth century and how nationalist
reformers articulated a new kind of membership in the state that had to be modernized.
As reformers confronted aggressive imperialist powers, their discourse constructed a
view of citizenship that was both collectivist and elitist, underscoring the people's
duty as being one of usefulness for strengthening the nation. In the second section, I
will discuss how the idea and practice of citizenship was depoliticized, becoming
more authoritarian under Japan's colonial rule (1910–1945), and how leftist
movements challenged these repressive tendencies. In the third section, I will focus
on the period of US Army Military Government (USAMG) rule (1945–1948), with
particular attention to the perpetuation of the authoritarian view and practices of
citizenship inherited from the colonial era. In the fourth section, I will discuss the
idea of citizenship and its practices in the era of authoritarian rule under Korean
civilian and military regimes (1948–1987), which show striking similarities to the
USAMG era. In the final section, I will highlight a significant rupture in the

authoritarian view of citizenship and its practices during the era of conservative democratization. Based on this historical analysis, I shall argue that the prototype of citizenship constructed from the nationalist discourse on building a modern nation is simultaneously collectivist and elitist. This prototype shows that individualistic assumptions implied in the liberal notion of citizenship were selectively modified and reinvented in the Korean context. This prototype became more authoritarian in the discourse of *kungmin*, and was at times challenged by a populist view among leftist thinkers and activists. But such challenges were usually unsuccessful in the face of power politics during the colonial rule, the USAMG rule, and the authoritarian rule by Korean civilian and military regimes, which had all suppressed grassroots leftist movements and organizations. The prominence of power politics in shaping the idea of citizenship and its practices in Korea reveals that citizenship has been a battleground between conservative forces trying to curtail political agency of grassroots men and women, and progressive forces trying to popularize such agency and empower people as political subjects. This type of battle has directly involved the wielding of political power, causing the specific characteristics of citizenship to be determined by complex power relations between the modernizing or modern state and social groups, within a given historical and social context.

2.2 The Enlightenment Era and the Prototype of Citizenship in Korea (1890–1900)

In many postcolonial societies, a broad spectrum of nationalist thinkers and politicians at the turn of the twentieth century encountered the idea of citizenship originating from the West and discussed how to adopt it to build a strong nation-state in the face of aggressive imperialism. In particular, nationalist thinkers in Korea introduced the idea of citizenship through Japanese and Chinese translations, partly because many of them were able to read and write these languages, and partly because they shared with their Japanese and Chinese counterparts the understanding that remaking the Korean people as a new people was the starting point in the creation of a new modern nation (Chŏn 2007: 400). Against the backdrop of a series of domestic and international events that heightened a sense of urgency to reform old Korea,[6] the Korean thinkers realized that the people were members of a nation that needed to be revived and modernized, and they published newspapers to educate them.[7] Newspapers became popular in the late 1890s as the medium of nationalist movements, but between 1899 (when the government forcefully closed the *Independent Newspaper*) and 1905 (when Japan turned Korea into its protectorate), publication of newspapers and other print materials drastically declined, increasing again between 1905 and 1910, when Korea was formally colonized (Chŏn 2007).

The *Independent Newspaper* (*Tongnipsimmun*), was published from April 1896 to December 1899,[8] and was the first vernacular Korean (and English) newspaper produced by Western-oriented reformers. The paper played a central role in articulating the novel idea of citizenship by recasting ordinary Korean people who used to be, at best, the object of benevolent rule. While it continued to use such old terms as *paeksŏng* or *inmin* (ordinary people who were ruled), mostly to refer to members of the state to be modernized (Ryu 2004: 55),[9] it redefined them as right-bearing and equal members – at least in abstract terms. Positing that this right would be free from the state's interference, the newspaper commonly paired this notion of right with the self (*chagi*).[10] Yet such inalienable rights were curiously confined to the right to property and life. As the newspaper repeatedly stressed these rights, it also often asserted that the government's primary duty was to protect life and property. At the same time, civil rights and political rights were clearly circumscribed in the discourse of citizenship in the newspaper, because the people were presumably not ready for these rights. A close reading of this newspaper for its entire duration shows that while it basically portrayed the Korean people, in reality, as being pitiful and ignorant – and therefore merely the objects of education and enlightenment – it repeatedly promoted diligent and productive people as new members of the nation, and emphatically touted economic independence as the basis of citizenship (Reading Group 2004). The newspaper only represented the people secondarily as watchmen who ought to monitor the government's activities and exercise their political right to elect their officials (Reading Group 2004: 177, 206, 425). With their political agency circumscribed, the people re-envisioned for citizenship were expected to be productive workers, property owners and educated members of the nation. Although they were entitled to some political rights – which was indeed a radical idea at the time – their citizenship was marked by a duty to be useful to the nation and follow enlightened leaders.

What is noteworthy about the economic concept of citizenship without full political agency is that the people who were identified to build the modern nation were not hailed as the autonomous and isolated individuals of Western liberalism. Instead, they were viewed as instrumental components of the nation who were to be awakened and mobilized. This utilitarian collectivism that suppressed the individual permeated the citizenship discourse as its main underlying tone. Even individual emotion was rechanneled into a collective resource to be mobilized for the nation. During 1898, when the *Independent* was deeply involved in organizing the "10,000 people's collaboration meetings" (*manmin' gongdonghoe*), it frequently published editorials that underscored the people's duty (*paeksŏngŭi chingmu*) for gaining national independence. Intriguingly, this duty was discussed in conjunction with "courage" (*yongmaeng*) as a form of political passion (Ryu 2004: 55–56). In this rhetorical style, the individual's feelings are recognized but his potential individuality is destroyed by his sacrifice to collective survival.[11] In this framework, the people's rights and equality were necessary not because they would foster independent individuals, but rather because they would strengthen the nation. It is no accident that the old collectivist terms, *paeksong* and *inmin*, were used most frequently to refer to new members of the nation-state, while such terms as "individual" or "citizen" were altogether absent in the discourse.

The discourse of citizenship in the *Independent* constructs a prototype of citizenship in modern Korea that prioritizes economic rights and agency but truncates political rights and agency. This concept resulted from the elitist nature of the nationalist discourse[12] and the political reality of dealing with a declined monarchy bolstered by conservative forces. Those nationalist reformers were the educated elite and their views were inevitably shaped by the old social order based on hereditary hierarchical status that kept the majority of the population illiterate and subservient. While the reformers' elitism can be justified to a certain extent because the populace was in need of education, this view fails to recognize the peoples' potential, as well as their wisdom and knowledge organically rooted in their own experiences. Since its foundation, the newspaper had to confront the hostility of Russia-oriented conservative aristocrats suspicious of its political motivation. As the newspaper's influence over society grew while it actively dealt with the urgent problems of the day, the hostility also grew until finally, co-founder and editor-in-chief Chae-p'il Sŏ (Phillip Jaisohn; 1864–1951), was forced to resign and leave Korea. Under the editorship of another co-founder, Ch'i-ho Yun (1864–1945), the newspaper continued its political and social engagement by organizing throughout 1898 the 10,000 people's collaboration meetings, the aforementioned mass protests, demanding that the Chosŏn government restore its independence from imperialist powers and modernize. The conservative forces accused the leaders of these protest gatherings of conspiring for a republican revolution. The last gathering was forcefully broken up and Yun was finally replaced by foreign editors, Henry Herbert Appenzeller, an American Methodist missionary, and later H. Emberly, an Englishman. By the end of 1899, the Korean government took over the newspaper and soon closed it (Chŏn 2004: 437–441). This political context highlights how the new idea of citizenship imported from outside the country was influenced by the power politics between the Chosŏn government and nationalist reformers; similarly, the elitist nature of the citizenship discourse alludes to grossly unequal power relations between these reformers and the grassroots population, which remained unorganized and voiceless.

In the decade following the demise of the *Independent*, the prototype of citizenship devolved into a discourse of *kungmin* (nationals or state's people), which displayed a reactionary and more authoritarian rendition of citizenship than was conveyed in the newspaper. This discourse of *kungmin* is very crucial to our understanding of the idea and practices of citizenship in Korea because, as already mentioned, this term has been the most commonly used to indicate citizen (as a member of the state) in Korea throughout the twentieth century. It is noteworthy that this term, being a Japanese translation of *Staatsvolk*, had been widely circulated throughout China and Japan since the 1870s, and referred to the new political community of a nation. In Japan, which later colonized Korea, *kungmin* (*kokumin* in Japanese) was characterized by self-sacrificing loyalty to the Emperor, and the imperial state consciously popularized *samurai* as the model of modern Japanese *kokumin* who would serve the nation (de Bary 2004: 181). While its German meaning conveyed an ethnic group that has sovereignty over a (nation) state that ruled a given territory, its Northeast Asian translations highlighted members' loyalty to a state (Pak 2004: 229).[13] In Korea, the term began to appear in nationalist newspapers and books in the 1890s and by the late 1900s it was more commonly used than the old terms *paeksong* or *inmin* (Kim 2004: 198).[14] *Kungminsuji* (*What Nationals Are to Know*; 1906) was arguably the most significant text among three books published on the subject of *kungmin* between 1894 and 1910; it was most widely circulated among the educated elite. Before its publication as a monograph, its contents were serialized in the conservative *Hwangsŏngsinmun* (from 15 July 1905 to 3 August 1905) under the generic authorship of "overseas traveler" (Kim 2004: 194, 202, 205). Its authorship is putatively linked to Kil-jun Yu (1856–1914), a reformer and politician who traveled to Japan and the U.S. to explore the modern world.

Focusing heavily on the state rather than its people, the book portrays *kungmin* as a natural component (along with land and government) of the state, and at best, the object of the government's benevolent rule, which echoes the Confucian notion of the sage ruler. This reactionary rendition of citizenship reveals a deeply contradictory position in its discussion of *kungmin's* duty and rights. It stresses the duty to pay taxes and perform military service for 3–4 years. In particular, it promotes universal male conscription because paid soldiers will not sacrifice their lives for the state. Regarding *kungmin's* rights, however, it vacillates between the modern notion of inalienable rights in the abstract and the acceptance of status hierarchy in reality. Hence, according to the book, sovereignty belongs to the monarch and the government is seen as the instrument to carry out his orders. Similar to the meanings of *paeksŏng* or *inmin* used in the discourse of citizenship in the *Independent*, *kungmin* – as the collectivity of people – are not sovereign subjects in reality, but objects to be mobilized to strengthen the state (Kim 2004: 207, 212–213). Unlike the newspaper discourse, however, the *kungmin* discourse does not address specific political rights to be exercised by the people. With its ironic title, this book obscures traditional paternalism in the relationship between the state and its members and fails to discuss what constitutes *kungmin*. This shows the contradiction inherent in the ruling elite that was in decline and forced to undergo change, but was unwilling to do so due to its vested interests in the status quo. Later, *kungmin* acquires a substantive meaning in an influential editorial in the *Taehanmaeilsinbo* (30 July 1908), which distinguishes *minjok* (a nation) from *kungmin*; while *minjok* refers to a naturally evolved community of people, *kungmin* signifies members of a political community deliberately bound by shared spirit and therefore ready to be mobilized, just like soldiers in military barracks (Pak 2004: 245–246).

The *kungmin* discourse disregarded individuals even more than the preceding discourse of citizenship did, due to its increasing emphasis on members' loyalty to the state to be modernized and to be preserved. This collectivism was indeed a dominant trend in the enlightenment era prior to the colonization of Korea. The trend was mirrored in two popular literary genres during the 1900s; biographies of heroes, and the fable. Especially after the Ŭlsa Treaty (1905), which entailed the loss of Korea's diplomatic sovereignty to Japan, nationalist writers published a series of biographies of Korean heroes and a foreign heroine who saved their countries from powerful enemies.[15] Although these books narrated the lives of exemplary individuals, they were not concerned with the inner world or particularity of an individual hero or heroine. Rather, the protagonists in these books served as a literary device for discussing ideal values and norms to be taught and promoted among the general public (Kwŏn 2003: 89). Similarly, fables published and circulated in this period used their major characters as literary devices to convey certain viewpoints concerning urgent social and political issues. This instrumental collectivism is evident in the common portrayal of individual characters and their actions and interactions which do not form a series of events that drive the underlying plots (as is the case in a modern novel), but merely function as a literary tool to convey social criticism (Ibid: 115). This dominant literary practice reflects the political exigency of mobilizing individuals for collective survival by disseminating nationalist messages and social criticism.

The discourse of *kungmin* reflects the political context characterized by the monarchical reaction to various reform movements in the midst of aggressive imperialism during the 1900s.[16] In a desperate attempt to assert itself against these domestic and international challenges, the Chosŏn court declared itself as the great Han Empire (*Taehanjeguk*) in 1897, disbanded in 1898 the Independence Club (*tongniphyŏphoe*) that cautiously promoted republicanism, and adopted absolute emperorship in 1899. This reactionary process harnessed political activism in general and in particular the discourse of citizenship, which explored new meanings of political membership. A major blow to this reinforcement of the monarchy was ironically the aforementioned Ŭlsa Treaty of 1905 (Kim 2004: 199–200). The further weakening of the Chosŏn court generated a political opening to re-galvanize reform movements; for example, *Mansebo*, a house organ of Chŏndogyo, a nationalist religion, promoted the individual's freedom to express his views through a legislative body and achieve upward mobility based on his ability, and reasserted the liberal idea of ordinary people as equal members of the nation who should be free from the hereditary status hierarchy and the gender hierarchy (Pak 2001: 63–64). In 1907, aforementioned Ki-t'ak Yang (1871–1938) and Ch'ang-ho An (1878–1938) founded *Sinminhoe* (New People's Association) and argued for a republican polity (Kim 2004: 201). But this type of revived effort could not halt Japan's colonization of Korea.

2.3 Depoliticization of Citizenship and Its Challenge During the Colonial Era (1910–1945)

Colonial rule not only relegated Koreans to second-class membership of the Japanese empire, it also facilitated the spread of the authoritarian view of citizenship previously adopted through the discourse of *kungmin*. The Japanese notion of the self-sacrificing *kungmin* loyal to the Emperor (see endnote no. 12) became the model to shape the colonized Koreans. As a result, citizenship in colonial Korea was depoliticized, especially during the first decade of colonial rule (officially called the era of "military rule") when the colonial state deployed very repressive measures to suppress political activism among the Koreans. We can see glimpses of such depoliticizing efforts in the aforementioned *Maeilsinbo*, the Governor General's newspaper and an important historical document that conveys the everyday lives of colonized Koreans in the 1910s. The newspaper encouraged Koreans to be diligent and productive members who could accumulate wealth incrementally and perform their duty to pay taxes, while in reality, basic civil and political rights were denied. This one-dimensional economic citizenship was coupled in the social realm with the lopsided focus on family and domestic affairs. This content was in stark contrast to the social section of *Taehanmaeilsinbo*, the predecessor to *Maeilsinbo*, which was commonly filled with reports on various voluntary organizations, including local schools, social reform groups and learned societies, which promoted national survival and the enlightenment of the Korean people (Kwŏn 2008: part 2). In addition, *Maeilsinbo*, the house organ of the colonial government, conveyed great hostility towards individualism, equating it with extreme selfishness (Pak 2004: 254).

The nation-wide uprising against repressive colonial rule on 1 March 1919 ended the era of military rule and ushered in the era of "cultural rule" during the 1920s, when the colonial state tolerated some limited civil rights for cultural activities in the press, publications, and associations. Taking advantage of this political opening, major newspapers with a national circulation were founded in early 1920, including the *Dong a Daily* and *Chosŏn Daily*, which still exist in South Korea as major conservative newspapers. Similarly, the Kaebyŏk company, financed by the Chŏndogyo church, published a series of new magazines for various groups of Koreans, starting with a monthly general magazine entitled *Kaebyŏk* (Opening or Creation) in June 1920; it began to publish a women's magazine *Puin* (Women) in June 1922, a children's magazine *Ŏrini* (Children) in 1923, a literary magazine *Pyŏlgŏngon* (Special World) in 1926, and a student magazine *Haksaeng* (Students) in 1929 (Kim 2007: 238). Along with the internal political change, the Russian revolution of 1917 and the spread of socialism and communism in the world also contributed to a new development in the discourse of citizenship in colonial Korea. It was around 1923 and 1924 that socialists emerged in the political landscape of colonial Korea and Korean nationalism was bifurcated into rightist and leftist camps (Yun 2007: 281). While *Dong-a Daily* often printed rightist viewpoints, *Chosŏn Daily* at times printed leftist viewpoints on various political and social issues. Embedded in the social context marked by the rise of leftist views, *Kaebyŏk*'s ideological orientation evolved from right to left by identifying itself as a "magazine for down-trodden Korean people" (Chosŏn *minjung*). At the same time it also functioned as a forum to advance these two different perspectives.[17] The Korean Communist Party (Chosŏn kongsandang) was established in 1925, but the colonial state forcefully disbanded it in 1928 (Ibid: 297).

On the one hand, conforming to the reality of colonial rule, right-wing "enlightenment intellectuals" continued the discourse of depoliticized citizenship. Instead of addressing the problem of citizenship in the colonial empire, they focused on Koreans' responsibility to cultivate morality and character through education and cultural activities (Kim 2007: 304–305). We can observe glimpses of this contradictory discourse in the aforementioned *Kaebyŏk* (1920–1926).[18] In their debate with emerging left-wing intellectuals about the controversy over the funeral ceremony of Yun-sik Kim (1835–1922),[19] such leading intellectuals as Ki-jŏn Kim, Ton-hwa Yi, and Kwang-su Yi affirmed the collectivist and elitist view of citizenship that essentially separated leaders from followers. They envisioned a modern society (not a modern state) where educated intellectuals like themselves lead the ignorant masses and shape public opinion through rational criticism and free discussion amongst themselves. They did not trust the masses' ability to articulate their own viewpoints and make decisions (Ibid: 310, 326). In particular, Kwang-su Yi (1892–1950), the major figure among this right-wing group, argued that sacrifice and service for the state and society would be more important than individual liberty and, paradoxically, asserted that "submission" (*pokjong*) is a genuine form of freedom. He also argued that equality between individuals would mean equality in terms of their human rights and humanity, but never equality of ability. Hence, he considered the distinction between leader and followers a natural aspect of human life (Yun 2007: 303–304). Ultimately, in his culturalist understanding of colonial Korea, Yi reduced political inequality to qualitative differences among individuals and failed to recognize that individual freedom and equality were political underpinnings of the modern society that its state had to institutionalize.

On the other hand, leftist intellectuals challenged the elitist view of depoliticized citizenship by anointing *minjung* (down-trodden people or grassroots people) as the subjects of politics and society. In the paucity of reliable documents on leftist movements during the colonial period, we can get glimpses of their views from the 1922 funeral controversy and the local autonomy controversy in the mid-1920s,[20] and the Korean Communist Party Manifesto published in 1926. In their opposition to observing a public ceremony for Kim's funeral, the leftist intellectuals clearly demonstrated that awakened *minjung* consciousness, and their sense of justice, were to be the source of public opinion and thus the people's ability to make decisions (Kim 2007: 307). Such leading leftist intellectuals as Chae-hong An and Nam-un Paek opposed the local autonomy movement supported by the colonial state by arguing that it obscured the colonial reality that reduced Koreans to laborers exploited by Japanese capitalists, and kept them deprived of basic liberty and rights to choose religion and political ideology, and to organize associations and participate in social affairs (Yun 2007: 298). The Korean Communist Party Manifesto (published in Shanghai, China in 1926) showed a similarly populist orientation, at least in principle. It pursued a democratic republic as the ideal polity where *kungmin* or *inmin* would enjoy not only the basic civil and political rights but also extensive social rights that would protect and nurture the working class (Yun 2007: 307, 308). These examples suggest that some leftist intellectuals embraced basic rights (largely ignored by the rightist intellectuals in their cultural and moral emphasis on enlightenment and characters) essential to modern citizenship. Yet these progressive ideas and their movements were suppressed by the colonial authorities; it is likely that such ideas became further marginalized as socialist and communist movements went underground in Korea and Korean communists outside Korea joined guerilla groups in Manchuria under the Chinese Communist Party to fight against the Japanese colonial empire.[21]

Outside the intellectual circle, socialism influenced local young men's movements across colonial Korea in the mid-1920s. Identifying with the labels such as "propertyless" (*musan*), "proletarian" (*pro*), "communist" (*kongsan*), or leftist (*jwaik*), local youth associations (*ch'ŏngnyŏnhoe*) mushroomed after the March First Movement (Chi 2007: 341). Initially, they were dominated by sons of local elite families, but as these young members of the elite were absorbed into the government's local bureaucracy in school committees, agricultural associations and credit unions, young leftist men, mostly hailing from humble backgrounds, filled the original youth associations. These associations carried out radical social reform activities by organizing night school programs and agricultural unions, performing plays, and addressing tenant farmers' problems. They were also opposed to the aforementioned issue of local autonomy supported by the colonial state (Ibid: 352, 353, 355). Owing to their subversive stance, the authorities monitored their activities and kept a file on their leaders. As revolutionary peasants and workers' movements grew in the early 1930s, the authorities suppressed them by force (Ibid: 373). The development and decline of this type of grassroots movement is significant to practices of citizenship because they reveal that the populist notion of citizenship spreads through the network of local organizations that try to solve serious problems ordinary people experience in their daily lives; the presence of such organizations induce people's willing participation in local politics. It also reveals that such grassroots movements are likely to trigger repression from the authoritarian state unless it desperately needs the grassroots population for its own political survival or to expand its power.

By the 1930s the authoritarian idea of citizenship that stressed unwavering loyalty to the state (without guaranteeing basic rights) was fully integrated into the militaristic expansion of the Japanese empire (de Bary 2004: 179–180). The colonial state tried to weaken the organizational structure of leftist grassroots movements, strengthen its own official administrative network, and tried to co-opt existing voluntary associations in local areas in order to turn them into its own instruments (administered mass organizations).[22] Faced with the persistent leftist movements that organized labor disputes, peasants' disputes, and night schools, the state in 1931 launched a nationwide repressive "rural village control policy" (*nongch'ont'ongjechŏngch'aek*) along with "ideological conversion" (*sasangsŏndo*) measures. Under these measures, the state closely collaborated with indigenous local elites to convert those left-leaning activists by offering monetary and status incentives (Chi 2007: 374, 376). Yet the spirit of protest survived in the 1930s in some local residents' movements in the Seoul area. Particularly in the second half of the 1930s, this type of local movement increased to address such mundane problems as garbage collection, running water and sewage systems, roads and transportation, education, public safety, housing, and assistance after natural disasters; each of these issues was made worse by increased migration to the city (Kim 2007: 223, 224–229). These residents used established mechanisms such as public grievances and petitions, which the colonial state allowed for after the March First Movement (Chi 2007: 364). Although these practices, along with mass rallies and local residents' associations, were corrupted by the collusion between the local authorities and local elite, especially in rural areas (Ibid: 368–371), the residents' movement in Sŏngbuk-dong, Seoul, shows an intriguing subversion of the state's control over informal local politics.[23] Its residents' association, under the leadership of an indigenous elite member, worked consistently to resolve an array of urban problems affecting the lives of its residents through the established channels (Kim 2007: 232–242).

It is noteworthy that public grievances and petitions filed by local residents in Sŏngbuk-dong and elsewhere mostly centered on problems with the state's distribution of public resources among local areas, stemming from administrative negligence and discrimination (Chi 2007: 369; Kim 2007: 230). The local residents' movement in Seoul suggests that some urban Koreans developed a sense of entitlement, demanding that the colonial government fulfill its responsibility. Although members of the states in pre-modern Korea used grievances and petitions to communicate their problems, there is a significant qualitative difference between the contents of these demands. The contents of problems addressed by the urban residents in colonial Korea included an array of modern expectations for the state's public service; they were not problems of food shortages, famine, or excessive extraction of people's resources by local officials, but those of education, housing, roads and transportation, running water and sewage systems, public safety, garbage disposal, and local development. In addition, the urban residents did not ask for benevolent aid or protection from the state, but asked for fair and professional handling of the public resources that they were entitled to. This is fundamentally different than the options that people had when they were wronged in pre-modern society: (1) appeal to officials for justice and remedy or (2) resort to self-help, including the extreme case of rebellion against the government. To be certain, the colonial state frequently did not respond to the urban residents' demands and this was why some petitions were repeatedly submitted and residents' movement at times became militant. Yet this line of development shows the emergence of a novel practice of citizenship that challenged the authoritarian and depoliticized mode that had been pervasive in the colonial era.

2.4 Perpetuation of the Authoritarian Citizenship Under the US Army Military Government Rule (1945–1948)

The abrupt end of colonial rule (15 August 1945) at the end of World War II and the subsequent US military occupation of southern Korea generated a political and social context that largely perpetuated the authoritarian view of citizenship, which promoted economic agency but restricted political agency. The very establishment of the USAMG (officially on 4 January 1946) indicated that in startling contradiction to the normative ideals of the modern state and citizenship, the US and its international allies saw decolonized Koreans as unfit for self-rule (which echoed the Korean Enlightenment intellectuals' distrust of the masses). Furthermore, the U.S.

considered the southern part of Korea to be "land without an owner".[24] As the occupying force, the US army treated Korean people as abject Orientals that it had saved from the tyranny of Japanese fascism, and certainly did not recognize them as modern citizens possessed of sovereignty.[25] The US promoted liberal democracy in Japan with serious plans and commitment, as a showcase to prove the superiority of the American political and economic system, but it had no interest in doing so in Korea, a colony it released from its former enemy. Instead, the US was primarily concerned with setting up an anti-communist regime that could serve its strategic interests in the midst of the escalating Cold War. Ironically, when it arrived in southern Korea with virtually no knowledge about the society, the US army encountered the nationwide network of the people's committee (*inminwiwŏnhoe*) and related leftist grassroots movements for the organization of farmers, workers and youth.[26] Although leftist movements in Korea grew organically out of anti-colonial resistance and had broad support from a majority of Koreans,[27] the USAMG perceived them as a competing political force and launched a militant attack against them in collaboration with right-wing Korean elite (Yi 2008: 131–132).

Throughout its rule, the USAMG prioritized the suppression and eradication of indigenous leftist movements and organizations, while sponsoring rightist movements and organizations. This political dynamic resulted in the reproduction of the authoritarian idea and citizenship practices in South Korea. It also left a lasting negative legacy for decades to come because the ultimate political priority influenced the way the USAMG designed and implemented its policies, and established the following paradoxical patterns of ruling. First, while claiming to eliminate the negative legacies of Japanese colonial rule, the USAMG continued to use colonial methods of ruling: (1) it utilized administered mass organizations (AMOs) created by the colonial state to implement its policy and exercise ideological control over various groups of the population, including peasants, workers, local residents, youth and women[28]; (2) under its informal but underlying tenet of anticommunism, the USAMG revived and strengthened its control over the press and broadcasting media, and consistently maintained censorship in the name of order and security (Yi 2008: 373–389); (3) although it ostensibly abolished the colonial system of state-licensed prostitution in 1947, in practice the USAMG incorporated military-regulated prostitution into the establishment and maintenance of US military bases throughout Korea (Moon 2010a). The persistence of these colonial methods of ruling indicates that the military government not only ignored basic civil rights, but also viewed its citizens as its instrument and, at best, the recipients of its benevolent rule. In particular, citizens who cannot exercise freedom of thought, expression, and conscience cannot be autonomous individuals but are arms of the state to be utilized.

Second, while the US ostensibly promoted "liberal democracy" in the world, the USAMG curtailed the exercise of democratic citizenship among Koreans – paradoxically in the name of promoting democracy against communism. On the one hand, the USAMG tolerated freedom of speech and the press in so far as it did not interfere with its policy and ultimate goal of establishing an anti-communist regime friendly to American interests, and increasingly denied freedom among leftists to the point of their complete annihilation. It commonly exercised such aggressive measures as stopping or closing newspapers and arresting journalists (Yi 2008: 374–376). On the other hand, the USAMG directly controlled broadcasting from the beginning of its rule. Using this most effective means of communication, it propagated the superiority of capitalist society and American democracy among various groups of Koreans (Ibid: 388). Similarly, in its education policy, the USAMG purged in the name of fostering the "patriotic democratic citizen" (*aegugjŏk minjusimin*) leftist teachers and students and indoctrinated other teachers and students to become conformist members of the state (Ibid: 415–417). These selective acts of tolerance and suppression of civil rights reveal that the ideal of democratic citizenship was easily compromised in the process of maneuvering power politics. Intriguingly, this echoes Japan's colonial state during the 1920s, which allowed for limited freedom of speech, press and assembly in cases that were not deemed to be political. It also mirrors attitudes of Korean Enlightenment intellectuals in the late nineteenth and early twentieth century; just like these intellectuals and the colonial authorities, in practice the USAMG promoted authoritarian citizenship that turned people into useful components of the state for carrying out its agenda; hence it promoted citizens' economic agency in capitalist society, but truncated their political agency, especially when it challenged the government authorities.

If we look for some positive legacy from the idea of citizenship from this period, the USAMG introduced political rights to vote and run for public offices and promoted gender equality, particularly in education. While this introduction of political rights was in itself a progressive departure from the authoritarian view of citizenship, it was deeply flawed in the absence of basic civil rights as discussed above. When citizens were not free to choose their political ideology, express their views in various media, and organize themselves, the exercise of universal suffrage and right to run for offices is easily reduced to formal trappings of procedural democracy. Regarding gender equality, although some nationalist reformers addressed this issue to strengthen the nation, the USAMG promoted gender equality as an element of democratic society (Yi 2008: 508). This ideal was put into practice in the areas of election and education. As a result, women participated as voters and candidates in the Constituent National Assembly (*chehŏngukhoe*) election in May, 1948, but not a single woman candidate was elected (Ibid: 448, 449). While it was a positive step to expand mandatory education – which had been severely limited during the colonial period – and introduce gender equality in education, specific aspects of education assumed gender hierarchy that naturalized women's roles as mothers and wives (Ibid: 417). In a nutshell, although this line of positive change undermined the elitist view of citizenship with popularizing political rights and promoting gender equality, it was more cosmetic than substantial. The methods of ruling used by the USAMG not only perpetuated the authoritarian view of citizenship, but also provided the model for the subsequent authoritarian regimes in Korea that promoted economic agency but curtailed the political agency of its own citizens.

2.5 Anti-communist and Productive Citizenship During Authoritarian Rule (1948–1987)

The establishment of the formally sovereign Korean state generated an impetus to integrate two existing ideologies, anticommunism and nationalism, so as to make Koreans into *kungmin*. Inheriting the legacies of colonial rule and USAMG rule, the Korean state officially adopted anticommunism as its ideology and maintained its fiercely anticommunist identity throughout its authoritarian rule and beyond. Especially after the internecine Korean War, anticommunism became synonymous with "liberal democracy", and being a citizen of the Korean state meant being an anticommunist. Building on the methods of ruling left by the USAMG, Syngman Rhee's civilian regime (1948–1960) supported right-wing organizations and activities and suppressed already weakened left-wing activities and organizations. In particular, Park Chung Hee's military regime (1961–1979) deployed the amalgamation of Foucauldian discipline and physical violence to remold its people into useful and docile *kungmin*. Compared with Rhee's regime, this combination became far more systematic because Park's regime extensively adopted modern instrumental rationality for effective ruling. On the one hand, it institutionalized such new disciplinary techniques as the "resident registration system" for effective surveillance over, and mobilization of, its people; it also introduced the ubiquitous display of anticommunist posters to exhort them to ferret out communists in their surroundings. On the other hand, the regime honed existing techniques such as using the administered mass organizations, education system, and the mass media to maximize its monitoring and indoctrination. Those who refused to fit into this anticommunist citizenship were punished under the National Security Law and the Anticommunism Law. These laws justified drastic curtailment of basic civil rights and political rights in the name of national security in the officially "democratic republic" (*minjugonghwaguk*). Throughout the authoritarian rule by civilian and military regimes, numerous political dissidents including labor activists and student activists as well as North Korean spies and their collaborators were persecuted and prosecuted for being communists or subversive "impure" elements (Moon 2005: 27–39).

Since it accentuated the anti-communist bent in the authoritarian mold of citizenship inherited from the past, the Korean state heightened the powerful ideology of nationalism to appeal to Koreans to be useful and loyal members of the nation. While this nationalist call was largely confined to becoming an anticommunist *kungmin* during Rhee's regime, Park's regime infused it with the economic duty for diligence and hard work. As discussed above, this collectivist call for productive citizenship was initially articulated in the *Independent Newspaper*, but its contemporary version came with the Korean state's actual power to transform its people into productive workers and managers and to build an industrial nation. The industrializing state mobilized its citizens on a massive scale to implement its industrial policies and carry out related campaigns. This economic duty was intricately coupled with military service for men and with fertility control and "rational" household management for women. This pattern of mass mobilization for economic growth continued during Chun Doo Hwan's regime (1980–1987), but the emergence of a consumer society in the 1980s began to undermine the power of the nationalist call for productive and diligent citizenship (Moon 2005: Chaps. 2 and 3).

Challenges to anticommunist and productive citizenship have existed since the beginning of the 1960s. College students, factory workers, and intellectuals (including scholars, writers, religious leaders, journalists and politicians) kept up dissident social movements against the dominant idea and practices of citizenship. Under the rubric of "democratization movements" (*minjuhwaundong*), these diverse groups of activists struggled to democratize citizenship directly and indirectly. As students and intellectuals protested against corrupted elections, the absence of elections, and violence against dissidents, workers and their intellectual supporters protested to obtain humane and fair treatment by their employers and government, who denied them decent wages, safe working conditions, and independent labor unions. Although these dissidents did not use the language of citizenship explicitly, their collective struggle demanded basic civil rights, political rights, and social rights, and their persistent demand for a humane and just society conveyed that they refused to become docile *kungmin* to be mobilized for the state's project with little personal entitlement (Moon 2005: 98–103).

2.6 The Emergence of Democratic Citizenship in Post-military Rule Korea

While the legacy of authoritarian citizenship is deeply ingrained in Korean society, the political transition to procedural democracy in 1988 and then the restoration of civilian administration in 1993 have permitted the development of some positive change in the hegemonic idea and practices of citizenship. With the restoration of political rights, Koreans have again voted to elect public officials at various branches and levels of the state. They have also experienced the expansion of civil rights to include the freedom of thought, expression and assembly. In particular, voluntary associations known as "citizens' organizations" emerged and became the agent of grassroots social movements to bring about "progressive" social change. These organizations popularized the term "citizens" (*simin*) as "masters" (*chuin*) of Korea who would monitor the state and other powerful institutions in society and demand their rights and justice. Using political and civil rights, different citizens' organizations have fought for social rights to guarantee minimum standards for wages, economic justice and a healthy environment free of pollution. In a nutshell, these organizations re-envision citizenship as a democratic relationship to the state (Moon 2005: 109–121). In the idea and practice of monitoring and ordering citizens, these organizations have undermined the essence of "Confucian governance" that authoritarian regimes in Korea, particularly Park Chung Hee's regime, evoked to culturally justify their authoritarianism (Moon 2003). They have challenged the Confucian views of politics as a moral exercise by rulers and the people's duty to follow, and introduced accountability for rulers through monitoring and checking by those governed.

These citizens' organizations, however, have been dominated by educated urban middle-class men, a relatively privileged social group among grassroots men and women. First, this class and gender cleavage has been apparent in the general membership and particularly the leadership of such major citizens' organizations as the Citizens' Coalition for Economic Justice (CCEJ) and People's Solidarity for Participatory Democracy (PSPD). This largely male-dominated and middle-class aspect can be read as a telling commentary on the centrality of socioeconomic power in the emergence of the political subjectivity of the democratic citizen. It is noteworthy that while the Korean Women's Associations United (KWAU), an umbrella organization of autonomous women's associations, has used the gender-specific term *women* (of different social strata) to identify the subject of its movement, the CCEJ has used the apparently gender-neutral term *citizen* as its subject. While middle-class women cannot but see themselves as gendered beings in the public sphere, middle-class men can see themselves there as gender-neutral citizens. Similarly, college-educated middle-class women tend to dominate the new type of women's organization. It is useful here to consider an insight from the postmodern critique of power and universalism, which highlights the following dynamic; it is often a dominant social group that attaches the mantle of universalism to its specific experiences, reducing subordinate groups' experiences to "special" ones.[29] Within this logic, a social movement organization dominated by men can claim the mantle of a gender-neutral citizens' organization, while a social movement organization dominated by women remains a women's organization. Equally, while a middle-class dominated organization can forget about its class, a working-class organization like a labor union cannot. Hence, some feminists reject the notion of citizen altogether as a masculinist category. Yet autonomous women's associations have fought for gender equality, including women's right to paid work for a lifetime and the elimination of the patriarchal family law. In practice, the term *women* as the agent of the social movement envisioned by the KWAU connotes the subjectivity of democratic citizens, who are equal to others and struggle to obtain and protect their rights (Moon 2005: Chap. 6; Moon 2002).

Second, the class and gender cleavage is also visible in the lingering division between autonomous labor union movements and the citizens' movements, and men's dominance in the labor movements. Some working-class men and their advocates reject the language of citizenship as a "bourgeois" notion because it has been embraced by the largely middle-class movements. Yet labor movements in Korea have strived to transform exploited and oppressed male workers into "masters" of their destiny who would enjoy the rights of democratic citizenship. At the same time, despite the recent history of the women workers' labor movement in the 1970s and 1980s, women workers have been marginalized in labor union movements dominated by male workers employed in high-paying heavy industry (Moon 2005: 130–143; Koo 2001: Chap. 4). The recurrence of class and gender cleavage confirms that social groups in more privileged positions in social stratification have better access to citizenship when there is a political opening.

While the citizens' organizations have contributed to the democratization of authoritarian citizenship conveyed for long by the term *kungmin*, ironically their practices have perpetuated the idea of grassroots citizens as objects of mobilization, rather than autonomous actors and decision makers. This problem is related to their organizational structures and focal activities; in this type of organisation, professional activist staff manages the daily routine and officers who are not usually elected by lay members make important decisions about short-term and long-term objectives (Kim 2006). As a result, lay members' voluntary participation in this type of citizens' organization is generally reduced to paying dues and supporting activities and events initiated by its officers and staff (Moon 2010b). In the Korean political context, where political parties have failed to identify and articulate the interests of different social groups,[30] the activities and events of the citizens' organizations tend to focus on monitoring and protesting against the state's policies and devising policy alternatives to fill the gap. Although these are extremely critical tasks, this quasi political party role relying on professional activists has stalled further democratization of citizenship. The phenomenon of the *Nosamo* movement deserves our attention for breaking with this pattern and raising a new possibility for a loose gathering of autonomous individual citizens who pursue their own interests in democratizing the political system in Korea.

Nosamo is an abbreviation of the "gathering of people who love Roh Moo Hyun," a former human-rights lawyer who was elected to be the 16th president of South Korea in December 2002. It began as a sort of fan club for the unusual politician, who ran for, and lost, in April 2000, the National Assembly election in a Pusan district. This was audacious behavior for a professional politician because he would easily have won if he had run for his original district in Seoul. He chose Pusan to prove that regionalism in Korean politics could be undermined. Although he lost, this experiment strengthened his appeal as a refreshingly different type of politician among certain voters who were deeply disaffected and repulsed by institutionalized politics in general, and elections in particular (No et al. 2002: 7–13). Because he had obtained his reputation as a courageous and conscientious politician over a decade,[31] the group of *netizens* posted their condolences and encouragement for Mr. Roh. This communication soon developed into an idea to create a cyber community to support him. Employing him as their totemic figure, this internet community rapidly expanded among individuals who hoped to bring about positive change in the established way of doing politics. By June 2002 its membership multiplied to 47,000, with some 200 local branches and 36 branches overseas (Ibid: 151).[32] Unlike existing major citizens' organizations, the *Nosamo* did not have a formal hierarchy and bylaws; instead, it was a loose gathering of individuals who shared diverse but overlapping interests in ending regionalism in Korean politics, just as Mr. Roh challenged in his own practice. In the cyber community, individual members are equal to one another in their right to cast Internet votes and in their responsibility for free and respectful discussion to form public opinion about issues raised by its members. As they got involved in Internet communication, members also organized regular off-line meetings for discussions and to socialize in person (Ibid: 96, 100, 249–250). During the 2002 presidential election, unlike other election campaign groups created by political parties and individual politicians, the *Nosamo* engaged in Mr. Roh's campaign without getting paid or using social connections based on hometown, school ties and kinship. Instead, its members volunteered for his campaign because they genuinely hoped to see a good politician like him succeed, and were excited about such potential. Indeed, the *Nosamo* played a crucial role in initiating the novel idea of selecting a presidential candidate of a political party through national elections (*kungminkyŏngsŏn*), making him the candidate of the Democratic Party in April, 2002, and in finally electing him to the presidency in December (Ibid: 123). According to self-descriptions and scholarly observations of the *Nosamo*, this success stems from the energy and dynamism of individuals who are transformed from "spectators" and "objects of mobilization" into "sovereign citizens" and "subjects with their own ideas" who can choose an egalitarian and communicative leader (Ibid: 61–62, 72). While the *Nosamo* has incorporated a continuing diversity of ideas and more elaborate bylaws since 2006, it has maintained its original spirit of being a loose community of ordinary individuals who choose to participate in realizing the ideal of sovereign citizens through mutual learning and engagement.[33]

Ever since he was catapulted to the pinnacle of power, primarily by a younger generation of voters who are looking for a principled and uncorrupted leader, Roh Moo Hyun himself made a far-reaching contribution toward the democratization of citizenship in Korea. During his "participatory government" (*ch'amyŏjŏngbu*; February 2003–January 2008), he took extraordinary steps in eliminating authoritarian conventions in the way the government dealt with its citizens, employees and business leaders. For example, he refused to use the repressive state apparatuses, including the police, intelligence agencies, and the prosecution, to monitor and check dissidents and his political competitors, which has been a very deeply entrenched practice in Korean politics. He also reduced the imperial power of the Korean presidency by replacing presidential appointments of high-ranking government officers with a system of open applications. He tried to end the insidious practice of extracting election campaign funds from big business firms. As repeatedly expressed in his own words and deeds, he worked as a president who served his *kungmins* as his "masters".[34] He communicated directly with ordinary citizens via the Internet and made government policy reports available to them. He also spread the culture of discussion and debate in the rigidly hierarchical circle of government officers.

However, his leadership with democratic intentions received far more criticism and even ridicule than praise and appreciation during his presidency. Such negative reactions came not only from powerful conservative forces in Korean society, but even from his own supporters who were critical of or disappointed by his policy decisions and mistakes. In a sense, these negative responses allude to various types of obstacles stacked against the democratization of citizenship and the enduring power of authoritarian citizenship in Korea.

2.7 Conclusions

The idea and practices of citizenship in Korea from the late nineteenth century to the early twenty-first century reveal certain recurring patterns in the power politics of citizenship. First, the enlightenment nationalists, the colonial authorities, the USAMG, and authoritarian regimes in Korea, all promoted collectivist and largely elitist versions of citizenship with relatively minor differences. In their total disregard for, or selective recognition of, basic civil, political and social rights, these social and political elites did not consider citizens as autonomous and free individuals, but as a collective resource to be tapped or an instrument to be employed in order to obtain their own objectives. In their emphasis on enlightenment and education, or the denial of education altogether, these elites treated citizens as ignorant or inferior, and therefore underscored their duty to follow the leadership of the elites themselves. Second, these social and political elites were far more ready to accept citizens' economic agency to be productive and accumulate wealth than to accept their political agency to think critically and act collectively. This capitalistic and authoritarian undercurrent in the collectivist and elitist versions of citizenship commonly resulted in de-politicization of citizenship in Korea. While the Constitution of South Korea has contained the modern rhetoric of the sovereignty of the people, in practice the de-politicization of citizenship makes political sovereignty the sole preserve of rulers and elites. This trend is not conducive to the growth of democratic citizenship that requires the popularization of the civic republican ideal of the citizen as a free and propertied political actor. Third, grassroots (leftist) movements have challenged the hegemonic idea and practices of authoritarian citizenship and reframed the collectivist orientation since the colonial era. Instead of highlighting the citizens' duty to contribute to, or even sacrifice for the collectivity of a nation, these popular movements have promoted the collective rights of downtrodden social groups. That is, in contrast to liberalism that anointed the individual as a free and isolated being entitled foremost to civil rights, these popular movements promoted the social rights of the collectivity of social groups such as the working class, peasants and women. When this type of movement is in its early stage and desperately needs mass support, it tends to display the idealistic balance between individual civil rights and collective rights; as the movement becomes more centralized or ideologically rigid, individual rights tend be ignored as a "bourgeois" trait. It is in this sense that the leftist-leaning *minjung* movement in contemporary Korea maintained an authoritarian strand in its populist orientation. Fourth, as the limitation of citizens' organizations that have pursued grassroots social movements in contemporary Korea suggests, democratic citizenship requires the liberal recognition of the individual in conjunction with the recognition of the collective rights of vulnerable social groups who cannot afford to be autonomous and free individuals.[35] Yet without specific leverage to win in actual power politics, grassroots men and women cannot enjoy democratic citizenship with full political liberty, civil rights and social rights as a lived reality.

If we accept democratic citizenship as an essential ingredient for making a good society, progressive movements and organizations need to accept the primacy of the family in Korean society, both as a powerful rhetorical metaphor and as a social unit in actual governance. The powerful symbol of the family as the prototype of the relationship between the state and its people stems from the enduring appeal of ethnic nationalism. This sense of nationalism views the Korean nation as a homogeneous family, and postcolonial sensibilities tend to embrace Korean "tradition" as a positive source of cultural identity. Because this seemingly unchanging tradition or culture can assuage uncertainty and anxiety caused by an extremely rapid pace of social change in the society, the state has expediently adopted policies of reinventing Confucian and other traditions, not only during military rule but also in the era of procedural democracy. As I discussed elsewhere regarding the notion of Confucian governance, democratization in Korea has largely been conservative in preserving this revived Confucian thought as the hegemonic framework for interpreting the relationship between ruler and ruled in terms of the family virtues of filial piety and respect for elders (Moon 2003).[36] In the democratization of Korea, the patriarchal family rather than the individual has been the actual unit of governance until recently. After several revisions of the family law since the 1950s, women's organizations in collaboration with other social movement organizations succeeded in eliminating the "household master system" (*hojujedo*) that reflected patrilineage in the Korean kinship system. In February 2005, the Constitutional Court ruled that this system was incompatible with the constitutional principle of gender equality. The obsolete system was replaced by the "family relations registration law" (*kajokkwangyedŭngnogbŏp*) in April 2007, which became effective on 1 January 2008. In contrast to the household master system, this new personal status law treats individuals as independent and equal entities. Now every individual has her or his own basic identification card containing just her or his dates of birth and death. Yet the basic card is supplemented by four related certificates which contain parental information, spousal information, adoption information, and biological and adoptive parent–child relations, respectively. These certificates show the continuing significance of the familial self in Korean society. It remains to be seen how Korean individuals situated in their familial relations will continue to develop their democratic citizenship.[37]

With the hindsight of observing an array of serious problems in society based on liberal individualism, we need to recognize the individual as the basic unit of democratic governance that can reduce arbitrary abuse of power and increase the possibility of treating people fairly, regardless of powerful social connections, such as those based on school, kinship and home town. This individual does not have to be the isolated and abstract individual of liberalism, but one who is situated in, and related to, other people in the family and beyond. At the same time the family does not have to be the only legitimate source of one's identity and relation to other people. Despite its affective appeal, the family metaphor often fails to accept that citizenship is predicated upon equality among members of the state, and glosses over the differences and conflicts that always exist among equal members. In line with Fred Dallmayr, here I would argue that the rapid transformation of East Asia, characterized by the rise of the impersonal market economy and the centralized modern state, requires us to build philosophical underpinnings that guide relationships among individuals as equal citizens in the public sphere of state politics, market economy and civil society. Dallmayr critically assesses that the Orientalist readings of the Confucian principles of the "five mainstays of human relationships" are merely static and hierarchical, and argues that ceremony and ritual, as well as the emphasis on the virtue of humaneness (*jen*), rechannel and temper such apparently asymmetrical human relations into ones based on reciprocity. Yet Confucian thought needs to develop an additional relation to the five mainstays of human relationships that are primarily concerned with familial relations, ruler-minister dyad, and friendship (Dallmayr 2004: 49–52). Certainly, there is serious tension between the social structural need to adopt democratic citizenship as an additional relationship among individuals (connected through the state), and the enduring emotional appeal of the family metaphor and its political expediency as the interpretive framework for all human relations in Korea. Here I wish to quote at length an interesting effort to interpret Confucian cultural underpinnings for the individual self that is commonly construed as the "Western" notion.

> One still hears, all too often, statements by supposedly educated persons, and even prominent intellectuals that the dignity of the individual is a peculiarly Western or Judeo-Christian idea and that people who do not recognize it cannot be expected to respect human rights. Conversely, those who claim to speak for Asian communitarian ideals charge concepts of human rights with being too individualistic, too Western, and too heedless of the claims that the community or state may make on the individual. In reality most Asian religions and philosophies, from the dawn of civilizations, have exhibited a self-awareness and a consciousness of individual responsibility predicated on a high evaluation of the human potential – variously expressed in languages that affirm this value in relation to the different ends of life that might be served by, or serve, individuals. In Confucian terms this could be the concept of personhood – the realizing through self-cultivation of a fully formed and developed person. (de Bary 2004: 231)

In conjunction with the philosophical underpinnings of equal human relationship, there are certain practical conditions required for the development of democratic citizenship. As I mentioned earlier, the autonomous individual is not a given but a product of enabling socioeconomic and political conditions. Economic independence or security is an essential precondition for democratic citizenship. The authoritarian versions of citizenship discussed above seem to touch upon this concern in their emphasis on economic agency, but this is different from actual efforts to ensure economic security for all citizens. Yet the economic conditions in Korea (and elsewhere) since the post-Asian financial crisis (1997–1998), have been very discouraging. The Korean economy has witnessed a drastic increase in irregular and temporary employment that has profoundly undermined economic security and independence among all of the working population, particularly for people in their twenties. Korea has the highest ratio of irregular or temporary workers in the world, and there were over eight million temporary workers in 2007 (Wu and Pak 2007: 21). The manufacturing economy of mass production and mass consumption was replaced by the information economy of flexible production for niche-market consumption. Despite this structural shift, the Korean economy has been unable to move radically away from the old model and embrace an education system that promotes individual creativity and independent thinking (Wu and Pak 2007). A neo-liberal economic regime and minimization of government regulation has accelerated a downward spiral for the majority of the population. It remains to be seen if this dire problem will galvanize a grassroots social movement that will contribute to the strengthening of democratic citizenship.

Endnotes

[1]For the rest of this chapter, Korea refers to South Korea unless noted otherwise.

[2]In my earlier work on citizenship in contemporary Korea (Moon 2005), I defined citizenship as membership in the democratic polity and traced its development in conjunction with social movements that challenged the authoritarian notion of *kungmin* (dutiful nationals). Although this relatively narrow definition was useful for my critical analysis of the gendered and classed trajectory of political membership in contemporary Korea, a broader definition used in this chapter allows us to recognize various paths in citizenship trajectories without making them as "aberrations".

[3]This usage of *simin* is similar to the Chinese word, *shimin*, whose meaning also changed over time (Zhiping 2004: 172).

[4]The current Constitution of the Republic of Korea still refers the members of Korean state as *kungmin*. Some equate *kungmin* with citizen and suggest that *kungmin*, as a specific category of *simin*, highlights the political membership of a nation, as opposed to other types of political communities (Cho 2009). However, given the history of citizenship in Korea discussed in this essay, this equation is problematic.

[5]I have observed these practices even among grassroots men and women who were involved in various types of citizens' organizations during my field work from 2004 to 2005 and in the fall of 2009.

[6]These events included the Kabo peasant rebellion (1894), the Sino-Japanese war (1895) triggered by this rebellion that resulted in the shocking defeat of Q'ing China, and the flight of Kojong (1852–1919), the *de facto* last monarch of the Chosŏn dynasty, into the Russian embassy (1896).

[7]In fact, the Chosŏn government noticed the political utility of newspapers before nationalist reformers and thinkers. It published *Hansŏngsunbo*, the first government newspaper printed entirely in Chinese characters (1883–1884) and *Hansŏngjubo*, a government newspaper in a mixture of Chinese characters and Korean alphabets (1886–1889), which succeeded *Hansŏngsunbo*. Later, old-fashioned intellectuals educated in Confucian classics published *Hwangsŏngsinmun* (September 1898–August 1910). Son, Pyŏng-hŭi, the third leader of Chŏndogyo, a nationalist religion, published *Mansebo* (later renamed *Taehanilbo*), a daily printed in Chinese characters and Korean alphabets (June 1906–June 1907). Yang, Ki-t'ak, a national

independence activist, founded *Taehanmaeilsinbo* (July 1904–August 1910) in collaboration with Bethel, an Englishman, which was later turned into *Maeilsinbo*, the house organ of the Japanese colonial government in Korea.

[8]With the use of full vernacular Korean not only for articles but also for commercials, the newspaper consciously set a broad boundary for its readership, including even rural residents and women. Initially, it published roughly 300 copies but soon its run rose to 3,000. More importantly, it was a newspaper that was read collectively. Readers commonly circulated it amongst their families, friends and neighbors. Literate people read it out to groups of illiterates in the era when ordinary Koreans showed great desires for new knowledge and information. It is estimated that each copy of the newspaper was read by 200–300 people (Chŏn 2004: 445–446).

[9]*Paeksŏng* was the most frequently used and its frequency steadily increased over time, whereas *inmin*'s frequency fluctuated. A far less frequently used term for the Korean people was *tongp'o* (those who share umbilical cords) as well as *kungmin* (national or state's people).

[10]Chu-wŏn Pak uses *kaein* (the individual) interchangeably with *chagi* (2004: 131, 146, 152). But this is misleading because the term *kaein* was not actually used in the newspaper and the term *chagi* does not necessarily mean *kaein*, the autonomous and isolated individual that liberalism promoted. Rather, in the context of late Chosŏn society, it is more likely to indicate the relational self that was embedded in the social network of family and kinship.

[11]This collectivist view of citizenship was quite dominant in East Asia during the era of high imperialism. In his *Outline of a Theory of Civilization* (1875), Fukuzawa Yukichi (1835–1901), a Japanese thinker and educator who significantly influenced Korean reformers, introduced a new idea of citizenship to Japan, but highlighted the collectivity of the nation as the subject of civilization, and subsumed individual members to it. He maintained that it is the spirit of an entire nation (rather than individual knowledge and cultivation) that determines the level of civilization (de Bary 2004: Chap. 8). Although there were some Japanese thinkers who embraced Western liberalism or saw its common ground with Confucianism, the political context of the Meiji government (1868–1911) resulted in the state-centered authoritarian interpretation of Confucian philosophy. In particular, it underscored the notion of self-sacrificing loyalty to the state. This was far more authoritarian than the nuanced notion of the loyal minister, who would be willing to risk death in remonstrating with the ruler, as Mencius advocated (Ibid: 181). Liang Qichao (1873–1929), a Chinese thinker who introduced modern ideas and concepts to East Asian societies through Chinese translation, took up the question of how Zhu Hsi's notion of "renewing the people" could be modified to create a new citizenry that would be active agents in a new Chinese nation. In his article, "Renewing the People", he argued that the Qing dynasty declined because it had only slaves, rather than people who were the subjects of a nation. Yet, like Yukichi, he also prioritized organic unity and order over individual freedom and equality (Chŏn 2007: 404, 408–409). For the English translation of "Renewing the People", see de Bary and Lufrano (2000: 289–291).

[12]This elitist view of citizenship is certainly not unique to Korean nationalists at the turn of the twentieth century. Yoshino Sakuzo (1878–1933), a Christian politician and educator, embraced many tenets of Western democracy and parliamentarianism. Yet he insisted on the following two prerequisites: the leadership of an educated (but not necessarily social) elite, and the leader's ability to embody public virtues and inculcate them in the people (de Bary 2004: 186). Even in the USA, popularly known for its mass democracy, the founding fathers were suspicious of the popularization of political liberty and rights and devised the system of the electoral college to control the outcome of universal (white male) suffrage. This legacy was conveniently forgotten in the U.S. until 2000, when the presidential election between George W. Bush and Al Gore was contested.

[13]Although popularly understood as a "legacy" of Confucianism in contemporary Asia and beyond, the idea of loyalty to ruler and the state did not exist in the original texts by Zhu Hsi (1130–1200), the founder of Neo-Confucianism. Rather, this idea was incorporated into the Meiji government's "Imperial Rescript on Education" (1890) and this innovation became a model for other Asian states that were desperately modernizing themselves (de Bary 2004: 179–180).

[14]For example, *Independent Newspaper* occasionally used it throughout its duration. The ratios of *paeksŏng* to *kungmin* in its articles were 447:24 (1896), 453:23 (1897), 762:39 (1898), and 814:12 (1899) (Ryu 2004: 41). It frequently appeared in the learned society newspapers that proliferated in the mid-1900s. It was used in the name of an organization (Kungminkyoyukhoe) founded in 1904 to promote national education, and the aforementioned *Hwangsŏngsinmun* also emphasized the distribution of national textbooks (*kungminkyokwasŏ*) (Kim 2004: 197).

[15]For example, Chi-yŏn Chang published the *Patriotic Woman's Biography* (aegugbuinjŏn) in 1907, an adaptation of Joan of Arc (Jeanne d'Arc). Ch'ae-ho Sin published *Ŭljimundŏk* (name of a famous general who defended Koguryŏ kingdom from Chinese invaders) in 1908, and *Yi Sun-sin's biography* (the name of a famous general who protected the Chosŏn Dynasty from Japanese invasions) in 1909. Ki-sŏn U published *Kanggamch'an's biography* (the name of a famous scholar-general of Koryŏ dynasty) in 1908 (Kwŏn 2003: 91).

[16]The notion of *kungmin* resembles that of *min* (people) in pre-modern China. First, it conveyed a contradictory duality between common people who are "private" entities (as opposed to government officials), and simultaneously public entities, in relation to the idea of territory under heaven, which is geographically larger, and morally higher, than the state. In China, the public has always been morally superior and prior to private in its value system, but the boundary between the two is relative and shifting. For example, a clan is private in relation to the state, but public in relation to its individual members. Second, the notion of *min* is open to two completely different evaluations: people as the source of the public, and the foundation of the state's legitimacy. At the same time, as individuals and individual groups acting in the concrete world, *min* is no more than an object of rule. Only after the establishment of the Republic (1911) new terms such as "*gongmin*" (public people) were coined to capture new citizenship in modern Chinese society (Zhiping 2004: 172).

[17]Its initial rightist orientation was expressed by its repeated emphasis on "remaking" (*kaejo*) Korea by achieving "enlightenment" (*kaehwa*) and "civilization" (*munmyŏng*). This cultural movement inherited the discourse of national reform during the period of Korean Enlightenment. Soon after, the colonial authorities permitted the publication of current affairs in November 1922. However, the magazine declared its solidarity with *minjung* (the down-trodden people or grassroots population) and published articles and editorials with a socialist orientation from 1923. Yet there was only one Leftist intellectual in its editorship throughout its existence, and the magazine became critical of both the right and the left in favor of cosmopolitan humanism in order to overcome selfish nationalism (Kim 2007: 240, 251, 257, 258).

[18]As the major Korean magazine during the decade, it published an average of 8,000 copies per month without missing a single issue, until it was forcefully closed by the colonial authorities. Although its main readership consisted of educated young men in the Seoul area, this record is significant in a society where almost 90 % of the population was illiterate and national readership of daily newspapers and monthly magazines barely reached 100,000. Its success is attributable to solid financial support from the Chŏndogyo church and its steadfast engagement with sociopolitical issues of the era (Kim 2007: 235).

[19]Yun-sik Kim was a renowned scholar of Chinese writing and government official of the Chosŏn Dynasty who became a moderate reformer during the Korean Enlightenment period and was involved in nationalist movements after colonization. His funeral was politicized in early 1922 by right-wing and left-wing thinkers who debated whether the ceremony should be made public or not.

[20]The issue of "local autonomy" for Koreans has a convoluted history under colonial rule. Initially, the local autonomy movement was promoted by the Kungminhyŏphoe (People's Association), a blatantly pro-Japanese organization, in order to demand Korean participation in the Japanese Parliament right after the March First Movement. The focus of the movement shifted to the formation of a core political force aimed at gaining political rights for Koreans under colonial rule after the *Dong-a Daily* published editorials articulating this necessity in 1922 and 1923. This topic became highly controversial, drawing support among the right and opposition among the left (Yun 2007: 281, 282).

[21]See Suh (1967) for a discussion of Korean communism in the 1930s.

[22]From the 1920 to 1945, there were 793 recorded "citizens' mass rallies" (*simindaehoe*), indicating rallies for residents of administrative units such as village (*li*), township (*myŏn*), county (*kun*), and province (*to*) (Kim 2007: 214). However, most of these rallies were organized by government officials and local elites in collaboration, and grassroots residents were merely mobilized. Mass rallies were commonly an integral part of handling public grievances by officials in collusion with local elites; when a petition was filed, a leader of a given local residents' organization formally or informally met with the government officials in charge and hammered out pseudo public opinion. Then both sides collaborated to form an association to carry out their plan (*kisŏnghoe*) or call a rally. In the next stage, the

local leader submitted a petition and bribed high-ranking officials with money and entertainment (Chi 2007: 370–371).

[23]What is noteworthy about Sŏngbuk-dong is that due to its beautiful natural environment, it drew a large number of educated intellectuals, artists, and the rich, and became an area with a nice cultural atmosphere (Kim 2007: 233). When the socialist youth movement weakened in this town in the late 1920s, the official resident organization led by the local elite became a central force in dealing with problems of everyday life in the 1930s (Ibid: 235, 237).

[24]See Fraenkel (361–362): re-quoted in Yi (2008: 127).

[25]For a more detailed discussion on such a perception, see Moon (2010a).

[26]Within a few days of Korean independence (15 August 1945), provincial people's committees were established in the 13 provinces and by the end of August, 145 local people's committees were set up throughout the country (Yi 2008: 108).

[27]The USAMG conducted a public poll in September 1946 to assess the political orientation among Koreans, including their preferences for societies based on capitalism, socialism and communism. According to this poll, 70 % of some 8,000 respondents answered that they prefer socialism, only 13 % chose capitalism, and only 10 % chose communism (Yi 2008: 110).

[28]More specifically, in early 1946 the USAMG revived the Agricultural Association (*nonghoe*) that the colonial state had created, controlling it on the basis of related colonial laws and expanding its organizational network to lower administrative units. In 1946, it established the Adult Education Associations (sŏnginkyoyu-khyŏphoe) under the Ministry of Education. Although this was formally a non-governmental organization, it had a national network based on the administrative hierarchy stretching from the government to city, province, county, town and village, for effectively reaching out to people and mobilizing them if need be (Yi 2008: 174, 180).

[29]A parallel can be made with different types of social minorities. For instance, people of color in the United States cannot forget their race because of their daily and personal experiences of racism, whereas it is easy for white people to forget their race because it rarely affects them negatively. Similarly, while it is convenient for heterosexuals to claim that sexuality is a private issue and to remain apparently neutral in public because their sexuality rarely affects them negatively in public, homosexuals cannot be oblivious to their sexuality as soon as it is known to other people.

[30]This major problem stems from the following factor: organizationally, political parties in Korea have functioned and been formed around a personal leader, and therefore lacked a rationalized system for representing interests of different social groups. This tendency has been further accentuated by pervasive anti-communism that has delegitimized an array of ideological views on various social issues.

[31]Since Roh Moo Hyun became a first-time legislator in 1988, he has shown this sort of exceptional behavior guided by his own principles, rather than expediently calculating his professional interest in getting elected. For detailed records of his activities as a human rights lawyer and then politician, see Kim, Yong-chŏl (1992),

Planning Committee (2002), Those Who Are With No Mu-hyŏn (2002), and Oh (2008).

[32]As of January 2010, its membership was approximately 110,000. See http://nosamo.org.

[33]See Nosamo's homepage at http://no174.nosamo.org/into/into_main.asp.

[34]For his own writings, see Roh (1989, 2001, 2009).

[35]As Georg Simmel argues in his essays on individuality, to be a free and autonomous individual is to obtain a position of power in society. Mainstream society tends to see a member of a minority social group as a representative of his or her collectivity rather than a unique individual; as a minority group gains more power in society, its members can move away from this imposing perception (Simmel 1971: 217–226). In addition, the free and autonomous individual is a product of specific social conditions and power politics, rather than a natural entity as liberalism assumes. It is a subject position that requires not only civil rights but also social rights including economic security, which can be achieved only through struggle.

[36]A telling example of the enduring power of the family metaphor in politics is a message that President Roh Moo Hyun (2003–2007) sent out to the Korean people on 8 May 2003. In this message, it is noteworthy that he reverses the metaphor of ruler-parents and the ruled-children and conveys that the people are like *his* parents because they enabled him to become President. This twist reflects his democratic sentiments as an exceptional politician who tried to live up to the democratic principle of people's sovereignty. See Yu et al. (2009: 11–15).

[37]The politics of family law reform shows the extent to which individual citizens, especially women, are treated as members of families, rather than autonomous individuals. Women's organizations with growing coalitions with other social groups led the Family Law reform movement from the late 1950s to the 2000s in order to create gender equality in actual family life. See Moon (2007) and Moon (2006).

References

Chi, Su-gŏl. 2007. Iljesigi ch'ungnam puyŏ, nonsangunŭi yuji jibdankwa hyŏksinch'ŏngnyŏnjibdan (Local elites and progressive young men's groups in Puyŏ and Nonsan counties, South Ch'ungchŏng Province during Japan's imperialist rule). In *Han'guk kŭndaesahoewa munhwa, III* (Modern society and culture in Korea, vol. 3), Ed. Kyujanggak Institute, Seoul National University, 335–395. Seoul: Seoul National University Press.

Cho, Han-sang. 2009. *Konggongsŏng'iran muŏsinga* (What is the public?). Seoul: Ch'aeksesang.

Chŏn, In-kwŏn. 2004. <Tongnipsinmun> ŭi chaehaesŏkkwa han'gugŭi sahoekwahak (Reinterpretation of the Independent Newspaper and social sciences in Korea). In *Paengnyŏnjŏn kŏulo onŭrŭl ponda: Tongnipsinmun tasi ilgi* (We look at today through an 100-year-old mirror: rereading the newspaper, Independent), Ed. Tongnipsinmun kangdokhoe (Reading group for the Independent Newspaper), 431–462, Seoul: P'urŭnyŏksa.

Chŏn, Tong-hyŏn. 2007. Taehanjeguksigi chungguk Yanggyech'orŭl t'onghan kŭndaejŏk minkwŏngaenyŏmŭi suyong: Han'gukŏllonŭi 'sinmin'kwa 'aegug' ihae (The acceptance of the modern concept of people's right interpreted by Liang Chi-chao during the Great Han

Empire period: Korean press's understanding of 'people' and 'love of the nation'). In *Kŭndaegyemonggi chisik kaenyŏmŭi suyongkwa kŭ pyŏnyong, 1895–1910* (The acceptance and changing usage of modern concepts during the Korean Enlightenment period, 1895–1910), Ed. Korean Culture Studies Center at Ewha Womans University, 393–435. Seoul: Somyŏng Publication Co.

Dallmayr, Fred R. 2004. Confucianism and the public sphere: five relationships plus one? In *The politics of affective relations: East Asia beyond*, Eds. Chaihark Hahm and Daniel A. Bell, 41–59. Lanham: Lexington Books.

de Bary, Wm. Theodore. 2004. *Nobility and civility: Asian ideals of leadership and the common good*. Cambridge, MA: Harvard University Press.

de Bary, Wm. Theodore, and Richard Lufrano, compiled. 2000. *From sources of Chinese tradition: from 1600 through the twentieth Century*, 2nd ed. Vol. 2. New York: Columbia University Press.

Kim, Chŏng-in. 2007. <Kaebyŏg> ŭl naŭn hyŏnsil, <Kaebyŏg> etamgin hŭimang (The reality that produced <Kaebyŏg>, hope contained in <Kaebyŏg>. In *Kaebyŏg'e pich'in singminji chosŏnŭi ŏlgul* (The face of colonial Korea reflected in Kaebyŏg), Eds. Kyŏng-sŏk Im and Hye-yŏng Cha, et. al., 235–264. Seoul: Mosinŭn saramdŭl Press.

Kim, Chun-gi. 2006. *Han'guk simindanch'eŭi naebuŭisagyŏljŏnge kwanhan yŏngu* (A study of internal decision-making processes in the citizens' organizations in Korea). Seoul: Seoul National University Press.

Kim, Hyŏn-ju. 2007. 3.1undong ihu purŭjuwa kyemongjuŭi seryŏgŭi susahak (Rhetorics of the bourgeois enlightenment camp after the march-first movement). In *Kaebyŏg'e pich'in singminji chosŏnŭi ŏlgul*, 297–334.

Kim, Tong-t'aek. 2004. <Kungminsuji>rul t'onghaesŏ pon kŭndae 'kungmin' (Modern 'nationals' seen through <What nationals are to know>). In *Kŭndaegyemonggi chisikkaenyŏmŭi suyongkwa kŭ pyŏnyong, 1895–1910* (The acceptance and changing usage of modern concepts during the Korean Enlightenment period, 1895–1910), Ed. Korean Culture Studies Center at Ewha Womans University, 193–221. Seoul: Somyŏng Publication Co.

Kim, Yong-chŏl. 1992. *No Mu-hyŏn non* (An essay on Roh Moo Hyun). Seoul: Sahoemunhwayŏnguso Publication Department.

Kim, Yŏng-mi. 2007. Iljesigi tosimunjewa chiyŏkjuminundong: sŏngbukchiyŏk sŏngbukdongŭi saryerŭl chungsimŭro (Urban problems and local residents'movements during Japan's imperialist rule: focus on the case studies in sŏngbukdong, sŏngbuk area). In Han'guk kŭndaesahoewa munhwa, III (Modern society and culture in Korea, vol. 3), 211–246.

Koo, Hagen. 2001. *Korean workers: the culture and politics of class formation*. Ithaca: Cornell University Press.

Kwŏn, Podŭre. 2008. *1910 nyŏndae, p'ungmunŭi sidaerŭl ilda: 'maeilsinbo'rŭl t'onghae pon han'guk kŭndaeŭi sahoe, munhwa k'iwŏdŭ* (Reading the 1910s, a period of rumor: social and cultural keywords of Korean modernity seen through a newspaper, Daily News). Seoul: Tongguk University Press.

Kwŏn, Yŏng-min. 2003. Kaehwagi sŏsayangsigŭi punghwakwa jŏngkwa pansingminjuŭi tamnonŭi sŏngnip: yŏngungjŏngiwa uwharŭl chungsimŭro (The process of differentiation in the epic story-telling style during the Korean Enlightenment period and the establishment of anti-colonial discourse: focus on hero's life story and fable). In *Han'guk kŭndaesahoewa munhwa*, I (Modern society and culture in Korea, vol. 1), Ed. Korean Culture Studies Center, Seoul National University, 87–121. Seoul: Seoul National University Press.

Marshall, T. H. 1950. *Citizenship and social class*. Cambridge: Cambridge University Press.

Moon, Seungsook. 2010a. Regulating desire, managing the empire: the U.S. military prostitution in South Korea, 1945–1970. In *Over There: Living with the U.S. Military Empire from World War Two to the Present*, Co-Eds. Maria Hoehn and Seungsook Moon. Durham, NC: Duke University Press.

Moon, Seungsook. 2010b. The interplay between the state, the market, and culture in shaping civil society: a case study of the PSPD in post-military rule Korea. *Journal of Asian Studies* 69 (2): 479–505.

Moon, Seungsook. 2007. *The rise of women in Korea: gains and obstacles, a special feature article commissioned by The Korea Herald* (a major English newspaper published in South Korea), 11 July 2007, 4 and 9.

Moon, Seungsook. 2006. Cambio social y situación de las mujeres en Korea del Sur: familia, trabajo y politica (Social change and women's position in South Korea: family, work and politics). In *Mujeres asiáticas: cambio social y modernidad* (Asian women: social change and modernity), Ed. Amelia Sááiz López, 24–48. Documento CIDOB-Asia, no. 12. Barcelona: Fundación CIDOB).

Moon, Seungsook. 2005. *Militarized modernity and gendered citizen ship in South Korea.* Durham, NC: Duke University Press.

Moon, Seungsook 2003. Redrafting democratization through women's representation and participation in the Republic of Korea. In *Korea's democratization*, Ed. Samuel S. Kim, 107–134. Cambridge: Cambridge University Press.

Moon, Seungsook. 2002. Carving out space: civil society and the women's movement in South Korea. *The Journal of Asian Studies* 61 (2), 473–500.

No, Hye-kyŏng, et al. 2002. *Yukwaehan chŏngch'iballan, Nosamo* (Pleasant political rebellion, Nosamo). Seoul: Kaemagowŏn.

Oh, Si-yŏng. 2008. *No Mu-hyŏn yech'annon* (A praise for Roh Moo Hyun). Seoul: Buknet.

Pak, Chu-wŏn. 2004. 'Tongnipsinmun'kwa kŭndaejŏk 'kaein', 'sahoe' kaenyŏmŭi t'ansaeng (The Independent Newspaper and the birth of the modern concepts of 'individual' and 'society'). In *Kŭndaegyemonggi chisikkaenyŏmŭi suyongkwa kŭ pyŏnyong, 1895–1910* (The acceptance and changing usage of modern concepts during the Korean Enlightenment period, 1895–1910), Ed. Korean Culture Studies Center at Ewha Womans University, 127–165. Seoul: Somyŏng Publication Co.

Pak, Myŏng-gyu. 2001. Hanmal, 'sahoe' kaenyŏmŭi suyongkwa gŭ ŭimich'egye (The acceptance of the concept of 'society' and its meanings in the late Choson period). *Sahoewa Yŏksa* (Society and history) 59, 51–82. Seoul: Korean Social History Association.

Pak, No-ja. 2004. Kaehwagiŭi kungmindamronkwa kŭ sogŭi t'ajadŭl (The discourse of kungmin and its internal others in the Korean Enlightenment period). In *Kŭndaegyemonggi chisikkaenyŏmŭi suyongkwa kŭ pyŏnyong, 1895–1910* (The acceptance and changing usage of modern concepts during the Korean Enlightenment period, 1895–1910), 223–256.

Planning Committee. 2002. *'Urisidaeŭi inmulilgi'* (Reading a person of our time). *No Mu- hyŏn sangsik hogŭn hŭimang* (Roh Moo Hyun: common sense or hope). Seoul: Haengbokhanch'aekilgi.

Reading group for the Independent Newspaper. 2004. *Paengnyŏnjŏn kŏulo onŭrŭl ponda: Tongnipsinmun tasi ilgi* (We look at today through a 100-year-old mirror: re-reading the newspaper, the Independent). Seoul: P'urŭnyŏksa.

Roh Moo Hyun. 1989. *Saram sanŭn sesang* (The world where human beings live). Seoul: Hyŏnjangmunhaksa.

Roh Moo Hyun. 2001. *No Mu-hyŏni mannan Lingkŏn* (Lincoln that Roh Moo Hyun met). Seoul: Hakgojae.

Roh Moo Hyun. 2009. *Sŏnggongkwa jwajŏl: No Mu-hyŏn taet'ongyŏng mot ta ssŭn hoegorok* (Success and despair: President Roh Moo Hyun's unfinished memoir). Seoul: Hakgojae.

Ryu, Chun-p'al. 2004. 19segi mal 'tongnip'ŭi kaenyŏmkwa chŏngch'ijŏk tongwŏnŭi yongbŏp: 'Tongnipsinmun' nonsŏrŭl chungsimŭro (The concept of 'independence' and its political mobilization in the late 19th century: focus on the Independent Newspaper). In *Kŭndaegyemonggi chisikkaenyŏmŭi suyongkwa kŭ pyŏnyong, 1895–1910* (The acceptance and changing usage of modern concepts during the Korean Enlightenment period, 1895–1910), 15–58.

Simmel, Georg. 1971. *On individuality and social forms: selected writings.* Chicago: University of Chicago Press.

Suh, Dae-Sook. 1967. *The Korean communist movement, 1918–1948.* Princeton: Princeton University Press.

Those who are with No Mu-hyŏn. 2002. *Kŭegesŏnŭn saramŭi hyanggiga nanda* (He smells fragrance of a human being.). Seoul: Yŏlŭmsa.

Yi, Hye-suk. 2008. Migunjŏnggi chibaegujowa han'guksahoe: haebang ihu kukka-siminsahoe kwangyeŭi yoksajŏk kujohwa (The ruling structure of Korean society during the period of the US Army Military Government: the historical making of the structure of state-civil society relations after the independence). Seoul: Sŏnin.

Yu, Simin, Chung-kwŏn Chin, and Se-hwa Hong, et al. 2009. *Irŏn pabo tto ŏpsŭmnida a! No Mu-hyŏn* (There is no other fool like this, ah! Roh Moo Hyun). Seoul: Ch'aekpose.

Yun, Tae-wŏn. 2007. 1920 nyŏndae sinjisiginŭi ,'singminji'wa ,'kŭndae' insik: chach'iundongŭl chungsimŭro (New intellectuals' understanding of ,'colony' and ,'modernity' in the 1920s: focus on self-rule movements). In *Han'guk kŭndaesahoewa munhwa*, III (Modern society and culture in Korea, vol. 3), Ed. Kyujanggak Institute, Seoul National University, 279–310. Seoul: Seoul National University Press.

Wu, Sŏk-hun and Kwŏn-il Pak. 2007/2009. *Chŏlmangŭi sidae'e ssŭnŭn hŭimangŭi kyŏngjehak: 88manwŏn sedae* (Economics of hope written in the era of despair: 880,000-wŏn generation). Seoul: Lediang.

Zhiping, Liang. 2004. Rethinking civil society in China: an interpretative approach. In *The politics of affective relations: East Asia beyond*, 169–199.

Chapter 3
Threats or Leverage for Korean Civil Society in Contesting Globalization

Hyun-Chin Lim and Suk-Ki Kong

Abstract This chapter examines the ways in which newly emerging threats or opportunities on multiple levels impact on national social movements. By comparing strategy shifts between environmental and human rights movements in Korea since the collapse of the military dictatorship in 1987, we find that international factors such as intergovernmental organizations, neoliberalism, and the Internet have collaboratively impacted on local activism in Korea. Paradoxically, political threats at both national and international levels could offer opportunities for local groups to form alliances around, across, and even beyond national borders. In contrast to human rights groups, environmental groups that develop transnational ties and domestic institutional channels are more likely to change from an insider strategy to an outsider one, and vice versa.

3.1 Introduction

This chapter aims to highlight key emerging factors for social movements such as a democratic policy-making process, neoliberalism and the Internet, and thus find out how these factors have collaboratively influenced Korean social movements since the collapse of the military dictatorship in 1987. Since favorable national political

H.-C. Lim (✉)
Asia Center and Deapartment of Sociology, Seoul National University,
599 Gwanak-ro, Gwanak-gu, Seoul 151-746, Korea

Olympic Apartment 318-1107, Oryoon-dong, Songpa-gu, Seoul 138-788, Korea
e-mail: hclim@snu.ac.kr

S.-K. Kong
Asia Center, Seoul National University, 599 Gwanak-ro, Gwanak-gu, Seoul 151-746, Korea

Mookungwha Kyung-nam APT. 308-1001, Shinchon-dong, Dongan-gu Kyungki-do
431-738, Korea
e-mail: skong@snu.ac.kr

M. Pohlmann et al. (eds.), *Citizenship and Migration in the Era of Globalization*,
Transcultural Research – Heidelberg Studies on Asia and Europe in a Global Context,
DOI 10.1007/978-3-642-19739-0_3, © Springer-Verlag Berlin Heidelberg 2013

opportunities have increasingly been intertwined with regional and international politics, the key factors indicate a close interaction between political opportunity structures (hereafter POS) across national borders. In response to this dynamic interaction, many local social movements in Korea have conducted transnational campaigns related to local issues by framing global norms, thus developing international ties via the Internet and international conferences over the last two decades.

These circumstances raise two contrasting questions: how can political threats offer opportunities for civil society to form various alliances to empower local movements, and how can favorable conditions such as institutional and financial support soften up their challenging voices toward the government's policymaking. We would like to answer these questions by comparing several cases from Korean human rights and environmental movements since the collapse of the military government in 1987.

3.2 Background: Theories and Experiences

Let us briefly address the topic of 'key threats to social movements'.

First, a strong state is a threat to local social movements. While the concept that local movements can mobilize transnational leverage to influence the state holds true in most cases, it must not overlook the importance of state-led transnational activities such as the diffusion of global norms (Spiro 1998, p. 808). In particular, strong states in the Third World argue that issues such as human rights and pro-environmental development belong exclusively to the countries' sovereignty (Risse et al. 1999). Despite pressure from supranational institutions like the UN, strong states defend their sovereignty by using the rhetoric of nationalism, anti-colonialism, pro-independence, and non-interventionism (Clark et al. 1998). As a result, transnational mobilization strategies within a strong state have had little effect on governmental policy-making because of its reluctance to accept the recommendations of transnational groups. Furthermore, strong states are much better prepared and equipped to deal with transnational impacts than social movements. In their spiral model, Risse and Sikkink (1999) have pointed out that states do not move along the path toward an improvement in human rights conditions in an evolutionary way, and that they may relapse into a previous phase of socialization in terms of international norms and ideas. The process of implementation within a domestic arena will be a slow, steady, and diluting or distorting process.

Second, increasing collaboration between transnational and local movement groups has brought about unbalanced power relationships between them. According to Scholte (2003), the key tasks for enhancing democracy vary as long as their location goes beyond the national arena to a transnational sphere. This transnational public sphere is where Non-Governmental Organizations (hereafter NGOs) gather to reform undemocratic decision-making processes by international financial institutions, including the IMF, the WTO, and the World Bank, which shape today's global economy. In addition, Bandy and Smith (2005) argue that just as with such undemocratic processes inside intergovernmental organizations, the relationship among NGOs begins to show an "unequal global north–south power relationship". Such an unequal relationship among NGOs in the transnational sphere often discourages global south NGOs from building sound transnational and local networks or forming global identities and movement frames in which small, local NGOs place great credence.

Third, counter-movements led by neoliberal business groups also develop strategies similar to NGOs in order to respond to emerging principles and norms, including ecological and human rights norms, with their ideology of neoliberalism. Neoliberal globalization networks, the so-called 'corporate global networks' participate in intergovernmental forums in which they develop terms favoring their interests such as 'wise use' and 'green-plus growing' to reduce international regulations (Rowell 1996, p. 101). For instance, they joined the trilateral partnership under UN guidelines, such as Global Compact, to support universal environmental and social principles. The master frame that the corporate actors rely on is neoliberalism, which increasingly threatens civil society, especially in the Third World. Since the mid-1990s, a number of regional protests have been shaped in terms of global justice, a collective action frame against neoliberal policies and institutions that are creating mounting inequalities between Western and Third World countries.

Consequently, civil society and activist groups have responded with increased networking, collective bargaining and political lobbying across a number of developing states, especially across Latin America and Southeast Asia, where, over the past decades, many states have transitioned to electoral democracies, namely procedural democracies. Local activism swiftly turned its attention to gaining new leverage in the neoliberal era. Let us briefly point out key leverages for local activism.

First, local movements began to understand the World Social Forums as a transnational reservoir. Social movements from the third world countries are becoming increasingly connected with Western movement organizations not only at world social-issue forums and counter-summits, but also through the Internet. In particular, "People's Summits" organized by NGOs have become venues for social activists to meet and share experiences, viewpoints, information, tactics, and strategies as well as to collectively align their national frames against the autocratic, sometimes tyrannical, hierarchical decision-making process and the intensifying global inequalities created by neoliberal policies and institutions (Ayres 2004; Bandy and Smith 2005). Various non-state actors, from grassroots groups and national social movement organizations to transnational groups, have met regularly in Seattle, Porto Alegre, Cancun, Chiang Mai, Mumbai, Bamako, Caracas, Nairobi, and Belém, in the name of the World Social Forum with the aim of developing alternatives to neoliberal economic globalization policies and solidarity networks, of supporting and encouraging each other, and of carrying out local activism against government trade and social policies based on neoliberal principles (Smith et al. 2007; Sen and Waterman 2009).

Second, a nation's domestic political structure influences the links between transnational and local activist organizations (Risse-Kappen 1995; Evangelista 1995). Lewis (2000) asserts that transnational environmental conservation groups can most easily affect the policies of politically "open" nations that have active domestic conservation movement organizations, because transnational groups can collaborate with domestic groups through networking. In keeping with this, Argentine human rights movements which mobilized transnational advocacy groups were able to produce a far-reaching and unexpected effect on the state and on society through the transformation of the society's norms, practices, and institutions that bore on domestic democratization. Argentine activists were thus able to achieve public and political recognition as well as much-needed reforms of social institutions and state structures (Brysk 1994).

Third, the Internet has played a pivotal role in spreading discourse across the public sphere. It has helped promote the concept of democracy and the importance of environmentalism across civil society, and has empowered democracy movements. However, Ayres aptly points out that although some evidence suggests it is a useful tool for those concerned with or committed to a particular cause, other evidence paints a picture of Internet users as lonely and isolated individuals, sinking ever deeper into depression while lost in a maze of chat rooms (Ayres 1999, p. 38). The Internet-based social movements need to be combined with the real world and real time social movements; because actual face-to-face contact helps people build and maintain relationships more effectively over a span of time. These very relationships form the fabric of activist networks. Also, there is a digital divide between the rich and the poor, both nationally and internationally. Such a digital divide causes inequalities based on knowledge and communication. By considering this double-edged aspect, those who are more likely to be devoted to cyber activism or 'click activism' need to combine on-line with off-line activism, which appears to be more effective.

In sum, there have been increasing shifts and changes in political opportunity structures in the form of threats or leverages which have affected local activism. Although there are some differences in the scale and scope of strategy shifts among local movement sectors, they all actively engaged in key processes of global framing and transnational networking. Both theoretical and empirical backgrounds raise the critical question of how Korean social movements have evolved and shrunk in contesting globalization.

3.3 Aims

The authors wish to answer the question of how the two Korean movement sectors – human rights and environment – have coped with new threats and opportunities since the collapse of the military dictatorship in 1987, with reference to insider and outsider strategies. As seen in Fig. 3.1, we believe that the movement sector responds more sensitively to new political conditions at various levels, as and

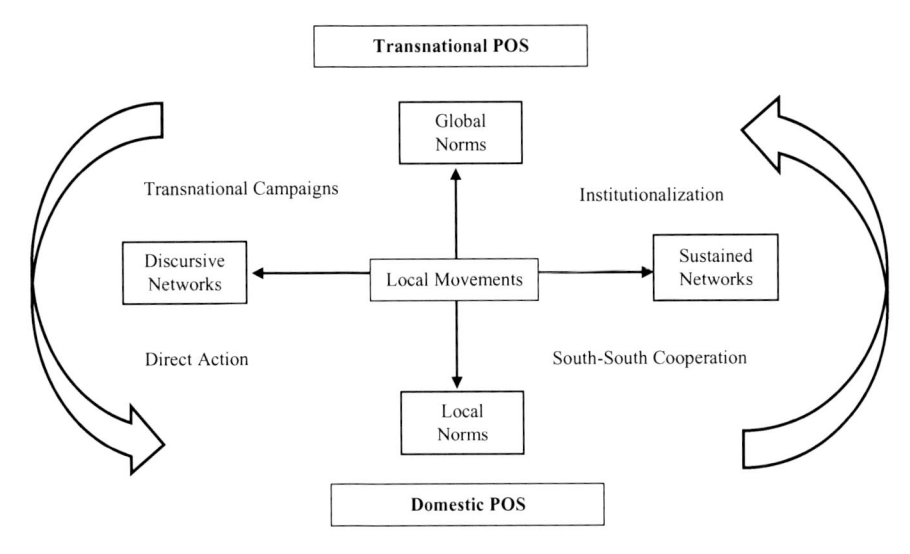

Fig. 3.1 Dynamic model of shifting strategy in local activism

when threats or opportunities lead to more frequent shifts in direction between insider strategy (such as the institutionalization of movements) to outsider strategy (like direct action), and vice versa.

Arguably, Korean environmental movements have been more likely to change with greater frequency between insider to outsider strategy, and vice versa, during two key processes: domestic democratization, and transnational mobilization since the collapse of the military regime in late 1980s and early 1990s. On the other hand, human rights groups are more likely to have kept their traditional strategy, i.e. direct action, because of the historical legacy of long contention with the government. However, they will find a new way of influencing the recalcitrant government by mobilizing the leverage of international institutions like the UN Human Rights Council and the UN Convention on Environment and Development. In the next section, we shall highlight the dynamics of strategy shifting in Korean social movements over the last two decades by comparing the two movement sectors.

In order to achieve a higher degree of reliability, we used three kinds of data gathering, namely: (1) interviews; (2) scrutinizing various documents published by movement groups, the government, and business groups; and (3) participant observation at Johannesburg World Summit on Sustainable development in 2002 and other national campaigns. In particular, the detailed tracing of various documents on key groups in each movement sector as well as in government reports enabled the authors not only to triangulate personal interviews, but also to map out how they change their movement strategies to adapt to a new political opportunity structure. In addition, national campaigns against government policies show how Korean human rights and environmental groups have consolidated the new emerging strategy of transnational mobilization, even while they were struggling with many new threats across national borders. We also analyzed the data by combining two supplementary methods: quantitative and qualitative analyses. Quantitative analysis was used to examine how differently the two movement sectors have mobilized both the insider and outsider strategies over time. The related data used here mainly stems from the Han'guk mingan tandche chongram (Directory of Korean NGOs, 2003), Han'guk siminsahoe yŏngam (Korea Civil Society Yearbook, 2003 and 2004), and Han'guk siminsahoe sipoyŏnsa (Korean Civil Society and NGOs from 1987 to 2002, 2004) as well as Ingwŏn harusosik (the Human Rights Daily News: 1993–2003).

3.4 Strategy Shifts in Environmental Movements

As for its relationship with the government, the Korean environment movement has swung between competition and cooperation since the Rio conference in 1992. Prior to the conference, environmental groups focused on various strategies to resist policies and to address various violations (incl. human rights and environmental violations) by the authoritarian government. After the collapse of Chun Doo-Hwan's military regime in 1987, environmental group leaders have had less significant confrontations with the government. And they have intervened and participated in government policymaking by sitting on various government committees. For example, key environmental groups such as the Korean Federation for Environmental Movements (KFEM), the Green Korea United (GKU), and Green Future have participated in the Consulting Committee of the Ministry of Environment, Presidential Commission on Sustainable Development (PCSD), and Green Civil Committee of Seoul, etc. Furthermore, the government has promptly initiated eco-friendly policies by strengthening the Ministry of Environment as well as by regulating companies that pollute the environment via the PCSD established in September 2000.

However, the government's cooperative atmosphere has fluctuated with regard to environmental issues. In May 2001, for instance, the government and majority party unilaterally decided to resume the Saemangeum land reclamation project, even though a year before the government and environmental groups had agreed to review and discuss the national project that had been initiated by the Roh government in 1991. This anti-environment trend continued to intensify with the advent of the IMF bail-out system in November 1997, followed by the neoliberal globalization of the Korean economic system. Paradoxically, such unfavorable POS, formed by the interaction of domestic and international political opportunities, did not discourage environmental groups from conducting various activities to protect the environment and to resist the government's policies.

In the following section, the dynamic relationship between POS and environmental activism is examined in chronological order, using case studies from national campaigns against the Saemangeum Land Reclamation Project.

3.4.1 State: A Strong Competitor in the Neoliberal Era

In order to achieve economic and environmental interests following the Rio world conference on the environment, the Korean government made concerted efforts to refine its diplomatic relationship with the UN and engaged actively in the UN resolution-making process in a more proactive way. Right after the Rio conference, the government hurried to establish a national taskforce to address environmental issues. This taskforce aims at effectively complying with global norms to promote high technology and laws, and forces industry to adopt eco-friendly processes and to conserve the environment. To enhance international cooperation in the human rights and environmental arenas, the Korean government established the Northeastern Asia Consortium on the Environment in 1992 and also participated in the follow-up meetings to the Rio conference, such as the UN Framework Convention on Climate Change (UNFCCC), the UN Convention on Biological Diversity (UNCBD), and the UN Commission on Sustainable Development (UNCSD). In addition, the government submitted an annual national report on the environment since 1993 in compliance with and to the UNCSD. The government also ratified various international conventions such as the Convention on International Trade in Endangered Species (CITES) in 1993, the UNCBD in 1995, and the RAMSAR Convention in 1997. Furthermore, in order to apply the Agenda 21 recommendation developed at the Rio conference, the central government fully supported the local government's initiative to establish a Local Agenda 21. Additionally, the government announced a new millennium plan to promote sustainable development when it launched the PCSD in September 2000.

In sum, the Korean government as a strong state coped with the transnational impact of the UN treaties and provided civil society with more access to policymaking as well as to developing its counter frame to compete with an eco-friendly one. But such open access to political power and new frames was still limited for environmental NGOs wishing to force the government to implement international treaties. And even so, this is not such a major accomplishment because NGOs are formally involved in government agencies and economic agencies have a monopoly of the decision-making process. As a result, environmental groups have developed a strategy of transnational activism that wavers between the insider and outsider strategy.

3.4.2 New Leverage: Transnational Campaigns

The Saemangeum land reclamation project had been neglected by environmental groups until they realized it would seriously destroy the eco-system near the Saemangeum tidal flat in the late 1990s. The environmental groups began to fight the project in 1998 after it had been constructed in 1991. In late May 2001, the Korean government, including the majority party, unilaterally decided to resume the project even though the government's Joint Committee for Evaluating the Saemangeum Project had not reached a final decision after a year-long evaluation. This unilateral decision prompted environmental groups to organize protests, to reconsider their options, and to carry out more organized and systematic resistance campaigns beyond the national border.

In fact, environmental groups followed the same strategy in the Saemangeum anti-land reclamation campaign as they had for the Tong River anti-dam campaign in which they strategically integrated insider and outsider strategies. As an insider strategy, NGO leaders and professionals not only participated in deliberations of the PCSD to influence the government's final decision on the Saemangeum project, but also recommended environmentalists to participate in the Joint Committee established to reevaluate the Saemangeum project. Unfortunately, these insider politics were not successful in influencing the government's decision because many pro-business, pro-development government agencies dominated the decision making process. Both NGO representatives on the Committee and NGO leaders affiliated with PCSD withdrew immediately from these committees and then intensified their criticism of the government for neglecting international conventions it had ratified, including RAMSAR and UNCBD.

Given this 'credibility gap', Korean environmental groups turned their focus to outsider politics, including mobilizing transnational leverage and conducting a nationwide campaign against this project. A Korean KFEM member describes the mobilization of transnational advocacy networks as follows:

> At the Reunion 2000 of the Goldman Environmental Prize at the San Francisco meeting from July 13–16, 2000, Yul Choi, Secretary General of the KFEM, appealed to his international colleagues who were Goldman Environmental Prize recipients in 1995 and then made a joint declaration, "Stop the Saemangeum Land Reclamation Project". Remarkably, by using his personal ties with transnational movement activists, he raised the urgent environmental issue – the Saemangeum project in South Korea – to the transnational sphere and afterwards invited famous transnational movement activists including Lester Brown, the former director of the World Watch Institute, and Ricardo Navarro, president of FOE International to visit the Saemangeum land reclamation area and to encourage the Korean local movements. (KFEM Kukjeyŏndae wiwŏnhoe 2001, pp. 344–368)

Transnational leverage politics such as this were unsuccessful in forcing the government to reverse either its attitude toward or policy on the environment due to various obstacles such as the President's and the local governor's pro-development stance, the cost of the ongoing project, and the lack of strong opposition from grassroots movements. Despite these huge barriers, environmental groups pursued a more fundamental approach to the project by forming an academic group, the Saemangeum Life Studies Association, composed of over 100 professionals and scholars seeking to develop alternatives to the national project and concrete plans to resist it.

During this campaign, in particular, a new transnational advocacy network emerged, which included KFEM, Global Response, Friends of the Earth International (FOEI), Third World Network, Australia Birds Network, and Japan Wetlands Action Network (JAWAN). These transnational advocates emailed thousands of

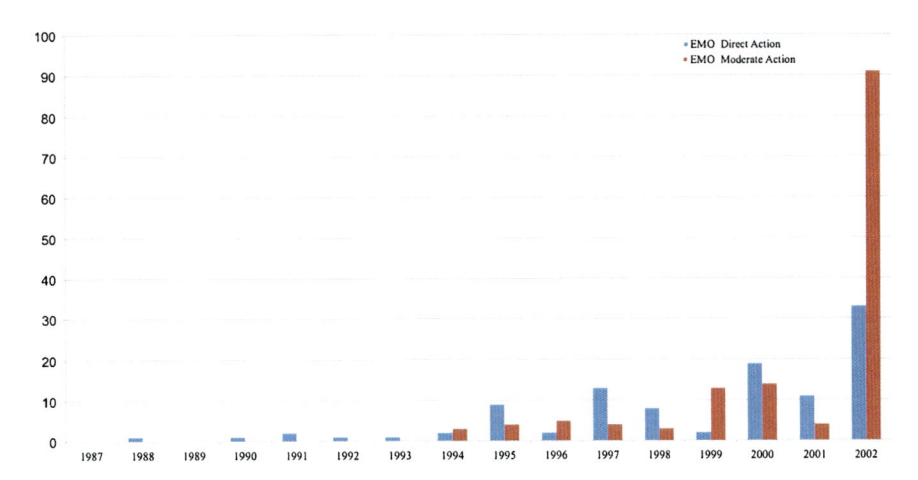

Fig. 3.2 Insider and outsider strategy in environmental activism (Source: Simin ŭi sinmun 2005, pp. 717–850)

letters to the Korean President Rho Moo-Hyun to preserve the Saemangeum tidal flat. In addition, the Global Response conference held in Boulder, Colorado, USA on 20 August 2003 also organized an international letter-writing campaign and encouraged the practice of 'Samboilbae', (three steps and one bow) in support of a Korean citizens' movement to stop the destruction of the Saemangeum tidal flats, the most important feeding ground for birds that migrate between Australia and Siberia (9,000 miles one way). Remarkably, this local Samboilbae practice facilitated transnational campaigns for supporting the Korean Saemangeum campaign and then was disseminated globally through the Internet (Simin ŭi sinmun 2004, p. 476).

As for the relationship between favorable POS and environmental activism, environmental groups actively cooperated with the government by engaging in various governmental committees, as mentioned above, especially since 1993. Figure 3.2 clearly shows the effect of favorable political opportunities given to environmental groups which led to them paying more attention to mobilizing moderate strategies.

But as seen in Fig. 3.3, direct actions or outsider politics have also increased due to the government's exclusion of NGOs in their decision-making processes. For example, hot-button environmental issues such as nuclear waste, the Tong River dam and the Saemangeum movements made environmental groups rely more on direct actions because of the government's unilateral top-down decision-making process. In contrast, most of the newly established environmental NGOs have preferred moderate actions (peaceful expressions), including environmental campaigns, public education, and policy development.

Quantitatively, the correlation between the adoption of moderate strategies and favorable POS is quite significant (.624, P < .01). It is important to note that the balance between insider and outsider politics is easily interchangeable in

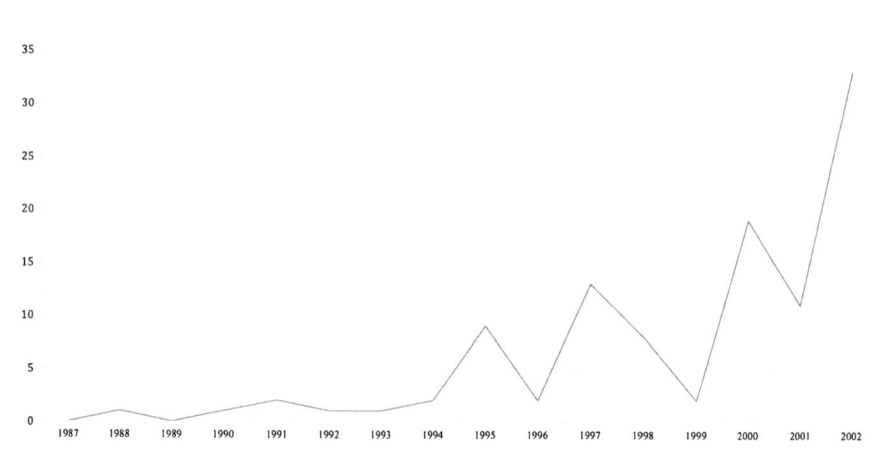

Fig. 3.3 Direct action in environmental activism (Source: Simin ŭi sinmun 2005, pp. 717–850)

environmental movements, as seen in Figs. 3.2 and 3.3. This suggests that the environmental movement sector is getting frustrated with the government's inconsistent policy orientation towards environmental issues because neoliberal globalization has intensified since the late 1990s.

3.5 Strategy Shifts in Human Rights Movements

Since Korean human rights movements have had far more difficulty in developing cooperative relationships with the Korean government, they have maintained a conflicting relationship with it. Although the government ratified international human rights treaties, such as the International Covenant on Civil and Political Rights (ICCPR), International Covenant on Economic, Social, and Cultural Rights (ICESCR) in 1990, and the Convention of the Rights of the Child (CRC) in 1991, it has not done much to enforce them. Instead, it has engaged in the UN reviewing sessions where it has shown off its adoption of international standards. Despite the recommendations of the UN Human Rights Committee (UNHRC) on the problems generated by the National Security Law (NSL) – in particular its infringement of the freedom of the press, speech, and association – the government continues to claim the NSL is necessary for national security, particularly to secure the country against the purported threat posed by North Korea. Fortunately, the National Human Rights Commission (NHRC), established in 2001, has played a brokering role between the Korean government and human rights groups. But the NHRC has been unable to compel the government to implement international human rights standards.

Given these limited opportunities, human rights groups have devoted their energies to developing alternatives to the government's logic of anti-human rights laws within the domestic context while reducing the transnational mobilization strategy to the minimum.

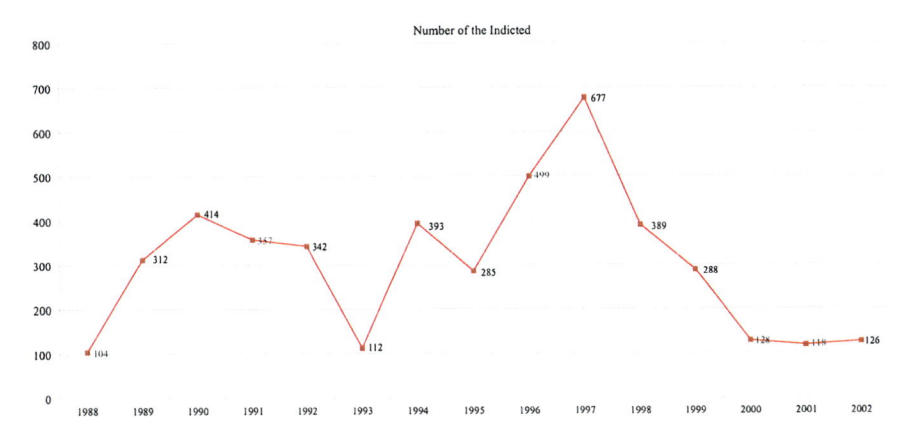

Fig. 3.4 Government coercion by the NSL, 1988–2002 (Source: NHRC 2004, pp. 24–66)

3.5.1 *Revolving Repression Concerning Security and Growth Frames*

The political context in Korea changed dramatically right after the collapse of the military regime. However, the favorable POS also changed into a repressive phase soon after. Figure 3.4 shows that the number of people indicted under the NSL increased immediately after a short-term drop and reached its peak in 1997. The government's zeal to get rid of remnants from the past – social activists, dissidents and outspoken political voices – waned, but the government still had a huge number of political prisoners. Under this harsh repression, human rights groups formed the National Solidarity Council to wage campaigns against the NSL in 1995 and 1998.

When President Kim Dae Jung, a supporter of human rights, was inaugurated in 1998, human rights groups expected major improvements in human rights. His stance on human rights created domestic POS, which had the potential to promote human rights more than at any other time. During the presidential election campaign in 1997, he promised to establish the NHRC to protect and promote the human rights of every individual residing in Korea. But it took quite a while to launch the NHRC after his inauguration in 1998. After many twists and turns, in November 2001 the NHRC was initiated and began to create laws and a judicial framework to protect and promote human rights in Korea through the persistent efforts of human rights groups, the determination of the government to keep its promise, and the pressure of international organizations (NHRC 2002). In the late 1990s, Korean human rights groups had a chance to move ahead with human rights reforms, as well as a new president who claimed to support human rights such as the NHRC. They also had a chance to advance their cause with new international support coming from the UNCHR by targeting the NSL under the ICCPR. However, they failed in their effort to move forward due to the government's reluctance to accept challenges from both domestic and international human rights groups. Unfortunately, this change of regime caused a reshuffling in domestic POS and resulted in limited changes in human rights issues. In particular, the NSL, periodically a tool of the government, remained in force and thus human rights groups continued to struggle for civil and political human rights by means of outsider strategies such as sit-ins, hunger strikes, and rallies.

3.5.2 New Leverage: Transnational Advocacy Networks

We would like to underline this overuse of outsider strategy in the human rights sector as 'delayed institutionalization' and an 'overload of freedom rights movements' by focusing on two national human rights campaigns: the anti-NSL and pro-NHRC movements. First, in the 1990s, defeating or amending the NSL had been one of the main goals for human rights movements as well as other movement sectors because of the effects it had on various movements. Fuel was added to national protests against the NSL by the first encounter with various international NGOs at the Vienna World Conference on Human Rights in June 1993. Later, Korean human rights groups organized another international conference on the NSL in 1995 and invited transnational activists to help them urge the recalcitrant government to abolish it. In particular, when President Kim Dae Jung and Rho Moo-Hyun, who supported the abolishment or reformation of the NSL, were inaugurated in 1998 and 2002 respectively, human rights groups threw all their energy into anti-NSL campaigns. For example, in 1999 and 2000, the People's Solidarity for the Abolition of the NSL emerged, which included about 200 civil and progressive movement organizations, which focused their efforts on abolishing the NSL. They mostly relied on direct action strategies: hunger strikes and street sit-ins, mass demonstrations, petitions to the Constitutional Court, and public opinion polls on the NSL (Simin ŭi sinmun 2005). In addition, they mobilized the leverage of Amnesty International (AI) to target the NSL. AI continuously urged the Korean government to abolish the NSL, a repressive tool used for years to support a corrupt government rather than ensure national security.

Second, the institutionalization process in human rights movements was slowed down and caught up by the NHRC established in November 2001. However, the Korean NHRC is essentially a "catch all" organization responsible for implementing new principles and recommendations agreed at the UNCHR. In spite of its autonomous status, the NHRC plays only a limited role in giving advice and addressing human rights violations. For example, although the NHRC enjoys absolute legal independence, just as a court does, it is bound to other administrative bodies including the Ministry of Government Administration and Home Affairs, the Ministry of Justice, and the Ministry of Finance and Economy in regard to recruiting, rule-making, and budgeting respectively. The constraints imposed on the NHRC regarding the promotion of human rights disappointed many human rights groups, which continue to demand a complete reformation of anti-human rights laws, practices, and law enforcement agencies by the NHRC.

We examined how Korean human rights groups mobilized either insider or outsider strategies between 1987 and 2002. As Figs. 3.5 and 3.6 show, human rights

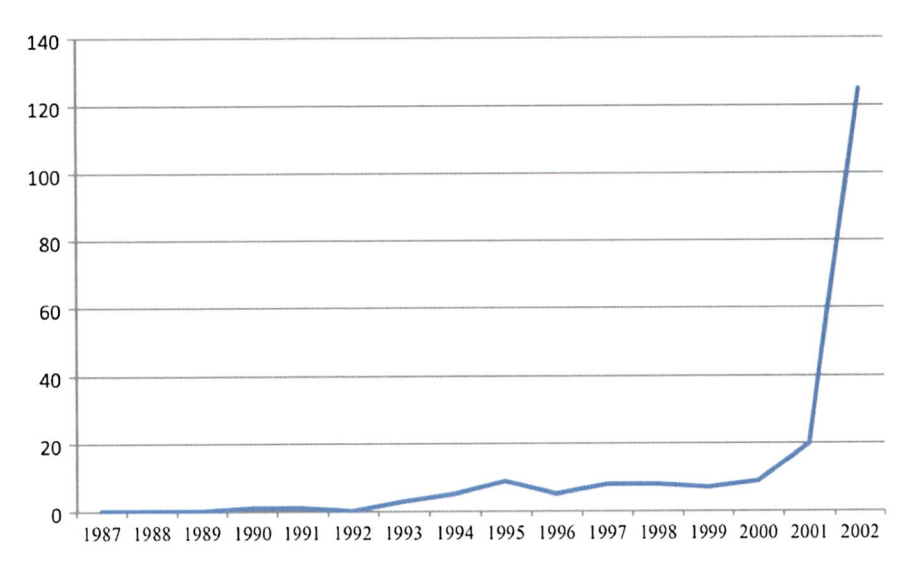

Fig. 3.5 Insider strategy in human rights movements (Source: Simin ŭi sinmun 2005, pp. 717–850)

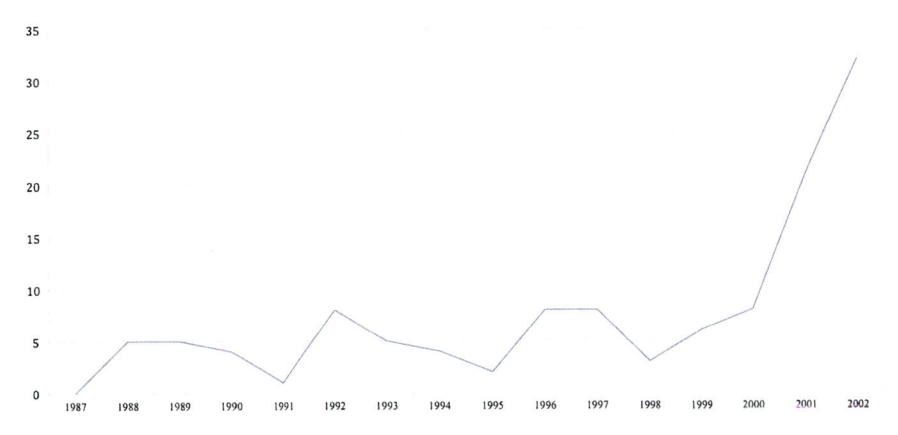

Fig. 3.6 Outsider strategy in human rights movements (Source: Simin ŭi sinmun 2005, pp. 717–850)

groups largely relied on outsider strategies and advanced insider activism when more favorable political opportunities arose. By contrast, the groups rarely mobilized a moderate insider strategy before the inauguration of the civil president, Kim Young Sam, in 1993. We can clearly see, however, that the largest increase in the use of insider tactics accelerated with the establishment of the NHRC in 2001, which can provide more institutional channels for human rights groups to access the government.

3.6 Conclusions: A Comparison Between Environment and Human Rights Sectors

We found that there are similarities and differences between the Korean environmental and human rights movements with reference to strategy shifts at both domestic and international levels throughout the contested globalization process.

First, immediately after the Rio World Conference in 1992, a greater range of channels of access to the government were opened up to environmental movements, thus allowing them to participate in the policymaking process. With that, environmental groups gradually adopted and carried out moderate insider strategies to influence government policies affecting the environment. With the advent of the IMF bail-out system, however, the government's economic and finance departments have gained more leverage due to the increasing impact of neoliberal policies and programs. In these unfavorable contexts, environmental groups have had to return to direct action strategies, such as the mass demonstrations and sit-ins of the late 1990s.

By contrast, human rights movements aim to challenge their target, "the state", which remains uncooperative and maintains a discordant relationship with the human rights groups. Even under the three civil presidents from 1993 to 2007, human rights groups have struggled to eliminate the state's repressive tool, the NSL. South Korea's so-called first human rights president, President Kim Dae Jung, barely kept his promise to establish the NHRC, which was created in response to the strong demands from human rights groups ever since the late 1990s. Furthermore, the NHRC has had limited authority to investigate, monitor, and recommend remedies for human rights abuses, but it does not possess the authority to direct the government agencies. Despite these constraints, the NHRC has served as a channel for human rights groups to work with government agents and to suggest pro-human rights policies.

Second, the two movement sectors found more opportunities to garner support at the international level through participation in world conferences in early 1990s. But, whereas environmental groups have continued to extend their participation in various international spheres on various issues, human rights groups have simply focused on the UNHRC and the related sessions to present their counter report to the government reports submitted to the Committee. In particular, human rights groups have become frustrated with the UNHRC mechanism, which seems to be controlled by the interests of the Western countries.

Although entry into the neoliberal world economy, following the IMF bailout system in the late 1990s, withered the dynamics of both movement sectors, the threats from the international level have prompted these sectors to turn their attention to the globalized issues, reframe their movement goals as global ideas, and join newly emerging global protests against neoliberal economic policies as well as the international financial organizations – WTO, IMF, and World Bank – that carry out these policies. Korean human rights groups have also joined anti-war protests against the US/UK-Iraq war because South Korea sent its troops to the Iraq war.

Third, despite such new opportunities as world social forums, the Internet, and transnational and local linkages, both the environmental and the human rights movement sectors in Korea have had difficulty in taking advantage of the new opportunities. One of the obstacles is the inability of Korean civil society to engage with NGOs from both the northern and southern hemispheres. For this reason, while seeking to overcome their marginal position in the transnational public sphere, as well as the dependencies of Global South NGOs upon the resources of Global North NGOs, the Korean environmental NGOs have begun to focus on regional networks as initiators for developing solidarity among Asian NGOs. By contrast, Korean human rights groups have realized the necessity of developing solidarity among Asian human rights groups, thus strengthening South-South NGO cooperation, because they have grown tired of the over-representation of a few star North NGOs in the transnational public sphere. Unfortunately, Korean transnational advocacy campaigns for human rights issues in neighboring countries such as East Timor have not attracted much attention from the general public.

As for the Internet, in point of fact Korea's well – developed information technology infrastructure made the Internet a promising tool for Korean movements to grow beyond the national and regional boundaries. However, while environmental groups have larger pools of volunteers with foreign language skills which are necessary to diffuse domestic activism globally and update the global community, human rights groups have had a somewhat smaller pool of volunteers with these skills. This means that human rights groups have had less success maintaining transnational networks and collaborations because of their small staffs and their lack of technical expertise and funding.

In sum, there have been an increasing number of threats and opportunities at multi-levels which have affected movement strategies in both movement sectors. Unlike human rights groups, environmental groups changed easily between the insider and the outsider strategy, and vice versa, throughout the 1990s – with dynamic changes arising between competing globalization networks. Interestingly, the threats have prompted both movement sectors to converge on the same issue, social justice or global justice, and to become interested in global issues by engaging in various transnational campaigns (Kong and Lim 2010). Future research should deal with this converging process and examine the ways that converging activism deploys on both domestic and international level.

References

Ayres, Jeffrey M. (1999). "From the Street to the Internet: The Cyber-diffusion of Contention". *Annals of the American Academy Political and Social Science*, 556, 132–143.
Ayres, Jeffrey M. (2004). "Framing Collective Action Against Neoliberalism: The Case of the 'Anti-Globalization' Movement". *Journal of World-System Research*, 10(1), 11–34.

Brysk, Alison. (1993). "From Above and Below: Social Movements, the International System, and Human Rights in Argentina". *Comparative Political Studies*, 26(3), 259–285.

Brysk, Alison. (1994). *The Politics of Human Rights in Argentina - Protest, Changes, and Democratization*. Stanford, CA: Stanford University Press.

Bandy, Joe. & J. Smith. (2005). "Factors Affecting Conflict and Cooperation in Transnational Movement Networks". In J. Bandy & J. Smith (eds.), *Coalitions Across Borders: Transnational Protest and the Neoliberal Order* (pp. 231–252). Lanham: Rowman and Littlefield.

Clark, Ann Marie, Elizabeth Friedman, and Kathryn Hochstetler. (1998). "The Sovereign Limits of Global Civil Society: A Comparison of NGO Participation in UN World Conferences on the Environment, Human Rights, and Women". *World Politics*, 51, 1–35.

Evangelista, Matthew. (1995). "The Paradox of State Strength: Transnational Relations, Domestic Structures, and Security Policy in the Russia and the Soviet Union". *International Organization*, 49(1), 1–38.

Juris, Jeffrey. (2008). *Networking Futures: the Movements against Corporate Globalization*. Durham, NC: Duke University Press.

Keck, Margaret & Kathryn Sikkink. (1998). *Activists Beyond Borders–Advocacy Networks in International Politics*, Ithaca, NY: Cornell University Press.

KFEM Kukjeyŏbdae wiwŏnhoe. (2001). *Kukjeyŏbdae hwaldong bogosŏ* (Report of International Collaboration), Seoul: KFEM.

Kong, Suk-Ki. (2006). "Transnational Mobilization to Empower Local Activism: A Comparison of the Korean Human Rights and Environmental Movements". Ph.D. dissertation, Department of Sociology at Harvard University.

Kong, Suk-Ki & Hyun-Chin Lim. (2010). "Segye sahoe p'orŏm kwa Han'guk Sahoeundong (The World Social Forums and Korean Social Movements: From Seattle to Belém)". The Korean Journal of International Relations, 50(1), 341–372.

Koo, Hagen. (1993). State and society in Contemporary Korea, Ithaca, NY: Cornell University Press.

Lewis, Tammy L. (2000). "Transnational Conservation Movement Organizations: Shaping the Protected Area Systems of Less Developed Countries". *Mobilization: An International Journal*, 5(1), 105–123.

Moghadam, Valentine M. (2008). Glo*balization and Social Movements: Islamism, Feminism, and the Global Justice Movement*, Lanham, MD: Rowman & Littlefield Publishers.

National Commission on Human Rights of Korea. (2003). Yŏnlebokosŏ (Annual Report), Seoul: NHRC.

National Commission on Human Rights of Korea. (2004). Kukgaboanbŏp jŏkyongesŏ nat'anan ingwŏn silt'ae (Report of Investigation into the Actual Condition of Applying the National Security Law), Seoul: NHRC.

Risse-Kappen, Thomas (ed.). (1995). *Bringing Transnational Relations Back In- Non-State Actors, Domestic Structures, and International Institutions*, New York, NY: Cambridge University Press.

Risse, Thomas and Kathryn Sikkink. (1999). The socialization of international human rights norms into domestic practices, In Risse, Thomas, Stephen C. Ropp, and Kathryn Sikkink, (eds.), The Power of Human Rights: International. Norms and Domestic Change. Cambridge, UK: Cambridge University Press.

Risse, Thomas, Stephen C. Ropp, and Kathryn Sikkink (eds.), (1999). *The Power of Human Rights: International Norms and Domestic Change*, New York, NY: Cambridge University Press.

Rowell, Andrew. (1996). *Green Backlash: Global Subversion of the Environmental Movement*, New York, NY: Routledge.

Sarangbang Group for Human Rights. (2003). *Ingwŏn harusosik (Human Rights Daily News: 1993–2003)*, Seoul: Sarangbang Group.

Scholte, Jan Aart. (2003). *Democratizing the Global Economy: The Role of Civil Society*, Centre for the Study of Globalization and Regionalization at University of Warwick.

Simin ŭi sinmun. (2003). *Han'guk mingandanche chongram (Directory of Korean NGOs)*, Seoul: The NGO Times.

Simin ŭi sinmun. (2004). *Han'guk siminsahoe yŏngam (Korea Civil Society Yearbook)*, Seoul: The NGO Times.

Simin ŭi sinmun. (2005). *Han'guk siminsahoe sipoyŏsa (Korean Civil Society and NGOs from 1987 to 2002)*, Seoul: The NGO Times.

Smith, Jackie and Hank Johnston. (eds.) (2002). *Globalization and Resistance*, Lanham, MD: Rowman & Littlefield.

Smith, J., M. Karides, et al. (2007). *Global Democracy and the World Social Forums.* Boulder, CO: Paradigm Publishers.

Spiro, Peter. (1998). Review Essay: "Non-state Actors and Global Politics". *The American Journal of International Law*, 92n4), 808–811.

Waterman, Peter and Jai Sen. (2009). *World Social Forum: Challenging Empires*, 2nd rev. ed., Montreal: Black Rose Books.

Part II

Chapter 4
The Migration of Elites in a Borderless World: Citizenship as an Incentive for Professionals and Managers?

Markus Pohlmann

Abstract This chapter examines whether migration patterns of professionals and managers sustain the assumption that these are transnational citizens. Instead of a braindrain/braingain pattern between countries, empirical findings based on data from the U.S., East Asia and Germany highlight the fact that the internationalization of management is rather a matter of "brain circulation". These findings are discussed against the backdrop of mainstream globalization theories that regard citizenship as an incentive for transnationals, yet empirical inquiry reveals that actual migration patterns require a sociological explanation based on cultural differences in career systems.

The twenty-first century has been proclaimed as the "Age of Mobility" (Papademetriou 2007) as well as an "Age of Migration" (Castles and Miller 2009). People from all over the world and with the greatest differences in social backgrounds are said to be moving and migrating increasingly around the globe. As for the developed countries, the populations' concerns and fears are growing with their perception that foreigners are pouring into their homelands. Politicians, scientists, journalists and others are responding in their own particular ways to this situation. In politics, the legal concept of citizenship has recently become one of the key issues for debates revolving around immigration policies. But citizenship is not merely a concept; it is also an emotional issue, because its changing legal status serves as a bureaucratic bottleneck for many other social policy issues that are formative aspects of any modern nation-state, especially the citizen's right to

M. Pohlmann (✉)
Department of Sociology, Heidelberg University, Bergheimer Str. 58, 69115 Heidelberg, Germany

Im Schulzengarten 20, 69151 Neckargemünd, Germany
e-mail: markus.pohlmann@soziologie.uni-heidelberg.de

M. Pohlmann et al. (eds.), *Citizenship and Migration in the Era of Globalization*,
Transcultural Research – Heidelberg Studies on Asia and Europe in a Global Context,
DOI 10.1007/978-3-642-19739-0_4, © Springer-Verlag Berlin Heidelberg 2013

vote. In recent times, science and politics have united in their efforts to understand the effects and consequences of citizenship status in a more profound manner. Consequently, this legal concept promises to become one of the most forceful mediums for the political integration of migrants, as well as their subsequent social integration.

In marked contrast, throughout the 1990s globalization has been said to have brought about a change in the concept of citizenship. Soysal (1994) even predicted that the emergence of post-national citizenship will replace traditional nation-based citizenship. Jacobson (1997) has also predicted the diminishing importance of citizenship, as related to nationality.

Are these predictions already coming true? Is our world actually composed of "transnational citizens"? This article tackles the issue by providing empirical evidence concerning the migration pattern of professionals and managers.

From a sociological perspective, citizenship is a mechanism of inclusion used by nation states. The nation state occupies a territory and assembles a majority of its carefully selected members on that territory.[1] Citizenship is a multidimensional concept that comprises membership of a specific nation-state and the formal rights and obligations that this membership entails. But citizenship can also be understood as a status and as an identity. According to Kymlicka and Norman (1995: 284), citizenship describes both a legal status and a desirable involvement in one's community. The principle premise of citizenship is that nation-states can set and control the parameters of membership (Gilbertson 2006). The words 'citizenship' and 'nationality' are often used interchangeably (i.e., dual nationality, dual citizenship). However, nationality is often used to signify membership of a community on the basis of common cultural characteristics whereas citizenship refers to membership conferred by a state. Citizens of a nation-state may include those who see themselves as part of a single nation based on a common culture or ethnicity, but more often include some groups who are seen as outside of national culture and incapable of inclusion (Gilbertson 2006).

In our research, we have focused on the formal concept of citizenship as a mechanism of inclusion used by nation-states. Here we are addressing the question "who's included and who's not?" Thus we are not focusing on national identity as an important factor in nation-states' decisions about citizenship (Choe 2006: 85). We are more interested in how citizenship has been used as an incentive to attract (talented) personnel all around the world. First we shall discuss whether the "brain-drain/brain-gain" pattern of migration between developed countries that are members of the Organisation for Economic Co-operation and Development (OECD) fits with the perception of an on-going "war of talents". Second, we ask whether transnational management is actually emerging and if this process is facilitated by the open-door-policies of OECD countries. Third, we suggest an explanation for the labour migration pattern that we have found and end with some conclusions.

4.1 Boundaryless Careers for High-Skilled People? The Brain Drain/Brain Gain Pattern

From the perspective of highly qualified employees, globalization is not merely a threat, but a chance to move across borders. Compared to the restrictions that low qualified employees are facing, national migration policies have opened up the doors for experts, professionals and managers (see Dreher 2003: 18; Chalamwong 2005: 488). A fierce competition for desirable jobs with high income and status is said to be taking place, as well as a "war of talents" between nations and between companies to hire the "best brains". Professionals and managers are said to be the pacemakers for borderless careers, in a world where money, goods and people are chasing each other around the globe (cf. Appadurai 1998: 15). Thus, globalization seems to foster the mobility of a new "jet set" of professionals and the establishment of a "world class" of management. Many others are reaching out to achieve a similar way of life. Crossing borders, staying abroad and demonstrating one's flexibility become necessary as well as sought-after prerequisites for meteoric careers. An unwritten law argues that the greater the mobility, the more rapidly young talent will rise above the competition. To this end, a lot of countries have paved the way for a greater influx of highly qualified personnel, in part by providing citizenship as an incentive.

Thus, recent years have witnessed growing competition for highly skilled migrants as many OECD countries have opened their doors to workers in the sector of Information and Communication Technology (ICT), along with other highly skilled professionals (see Chalamwong 2005: 489). The globalization constellation has changed for highly qualified people. Citizenship has been used more extensively to attract top skills. But according to Chalamwong, most OECD and developed Asian countries have not introduced special measures to recruit highly skilled foreign workers. They continue to rely on their existing work-permit systems. The schemes that have been introduced invariably aim at ICT and health staff (especially care givers or nurses) and intra-company transfers for skilled workers (see ibid 515).

German students are a role model in this sense; never before in history have so many of them studied in foreign countries. Compared with other European countries, German students rank at the top in terms of mobility. As a sending country, Germany ranks fifth following China (1), India, the Republic of Korea and Japan (BMBF 2005: 9f). A year or an even longer period spent abroad appears to be a reliable jump-start to a career, not least due to language proficiency acquired along the way. Not surprisingly the number of expatriates is on the rise as well. Corporations send their employees to their foreign subsidiaries with similar intentions, thus creating a new form of migration that obviously obeys different rules compared to traditional emigration patterns (cf. Kolb et al. 2004). These different rules, rules of intensified and globalized competition, imply international and transnational career paths. Consequently, in addition to the emphasis on the role of TNCs in the world economy, the rise of "global elites" has become one of the central assumptions of mainstream globalization theories. Along with the internationalization of production chains, a transnational management seems to be emerging that is forming a new world class of business elites (see Hartmann and Kopp 2001). As described by Ulrich Beck (1997: 17), these people are able to produce their goods where costs are minimal, settle and work where life is most comfortable, and pay taxes where rates are lowest. But as elites they are also responsible for many of the decisions that shape the world's economy.

The sociology of migration has widely ignored these new movement patterns among highly qualified labour. Controversies associated with the international migration of labour are often subjected to a debate about problems of integration in recipient countries. Discussion of these problems is usually restricted to the analysis of ethnic minorities, or focuses on low skilled workers migrating between specific world regions (cf. Pries 1998: 71; 2003, 2005a, b; Kolb 2006). In the case of managers and highly skilled labour, it is assumed that a new international labour market is developing (cf. Pries 1998; Castles and Miller 1993; Rodriguez-Pose 2003). But although a new form of migration among companies has been observed, it has not been systematically taken into account. Even in the literature of business economics, where transnational strategies for transnational management are an important subject, the careers of executives have not been carefully analyzed.

To examine how the migration pattern of high skilled labour is related to the citizenship issue, we shall first discuss whether a brain drain/brain gain pattern is emerging between developed countries. According to Chalamwong, the concept of brain drain first emerged in the 1960s when it was used to describe the migration of British intellectuals and scientists to the United States. Mostly, the debate concerning brain drain has taken the perspective of the human capital approach. Chalamwong writes: "Governments invest in this human capital through training and education and expect a return on their investment when the individual becomes economically active, starts paying taxes, etc." (Chalamwong 2005: 502f). From this perspective, the migration of highly skilled human resources represents a "loss" to the sending country, which does not reap the returns on its investment in these people. The International Labour Organization (ILO) "indicates that there is considerable evidence that the average level of human capital in a society has positive effects on productivity and growth. Conversely, low levels of education resulting from high levels of skilled emigration can slow the growth rate of the economy and adversely affect those who remain" (Chalamwong 2005: 503).

Although this point of view is corroborated by statistics on the mobility of students and university graduates (cf. BMBF 2005; Han 2005: 38ff), images of warlike competition and exodus are exaggerated. Statistics of the European Union show that only 4 % (1.2 million people) of all highly skilled people in its member states are foreigners (cf. Jahr et al. 2002: 321). Jahr et al. (2002) draw the conclusion that the mobility of young European graduates is moderate and not alarming, according to a survey of 36,000 graduates, comparing 11 European countries and Japan. Of those people who graduated in their country of citizenship, 4 years later only 3 % had decided to work abroad (cf. Jahr et al. 2002: 329). For example, although German students are relatively mobile during their studies, it is a remarkable fact that their eagerness to take a job abroad is below average compared to students from other countries.

Table 4.1 Growth of the foreign-born US-population by country of birth 1995–2006

	1995	2006	Decrease/increase
Japan	358,000	235,000	−123.000
Korea	710,000	304,000	−306.000
China	690,000	1,386,000	+696,00
Germany	586,000	594,000	+8,000
England	608,000	528,000	−80,000
Italy	446,000	409,000	−37,000

Source: Migration policy institute, data hub (2007)

Table 4.2 Foreign population in the Republic of Korea by level of qualification and position

2008	Total	High qualified	Workers	Art and sports
Foreign born	531,133	29,844	496,672	4,617

Highly qualified personnel	Total	Legal	Illegal (age: 16–60)	Illegal (total)
Total	29,844	28,630	1,158	1,214
Teacher, Professor (E-1)	1,564	1,516	36	48
Language teaching (E-2)	17,970	17,408	548	562
Research (E-3)	2,231	2,139	85	92
Teaching of technology (E-4)	163	151	12	12
Professionals (E-5)	451	425	17	26
Special tasks (E-7)	7,465	6,991	460	474

All studies that have investigated a possible brain drain from Germany and selected other OECD countries to the USA concluded that it has not been of considerable magnitude. Only a few Germans have permanently settled in the US, and the size of this population has remained consistently low (approximately 0.8 % of the total German population) (cf. Table 4.1). Thus, temporary residence has prevailed as the dominant form of migration (cf. Diehl and Dixon 2005: 714ff). In the case of the Republic of Korea, there has actually been a substantial decline in the number of US residents. The only exception to this trend is the People's Republic of China, from which emigration to the US has remained high.

The share of people with a university degree and in professional or managerial positions has not changed considerably over time. Thus a brain drain is not apparent, neither in terms of population structure nor with regard to the international variance in this realm. The large-scale import of labour into Japan and Korea has been mostly restricted to low skilled workers, with only low numbers of highly qualified personnel from OECD countries (cf. Chalamwong 2005).

According to this line of research, brain drain and brain gain have a negligible role in the contemporary world economy. The easing of restrictions on Japan's migration policy has caused the foreign population to grow from 85,500 in 1992 to 154,700 in 2000 – across all qualification levels. Notwithstanding that a similar trend is visible in the Republic of Korea, but both countries still host a low proportion of foreigners: 1 % and 0.3 % respectively of their entire population.

Table 4.3 Foreign population in Japan, Republic of Korea, USA and Germany by level of qualification (2006)

| | Qualification level and origin | | | | | |
| | High | | Medium | | Low | |
	OECD	Non-OECD	OECD	Non-OECD	OECD	Non-OECD
Japan	134,132	137,675	196,569	211,291	114,217	125,330
Korea	18,406	20,982	6,866	48,887	1,445	29,478
USA	1,287,614	2,235,188	2,381,200	2,659,979	5,084,499	2,934,046
Germany (2001)	1,132,000		3,590,000		4,906,000	

Source: OECD-Data (2006)
Note: Since there was no data available for Germany in 2006, the reported numbers originate from the *Source OECD International Migration Statistics* (2001)

Most of those migrants originate from non-OECD countries such as the Philippines and China (cf. OECD Migration Report 2004). In 2006, Japan hosted 271,807 highly-skilled foreigners (134,132 from OECD countries) compared to 647,407 migrants with a low or intermediate skill level. In Korea in 2006, there were 18,406 highly skilled foreigners from OECD countries and 20,982 from non-OECD countries compared to 86,676 migrants with a low or intermediate skill level (Table 4.2).

In the USA, the numbers are greater but the proportion is similar. There are 13 million migrants with a low or intermediate skill level and more than 2.2 million highly skilled foreigners from non-OECD countries. Germany has roughly the same ratio of high-skilled to medium- and low-skilled workers (Table 4.3).

We are able to conclude that, if measured in quantitative terms, there is increased mobility in the workforce but there has not been any appreciable brain drain that might deplete necessary resources in OECD countries. Although there are serious methodological difficulties in obtaining the necessary data, the evidence is straightforward; taking up residency abroad is mainly temporary and marginal in nature. The argument that mobility may cause "brain circulation", or "brain exchange" rather than "brain drain" will more likely hold for the mobility of skilled workers among developed countries, and not among developing countries (see also Chalamwong 2005: 505). Martin (2002) points out that a new era of "brain circulation" may have begun between Asian countries and the United States.

The above analysis discussed high-skilled workers as a single group. We shall now examine whether our conclusions extend to top-management personnel.

4.2 Internationalisation of Management: "Brain Circulation"

There are two forms of internationalisation that we will subject to critical scrutiny in this section. At issue is the question of whether domestic leaders pursue their careers abroad and whether they are able to reach the top positions. But it is also contestable whether staying abroad as a student or in a leadership position is of any

Table 4.4 Foreign top managers among the board of directors of top 100 companies in China, Japan and Korea (Chaebol)

Top industrial enterprises	CEO China N = 100, 2005	CEO Japan N = 100, 2006	CEO Korea[a] N = 100, 2008
Foreigner	0	4	4
Has studied abroad	7.1 %	21.8 %	30 %
Has worked abroad ≥ 1 Y	9.1 %	40 %	43.3 %

Source: Own Research

Notes:

[a]CEO Korea: If one looks at the *chaebol* instead of solely focusing on industrial enterprises, then there are six CEOs with foreign citizenship

2. This research received the support of Isabel Burkert in the case of Japan (cf. Burkert 2007), in the case of China support came from Yuan Yuan Liu and in the case of the Republic of Korea it was Jong-Hee Lee who aided in acquiring the data

relevance to actual career paths (cf. Mense-Petermann and Wagner 2006; Klemm and Popp 2006).

According to the data of Germany's "microcensus" there is a considerable increase in the number of foreign entrepreneurs, managers and heads of department. But their overall share amounted only to 6 % in 2004 and 7.3 % in 2006 respectively. That is not as much as mainstream globalisation theories would have led us to expect, since the statistics include a multitude of foreign small and medium-sized enterprises (SME) and executives who had a temporary assignment in an SME in a foreign country. And even in the top ranks of German companies the picture does not change, according to the data from Michael Hartmann's studies. He reports (Hartmann 2007a: 59) similarly low percentages of foreign personnel in top management positions. In between 1995 and 2005, the absolute number of foreign top managers in Germany's top 100 companies has risen from 2 to 9, but many of those come from neighbouring Austria or Switzerland. There are no British or US-American citizens at the top of a German company. And the 10 % of foreign citizens among the 416 board members in 2005 had usually remained in the corporation after a takeover (cf. Hartmann 2007a: 59f).

If one is to assume a global market for top managers, the German segment is typical in international comparison. The share of foreign top managers in France's 100 biggest enterprises has remained steady at 2 % between 1995 and 2005. In the case of the USA, according to Hartmann, only 5 % of CEOs have been raised abroad (cf. Hartmann 2007b). The SpencerStuart CEO-report counts 16 foreign CEOs in the USA's 100 biggest enterprises in 2008. Surveying East Asian countries produces similar results, in some cases with even lower shares of foreign personnel than in German companies (Table 4.4). The results seem pretty homogenous, the only exception in the sample being the case of Great Britain with a remarkable rate of foreign top managers amounting to 20 %. However, this portion consists mostly of people from Commonwealth countries.

On the Chinese mainland the top 100 industrial enterprises are by and large state-owned. Roughly 76 % of these enterprises have a CEO who is at the same time board member of an important subcommittee of the communist party. That is one of the reasons why foreign personnel cannot be selected for these positions. In Korean *chaebol*, the influence of family clans prevails and secures their dominion of the companies' boards by building informal networks between formally autonomous enterprises. Measures of the International Monetary Fund (IMF) introduced in the wake of the Asian financial crisis in the late 1990s have been quite unable to change this fact. And similarly in Japan the modernization of industrial consortiums has not led to the assignment of international personnel to top domestic positions.

With regard to middle management, our case studies of German industrial companies show the same pattern as reported above. So-called "inpatriates", the residing foreigners, are largely employed as professionals, not as executives. In our case studies we found a quota effectively ranging from 4 % to 6 % of inpatriates in middle and upper management positions. Once again these people come to a great extent from EU countries, especially from Austria and Switzerland. Thus, considering middle management positions there are no signs of an international market for executives of any significant proportion or of any relevance to career paths. Preliminary data gathered from case studies in the U.S. chemical industry show a quota of foreign citizenship in senior management positions of approximately 8 %. 2 out of 25 senior managers in the sample had actually moved to the U.S. According to our case studies of big business conglomerates in Korea, they have established think tanks that include international talents with staff functions, but those recruited from abroad remain outside the line organisation (cf. Pohlmann 2002). The same applies to Japanese consortiums.

These findings lead to the conclusion that that national career patterns prevail with regard to top managerial positions. There is little reason to believe in the significance of either brain drain or brain gain. Our data is consistent with the idea that the internationalisation of management is a matter of brain circulation, which is to say: temporary residency abroad. In terms of international student exchanges between universities and the number of expatriates sent abroad, a substantial rise can be seen both in numbers and in importance for national career paths (cf. Diehl and Dixon 2005: 715f). This also holds true for the cases of Japan and Korea. Studying or working abroad is a means of internationalising one's career profile.

Hence, the chances of staying abroad are limited. A longer duration bears risks of missing important domestic opportunities, especially of missing opportunities for advancement in the national domain. Thus, in view of the descriptive data above, the main mechanism of internationalisation is a temporary assignment.

4.3 Domestic Careers Instead of International Markets

The picture that mainstream globalisation theories suggest is an exaggeration of actual results regarding the internationalisation of management. Although management experiences in a foreign country gain in relevance, the majority of careers are pursued exclusively in the national domain. An international executives' market

Table 4.5 Domestic careers of CEOs in top 100 industrial enterprises in China, Japan and Korea

Industrial enterprises	CEO China N = 100, 2005	CEO Japan N = 100, 2006	CEO Korea N = 100, 2008
Domestic careers	81.8 %	79.2 %	74 %
Job tenure	18.7 years	27 years	24.7 years
Age	55.3 years	62.7 years	59.7 years

Source: Own Research
Notes:
1. CEO Korea: The data refer to the total top 100 consortiums in the Republic of Korea
2. This research received the support of Isabel Burkert in the case of Japan (cf. Burkert 2007), in the case of China support came from YuanYuan Liu and in the case of the Republic of Korea it was Jong-Hee Lee who aided in acquiring the data

among OECD countries has yet to be established. The reason for this is that in all three world regions under scrutiny, there is a strong preference for domestic careers.

Whereas in Germany their relevance is lowest, accounting for roughly half of all CEO positions in 2005 (cf. Hartmann 2007a), data from Spencer Stuart show that in more than 80 % of all cases newly appointed CEOs in the top 500 U.S. companies were "insiders" in 2008. Such domestic careers are absolutely predominant in East Asia, accounting for roughly 74–82 % of all career paths (Table 4.5).

Especially in Japan and South Korea, averages for age as well as for job tenure of CEOs exceed even high expectations. Reforms and restructuring were not able to change such a clear preference for insiders. The recruitment of outsiders to an extent as in Germany is exceptional in international comparison. But if conglomerates recruit outsiders their selection favours the candidates of dominant coalitions and networks, according to our research. Thus, neither external nor the internal labour markets of organizations can account for these decisions.

The hypothesis that a new transnational management has emerged cannot be sustained by our empirical findings. Citizenship neither works as an incentive for the high skilled workers of OECD countries nor for the economic elites of developed countries, yet. The "war of talents", fought with "open door" migration policies on international markets is an exaggerated as well as misleading depiction, if not a myth, of mainstream globalization theories.

4.4   Conclusions

Does globalisation lead to global markets for managers and international careers? The hypothesis of the globalisation literature that a transnational management is emerging out of a global "war of talents" was examined in this article by using data on the migration of managers from the U.S., East Asia and Germany. The data show that no significant brain drain between these countries is taking place; "brain circulation" of insiders with short-term stays abroad is the dominant career pattern. The less likely the exchange of an installed CEO, the more the career systems are used for status achievement by clans, and the stronger the influence of informal cultural rules, the higher the rate of insiders. Thus, between the U.S., Germany and East Asia no significant global markets for managers have evolved as yet.

The open-door policies of nation-states do not change that picture. Citizenship does not work as an incentive. It cannot attract talented people all round the world because they still face substantial disadvantages by continuing their careers abroad. The underlying career systems within specific firms and the role of internal labour markets for high-skilled personnel have not changed in line with the expectations of the globalisation literature. To deal with global issues inside and outside of those groups of globally operating firms makes it even more necessary to rely on trust, loyalty and informal cultural rules inside a firm's networks. Thus, globalisation is fostering the importance of insider career systems for global firms' recruiting practices instead of opening them up to outsiders.

Endnotes

[1]Attribution and acquisition of citizenship are structured according to two principles: *jus soli* (the conferral of citizenship on persons born in the state's territory, or soil) and *jus sanguinis* (the conferral of citizenship on persons with a citizen parent or parents, viz. by blood). Most nation-states base their citizenship laws on a combination of *jus soli* and *jus sanguinis* (see Gilbertson 2006).

References

Appadurai, Arjun. 1998. "Globale ethnische Räume. Bemerkungen und Fragen zur Entwicklung einer transnationalen Anthropologie". In *Perspektiven der Weltgesellschaft*, Ed. Ulrich Beck, 11–39. Frankfurt/M.: Suhrkamp.

Beck, Ulrich. 1997. Was ist Globalisierung?. Frankfurt/M.: Suhrkamp

Bundesministerium für Bildung und Forschung (BMBF). 2005. *Internationalisierung des Studiums: Ausländische Studierende in Deutschland, Deutsche Studierende im Ausland.* Bonn, Berlin: BMBF.

Bundesamt für Migration und Flüchtlinge (ed.). 2008. *Ausländerzahlen 2008.* Nürnberg: Bundesamt für Migration und Flüchtlinge.

Bundesanstalt für Arbeit (ed.). 2002. Jahresbericht 2002: *Die berufliche Situation von jugendlichen und erwachsenen Migranten in Deutschland.* Nürnberg: Bundesanstalt für Arbeit.

Burkert, Isabel. 2007. "Die ökonomische Elite Japans – eine Untersuchung der Rekrutierungsmechanismen der Inhaber wirtschaftlicher Spitzenpositionen". Magisterarbeit im Fach Soziologie, Heidelberg: Universität Heidelberg.

Castles, S. and Miller, M.J. 1993. *The age of migration: international population movements in the modern world.* London: Macmillan.

Chalamwong, Yongyuth. 2005. "The Migration of Highly Skilled Asian Workers to OECD Member Countries and its Effects on Economic Development in East Asia". In *Policy Coherence Towards East Asia, Development Challenges für OECD Countries, Development*

Center Studies, Ed. Kiichiro Fukasaku, Masahiro Kawai; Michael G. Plummer and Alexandra Trzeciak-Duval, 487–526. Paris: OECD.

Castles, Stephen, and Mark Miller. 2009. *The Age of Migration. International Population Movements in the Modern World*, 4th ed. Basingstoke, London: Macmillan Press.

Choe, Hyun. 2006. "South Korean Citizenship: The Institutional Changes since 1987 and their Effects on Citizen's Consciousness (in Korean)". In *Democracy and Human Rights* 4, 172–205.

Deutschland Statistisches Bundesamt (ed.). 2006. *Datenreport*. Wiesbaden: Statistisches Bundesamt.

Deutschland Statistisches Bundesamt (ed.). 2006. *Strukturdaten zur Migration in Deutschland*. Wiesbaden: Statistisches Bundesamt.

Diehl, Claudia, and David Dixon. 2005. "Zieht es die Besten fort? Ausmaß und Formen der Abwanderung deutscher Hochqualifizierter in die USA". *Kölner Zeitschrift für Soziologie und Sozialpsychologie* 57, 714–734.

Dreher, Sabine. 2003. "Vom Wohlfahrtsstaat zum Wettbewerbsstaat? Die Bedeutung der Migration für die Globalisierungsdebatte". In *Migration im Wettbewerbsstaat*. Ed. Uwe Hunger und Bernhard Santel, 13–32. Opladen: Leske + Budrich.

Gilbertson, Greta. 2006. *Citizenship in a Globalized World, Migration Information Service*. Washington: Migration Policy Institute.

Han, Petrus. 2005. *Soziologie der Migration*. 2nd ed. Stuttgart. Lucius & Lucius/UTB.

Hartmann, Michael, and Johannes Kopp. 2001. "Elitenselektion durch Bildung oder durch Herkunft?" *Promotion, soziale Herkunft und der Zugang zu Führungspositionen in der deutschen Wirtschaft, in: Kölner Zeitschrift für Soziologie und Sozialpsychologie* 53, 436–466.

Hartmann, Michael. 2007a. Soziale Selektion, Hauskarrieren und geringe Internationalisierung. *Personalführung* 1, 54–62.

Hartmann, M. 2007b. *Eliten und Macht in Europa – Ein internationaler Vergleich*. Frankfurt/M., New York: Campus.

Jacobson, David. 1997. *Right across Borders: Immigration and the Decline of Citizenship*. Baltimore: The Johns

Jahr, Volker et al. 2002. "Mobilität von Hochschulabsolventen und –absolventinnen in Europa". In *Arbeitsmärkte für Hochqualifizierte, Beiträge zur Arbeitsmarkt und Berufsforschung, BeitrAB 256, IAB der Bundesanstalt für Arbeit*, Ed. Lutz Bellmann und Johannes Velling. Nürnberg.

Kolb, Holger et al. 2004. "Recruitment and Migration in the ICT Sector". In *Organisational Recruitment and Patterns of Migration. Interdependencies in an Integrating Europe*, Eds. Michael et al., 147–177. Osnabrück: IMIS-Beiträge.

Kolb, Holger. 2006. "Internationale Mobilität von Hochqualifizierten – (k)ein Thema für die Migrationsforschung". In *Neue Zuwanderergruppen in Deutschland*, Ed. Frank Swiaczny und Sonja Haug. 159–174. BIB Materialien zur Bevölkerungswissenschaften 118: Wiesbaden.

Klemm, M., und M. Popp. 2006. "Nomaden wider Willen: Der Expatriate als Handlungstypus zwischen Alltagswelt und objektiver Zweckbestimmung". In *Wissensformen und Denkstile der Gegenwart*, Eds. W. Gebhardt, W. und R. Hitzler, 126–139. Wiesbaden: VS Verlag.

Kymlicka, Will, and Wayne Norman. 1995. "Return of the Citizen: A Survey of Recent Work on Citizenship Theory". In *Theorizing Citizenship*, Ed. R. Beiner Albany. New York: State University of New York Press.

Martin, P.H. 2002. Highly skilled Asian workers in the US. Paper prepared for the Workshop on International Migration of Highly Skilled Workers: Its Current. Situation, Problems and Future Prospects in Asia, Tokyo, 4–5 February.

Mense-Petermann, Ursula, and Gabriele Wagner (ed.). 2006. *Transnationale Konzerne: Ein neuer Organisationstyp?* Wiesbaden: VS Verlag.

Papademetriou, Demetrios G. 2007. *The Age of Mobility. How to Get More Out of Migration in the 21st century*. Migration Policy Institute.

Pohlmann, Markus. 2002. *Der Kapitalismus in Ostasien. Südkoreas und Taiwans Wege ins Zentrum der Weltwirtschaft*. Münster: Westfälisches Dampfboot.

Pohlmann, Markus. 2004. "Die Entwicklung des Kapitalismus in Ostasien und die Lehren aus der asiatischen Finanzkrise". *Leviathan* 3.

Pries, Ludger. 1998. "Transnationale soziale Räume". In *Perspektiven der Weltgesellschaft*, Ed. Ulrich Beck, 55–88. Frankfurt/M.: Suhrkamp.

Pries, Ludger. 2003. "Gespaltene Migration – gespaltene Gesellschaft? Migranten-Inkorporation in Zeiten der Transnationalisierung". In Gespaltene Migration, Eds. Wolfgang Schröer and Stephan Sting, 111–126. Opladen: Leske + Budrich.

Pries, Ludger. 2005a. "Migration und transnationale Oekonomie". In *Projekt Migration*, Eds. Kathrin Rhomberg and Marion von Osten. Köln: Kölnischer Kunstverein.

Pries, Ludger 2005b. "Arbeitsmigration und Inkorporationsmuster in Europa". In *Zwischen den Welten und amtlichen Zuschreibungen. Neue Formen und Herausforderungen der Arbeitsmigration im 21. Jahrhundert*, Ed. Ludger Pries, 15–41. Essen: Klartext.

Rodriguez-Pose, Andrés. 2003. *The European Union. Economy, Society, and Polity*. Oxford: University Press.

Seol, Dong-Hoon. 2005. "Comparative Analysis of the Foreign Labour Policy in Japan and Korea". *The Korean Journal for Japanese Studies* 21, 201–317.

Soysal, Yasemin Nohoglu. 1994. *Limits of Citizenship: Migrant and Postnational Membership in Europe*. Chicago: University of Chicago Press.

Chapter 5
A Comparative Analysis of Foreign Workers and Citizenship in Korea and Germany

Jong-Hee Lee

Abstract The number of foreign workers has increased in both Korea and Germany as part of globalization, and there has been a liberalization of the concept of citizenship. Korea and Germany have maintained the tradition of nation-states based upon ethnic and racial homogeneity. With respect to citizenship, these two countries are comparable and have cross-case validity in that both of them have accepted immigrant workers on short-term contracts. Both countries actively provide incentives to attract foreign professionals, while the "return home" policy towards unskilled workers is closer to exploitation. Korea gives priority to the employment of Koreans, and Germany does so to citizens of the European Union. In this respect they are similar, with each country importing a minimum number of foreign workers based on the principle of complementarity in the labor market. There are also several important differences between the two countries. This paper seeks to analyze migrant worker policy and institutions and the characteristics of foreign workers' civic status in Korea and Germany. Chapters 2 and 3 analyze the history and current status of foreign workers in Korea and Germany, respectively. Chapter 4 conducts a comparative analysis of foreign workers and citizenship in Korea and Germany. Chapter 5 draws lessons from the example of Germany that may benefit Korean immigration policy.

This paper is an edited version of an article published in *Zeitschrift der koreanisch-deutsche Gesellschaft für Sozialwissenschaften* 20(4) (Winter 2010). I would like to thank Dr. Christoper Fiorillo for comments on the manuscript.

J.-H. Lee (✉)
National Election Broadcasting Debate Commission, 17, Backjae-gil, Gwanak-gu, 23, Nam-bu sun-hwan-ro 272 gil, Gwan-ak-gu, Seoul 151-800, Korea

Silim-ro 58 ga gil 64-3(601), Gwan-ak-gu, Seoul 151-015, Korea
e-mail: doreaner@hanmail.net

M. Pohlmann et al. (eds.), *Citizenship and Migration in the Era of Globalization*, Transcultural Research – Heidelberg Studies on Asia and Europe in a Global Context, DOI 10.1007/978-3-642-19739-0_5, © Springer-Verlag Berlin Heidelberg 2013

5.1 Introduction

Korea has undergone dramatic social changes in the age of information and globalization, including a rapid increase in the number of foreign workers, from 6,000 in 1987 to 6,000,000 in 2009. In this respect, Korea resembles the Germany of a few decades ago. Germany encouraged the entry of foreign workers in order to promote its industrial and economic development after the Second World War. Accordingly, the number of foreign workers was around 630,000 in 1962 (3.1 % among total employees) and skyrocketed to 2.6 million in 1972 (10.5 % of the total work force).

But economic recession led to rising unemployment in the early 1970s, causing the German government to stop importing foreign labor in 1973. This policy is still effective today. However, through an exemption clause aimed at filling the manpower gap in specific types of jobs, some foreign workers are still admitted into Germany. For example, seasonal workers and factory-contract workers are included in the exemption (ASAV for Anwerbestoppausnahmeverordnung in German). As of 2008, 8.8 % of the German population is foreign.

Globalizaiton brought with it a change in the concept of citizenship, which in the past was closely connected to the nation-state. Soysal (1994) predicted that the emergence of post-national citizenship will replace the traditional nation-based citizenship. Jacobson (1997) also predicted the diminishing importance of citizenship related to nationality.

According to Kymlicka and Norman (1995: 284), citizenship describes both a legal status and a desirable involvement in one's community. Citizenship is an important concept in contemporary democratic thought and in institutions dealing with the relationship between citizens and between the citizen and the state. Citizenship often refers to civic status guaranteed by the community and including civic rights and responsibilities. It can also be defined as civic consciousness, civic virtue, and civic participation (Choe 2006; Klusmeyer 2001).

There are conflicting predictions about the influence of international labor turnover and globalization on citizenship. Some scholars (Joppke 1998; Soysal 1994; Jacobson 1997; Hollifield 1992) argue that globalization weakens the nation-state. They predict that phenomena such as international labor turnover will cause many nations to become multi-ethnic societies, and that as a result, those nations will no longer form a culturally homogeneous community. However, Brubaker (1992, 1994) argues that citizenship will not be greatly changed in spite of globalization and mass immigration in that citizenship has a close relationship with national identity. Foreigners' residence status and citizenship are emerging as social issues, because an increasing number of immigrant workers become permanent residents.

Korea and Germany have maintained the tradition of nation-states based upon ethnic and racial homogeneity. With respect to citizenship, these two countries secure equivalence in comparative research and cross cases validity in that both of them have accepted immigrant workers on short-term contracts while maintaining a Principle of Nationality Act based on jus sanguinis.

This paper seeks to analyze migrant worker policy and institutions and the characteristics of foreign workers' civic status in Korea and Germany. Chapters 2 and 3 analyze the history and current status of foreign workers in Korea and Germany, respectively. Chapter 4 conducts a comparative analysis of foreign workers and citizenship in Korea and Germany. Chapter 5 draws suggestions from Germany's policy of foreign immigrant assimilation that may be applied to Korea because the history of immigrant workers in Germany is longer than that of Korea.

5.2   The Employment System for Foreign Workers in Korea

As of December 2008, the total number of foreigners working in Korea amounted to 1.16 million. These included about 559,000 Chinese, 121,000 Americans, 90,000 Vietnamese, and 46,000 Filipinos. Among them, over 177,955 were illegally living in the country (15.2 % of all foreigners) (Fig. 5.1).

There was an increasing demand for foreign workers in Korea to fill the manpower shortage in low-wage unskilled sectors as the Korean economy went through structural and social changes. A small number of foreign workers came to Korea in the mid-1980s, and in 1987, there were about 6,000. But the number of foreign workers skyrocketed to 600,000 in 2009. Among them, most were unskilled laborers (508,436) (Table 5.1).

In terms of their status, 307,329 (57 %) were in the visit-cum-employment category, with unskilled employees numbering 183,997 (33 %). The rest were composed of foreign language teachers (22,723, 4 %), trainee-cum-employment workers (12,393, 2 %) and others (22,840, 4 %) (Fig. 5.2).

The percentage of unregistered foreign workers in Korea is very high. This suggests that their working conditions are likely to be poor compared with those of average workers, and even their basic human rights may be at risk. Indeed, beyond poor working conditions (including excessive working hours), abuses such as wage arrears, beatings, imprisonment, and confiscation of ID cards have led to a serious breach of the basic human rights of guest workers in Korea.

This was reformed through an employment permit system, which was introduced in 2004 at the request of non-governmental organizations. The permit system regards foreign workers as employees in order to guarantee their basic rights. From 2007 onwards, the industrial trainee system was abolished and replaced entirely by the employment permit system (Table 5.2).

There have been four distinct policies for dealing with the employment of foreign workers in Korea since 1990: an industrial trainee system for Korean companies that invest in foreign countries, a modified and expanded industrial trainee system, a trainee-cum-employment system, and now an employment permit system.

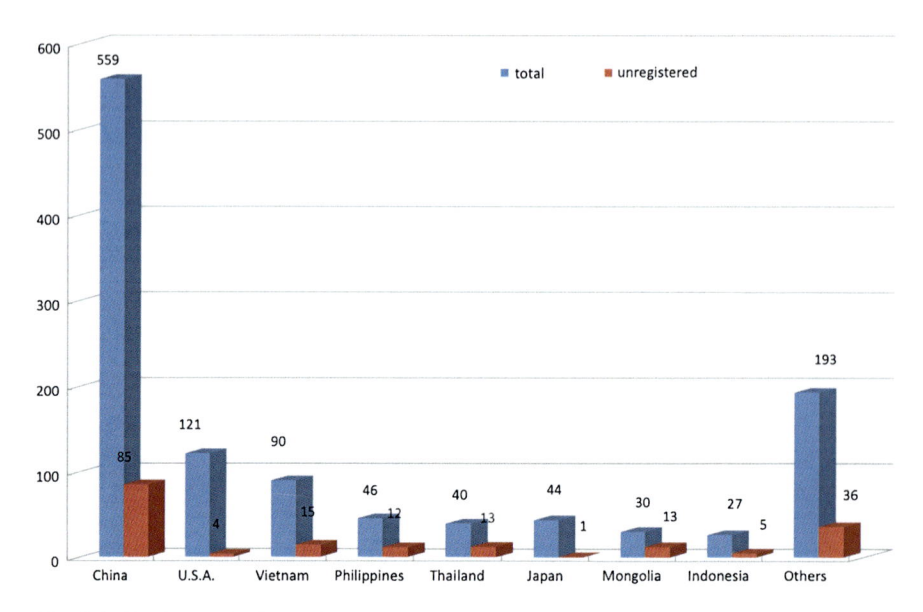

Fig. 5.1 Foreigners in Korea by nationality year 2008 (in thousands) (Source: http://www.immigration.go.kr (accessed 23 January 2010))

Table 5.1 Total foreign workers in Korea as of December 2009

Classification		Total number of foreign workers	Professional	Unskilled laborers
Total		549,282	40,846	508,436
Legal residents		499,635	38,635	461,000
Unregistered foreign workers	(age: 16–60)	47,260	2,182	45,078
	Total	49,647	2,211	47,436

Source: http://www.immigration.go.kr (accessed 23 January 2010)

In November 1991, the government initiated an industrial trainee system for Korean companies which invested in foreign countries. Trainees were allowed to stay in Korea for up to 6 months, with the possibility of an extension for another 6 months. In addition to transferring technical expertise, it also enabled firms to utilize foreign labor to fill the shortage of Korean workers (Yoo et al. 2004: 5).

The industrial trainee system was expanded in 1993, increasing the number of types of industry that could employ foreign workers from 10 to 21, and increasing the maximum period of training from 1 to 3 years. The Ministry of Labor was charged with directing and supervising working conditions among guest workers. Under this industrial trainee system, foreign workers were deemed to be interns rather than regular employees. Therefore, their human and other rights were a major issue.

The introduction of the trainee-cum-employment system in 1998 allowed trainees who went through a 2-year industrial internship to receive certification and to become normal workers. But this system still had the shortcomings of the

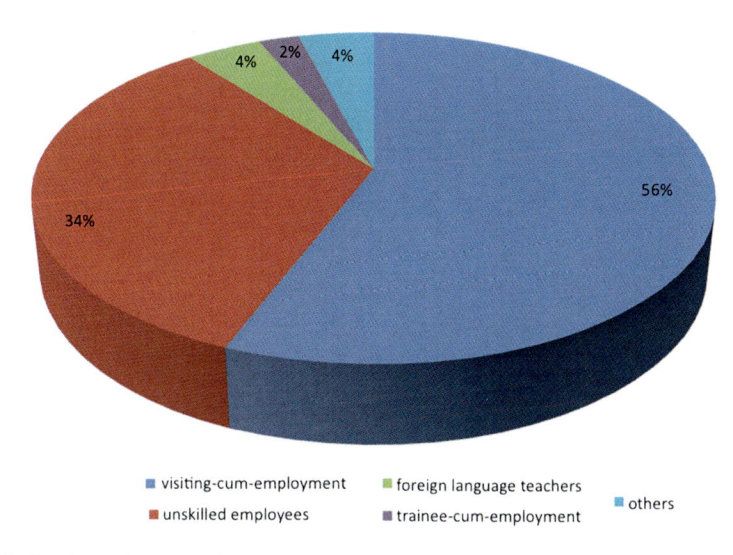

Fig. 5.2 Foreigners in terms of their status, December 2009 (Source: http://www.immigration.go. kr (accessed 23 January 2010))

previous industrial traineeship system. Revised in 2001 and 2002, the system was modified to allow 1 year of traineeship followed by 2 years of employment. The Policy Deliberative Committee of Foreign Industrial Manpower was given the authority to select the countries from which foreign workers would be allowed, and to set quotas restricting the number of workers from each country. The Committee was also charged with limited oversight of the agencies which sent and received trainees. In addition, the Committee was to estimate the number of illegal workers and to take this number into consideration in determining the next year's quotas. The system provided ethnic Koreans (mostly from China) with the status of workers, allowing them to work in service industries.

The current employment permit system allows the employers to hire foreigners and thus enables the workers to apply for visas. Differences between the industrial trainee system and the employment permit system involve the status of workers. The employment permit system recognizes foreigners as workers, not as trainees. It also restricts the involvement of private agencies in managing foreign workers. Finally, in contrast to previous policies, the employment permit system explicitly gives priority to the employment of Korean workers. Thus the number of foreign workers is kept to a minimum (Table 5.3).

Visit-cum-employment is targeted at ethnic Koreans living in China and the former Soviet Union. Visit-cum-employment (H-2) status allows visitors to seek employment, and it streamlines the employment procedures that are required of the employers. Visas for visit-cum-employment are valid for up to 5 years and allow multiple visits to Korea. Once in Korea, visa-holders can work there for up to 3 years.

Table 5.2 Foreigners in terms of their status since 1987

| | | Legal residents | | | | | | | |
| | | Holders with employment visas | | | | Industrial trainee | | |
Year	Total	Total	Professionals	Unskilled labourers	Trainee-cum-employment	Sailors in Korean waters	Those recommended by the industry	Industrial trainees from Korean companies investing	Unregistered foreign workers
1987	6,409	2,192	2,192	0	0	0	0	0	4,217
1988	7,410	2,403	2,403	0	0	0	0	0	5,007
1989	4,610	2,474	2,474	0	0	0	0	0	12,136
1990	1,235	2,833	2,833	0	0	0	0	0	18,402
1991	45,449	3,572	2,973	0	0	0	0	599	41,877
1992	43,664	2,765	3,395	0	0	0	3,932	5,438	30,899
1993	8,500	3,992	3,767	0	0	0	3,759	6,466	54,508
1994	1,824	3,593	5,265	0	0	0	18,816	9,512	48,231
1995	128,906	7,040	8,228	0	0	0	23,574	15,238	81,866
1996	210,494	81,440	13,420	0	0	0	38,296	29,724	129,054
1997	245,399	97,351	15,900	0	0	0	48,795	32,656	148,048
1998	157,689	58,152	11,143	0	0	0	31,073	15,936	99,537
1999	217,384	82,046	12,592	0	0	0	49,437	20,017	135,338
2000	285,506	96,511	17,000		2,063	0	58,944	18,504	188,995
2001	329,555	74,349	19,549	0	8,065	0	33,230	13,505	255,206
2002	362,597	73,358	21,506	0	12,191	0	25,626	14,035	289,239
2003	388,816	250,760	20,089	159,706	20,244	0	38,895	11,826	138,056
2004	420,702	232,219	20,272	126,421	48,937	34	28,125	8,430	188,483
2005	345,911	165,119	23,609	52,305	50,703	212	32,148	6,142	180,792
2006	423,481	195,569	27,221	113,524	54,517	307	38,187	5,831	186,894

Source: Seol (2007: 389)

Note: (1) Professionals refers to professors, foreign language teachers, technical experts, people in the entertainment field and visa holders with specific occupations

(2) Industrial trainees recommended by industrial organizations, including the Korean Federation of Small and Medium Business, the Construction Association of Korea, the National Federation of Fisheries Cooperatives, and the Korean Agricultural Cooperatives. Industrial trainees recommended by the industry were referred to the Ministry of Industry and Commerce

(3) Illegal migrant workers do not include the economically inactive (below age 15 and above age 61)

(4) Starting month in each year is December

Table 5.3 Qualitative comparison between the two systems

Classification	Industrial trainee system	Employment permit system
Status of foreign workers	Trainees, not workers	Workers
Introduction and management	Private employers organization	State or public agencies
Quota system	Compulsory	Employer's choice of foreigners and work contract
Priority of hiring Koreans	None	Yes

Source: Yoo et al. p. 14

There are two additional features of Korea's policy towards migrant labor that should be noted. First, the recruitment and management of foreign workers is based on bilateral agreements between Korea and a number of other countries. Second, Korea has an open door policy on skilled foreign workers. But unskilled workers must return to their native countries, and the Korean government then allows another pool of foreigners to be hired.

5.3 The Employment System for Foreign Workers in Germany

Germany began to accept foreign workers at the close of the 1880s due to industrialization and shortage of manpower. Approximately more than 1.2 million seasonal foreign immigrant workers filled labor shortages in Germany before World War I. Polish people occupied one of the biggest foreign groups in Germany pre-1914. In those days, the German government permitted foreign workers' employment in Germany, but it did not allow them permanent residence in Germany or naturalization as Germans (Oltmer 2005). The German government imposed forced labor on foreign workers during World War I. Foreign forced laborers likewise played a part in taking the place of German male labor during World War II. The German government also adopted a policy of having a great many German people emigrate to Middle and Eastern Europe (Oltmer 2005).

Foreign workers began arriving in West Germany in large numbers in the 1960s, in order to promote its industrial and economic development after the Second World War.

Germany accepted foreigners through a work permit system, and limited the stay of workers by limiting their period of employment.

Migrant workers were recruited mainly from a number of countries in southern Europe. The number of foreign workers was around 630,000 in 1962 (3.1 % of the total labor force) and had increased to 2.6 million by 1972 (10.5 % of the total labor force) (Table 5.4).

The German government stopped the import of foreign labor in 1973 at the onset of a worldwide recession. This policy is still in effect today. However, through an exemption clause aimed at filling the manpower gap in specific types of jobs, some foreign workers are still admitted into Germany.

Table 5.4 Number of foreign workers in Germany (1962–1972)

Year	Number of foreign workers	Percentage of foreign workers among total employees
1962	629,022	3.1
1963	773,164	3.7
1964	902,459	4.3
1965	1,118,616	5.3
1966	1,243,961	5.8
1967	1,013,862	4.7
1968	1,018,859	4.9
1969	1,365,635	6.5
1970	1,806,805	8.6
1971	2,128,407	9.8
1972	2,284,502	10.5

Source: http://www.auslaender-statistik.de/bund/gast_1.htm (accessed 20 January 2010)

Many foreign workers have opted to remain in Germany and subsequently brought their families there to live. As a result, and owing to higher birth rates, the foreign population in Germany has increased substantially. As of 2005, the number of recent immigrants and their families totaled 15.3 million, about 19 % of the total population.

According to 2005 statistics, 14.8 million people (approximately 96 %) of immigrants live in the former West German area and Berlin. The proportion of immigrants is particularly high in big cities, such as Stuttgart (40 %), Frankfurt (39.5 %) and Nuremberg (37 %). The proportion of immigrants is even higher among children, with approximately a third of children under the age of 5 coming from immigrant families (Bundesamt für Migration und Flüchtlinge (ed.) 2005). And again, the proportions are higher in some large cities (Nuremberg 67 %, Frankfurt 65 %, Düsseldorf 64 % and Stuttgart 64 %).

As of 2008, there were 6.73 million foreigners in Germany (excluding ethnic German immigrants) (Table 5.5). Of these, 24.3 % were citizens from the 14 long-standing member states of the EU. Another 10.7 % were citizens of countries that joined the EU since 2004. The other 65.0 % were from non-EU countries (Table 5.6).

Turks made up the largest group (1.7 million), followed by immigrants from Italy (528,000), from the former Yugoslavia (330,000), Poles (260,000), Greeks (294,000), and Croatians (225,000) (Table 5.7).

According to the 2007 statistics, foreigners who stay for more than 20 years, more than 10 years, and more than 5 years accounted for 35.4 %, 64.5 %, and 49.4 % respectively, of all foreigners in Germany. The average length of a foreigner's stay in Germany is 17.7 years.

The number of workers with work permits has declined since 2002. However, this simply reflects revised immigration laws that allow citizens of the EU to work without a permit (Table 5.8).

Foreigners are required to obtain a residence and work permit before they are allowed to work in Germany. However, an exception is made for nationals of the long-standing EU member states, who can work freely in Germany without

Table 5.5 Number of foreigners and the total population in Germany (1951–2008)

Year	Population in Germany	Foreigners total	Percentage of foreigners in the German population
1951	50,808,900	506,000	1.0
1961	56,174,800	686,200	1.2
1970	61,001,164	2,737.905	4.5
1980	61,657,945	4,566,167	7.4
1990	79,753,227	5,582,357	7.0
2000	82,259,540	7,267,568	8.9
2001	82,440,309	7,318,263	8.9
2002	82,536,680	7,347,951	8.9
2003	82,531,671	7,341,820	8.9
2004	82,500,849	7,289,980	8.8
2005	82,437,995	7,389,149	8.8
2006	82,314,906	7,255,949	8.8
2007	82,217,837	7,255,395	8.8
2008	82,098,534	7,246,558	8.8

Source: Bundesamt für Migration und Flüchtlinge (Ed.) (2008: 4–5)

Table 5.6 Foreigners in Germany and their country of origin (2008)

Total	6,727,618	100 %
Old EU member states	1,638,110	24.3
New EU member states (joined the EU since 1 May 2004)	575,039	8.5
New EU member states (joined the EU since 1 January 2007)	148,310	2.2
Non-EU countries	4,366,159	65.0

Source: Bundesamt für Migration und Flüchtlinge (Ed.) (2008: 10)

Table 5.7 Foreigners in Germany and their country of origin (person, %, 31.12.2007)

Total	6,755,811	100 %
Turkey	1,713,551	25.4
Italy	528,318	7.8
Poland	384,808	5.7
Serbia and Montenegro (former Yugoslavia)	330,608	4.9
Greece	294,891	4.4
Croatia	225,309	3.3
EU Countries except Italy, Greece and Poland	1,128,130	16.7
Other countries	2,139, 264	31.7

Source: Bundesamt für Migration und Flüchtlinge (Ed.) (2008: 8)

residence or work permits. Citizens of newer EU member states[1] still do need work permits (although this requirement is only intended to apply during a transition period). These countries include the Czech Republic, Estonia, Latvia, Lithuania, Hungary, Poland, Slovenia and Slovakia, all of which joined the EU in May 2004, and Romania and Bulgaria, which joined in 2007. Although Malta and Cyprus

Table 5.8 Status of foreign workers who receive a work permit (unit: person)

	2002	2003	2004[a]	2004[b]	2005	2006
Total	945,073	886,386	873,470	497,298	364,069	284,139
Initial recipient	529,581	502,725	503,485	333,482	291,794	251,043
Those who extended	197,498	182,575	173,909	102,390	52,027	23,757
Already received	217,994	201,086	196,076	61,426	20,248	9,339
Declined	48,182	44,126	42,890		6,253	7,684

Source: Bundesagentur für Arbeit (Ed.) (2006: 40)
Note:
(1) 2004[a] and 2004[b] resulted from the revision of the immigration laws in 2005
(2) Starting January 2005, rules relating to work permit for the nationals of the EU were revised

joined the EU in 2004, their citizens do not need permits to work in Germany (Bundesagentur für Arbeit 2006: 33).

Since 1973, the policy of the German government has been to restrict the import of foreign labor to specific areas in which German labor is deemed insufficient. However, there are four exemptions to the ban on foreign labor (as specified in the ASAV, or Anwerbestoppausnahmeverordnung in German). One is for seasonal work in sectors such as farming in which demand for labor rises sharply for a few months each year. Also covered by this exemption are workers in the entertainment sector (Schaustellergehilfe). Foreign seasonal and entertainment workers are allowed to work for no more than 4 months per year.

A second exemption is for factory-contract workers (Werkvertragsar-beitnehmer). Germany has an agreement with 13 central and eastern European countries[2] that allows foreign companies in partnership with German firms to employ a limited number of foreign workers in Germany.

A third category of exemption is for "guest" workers (Gastarbeitnehmer). Germany has an agreement with 10 EU states plus Albania, Russia, and Croatia that allows workers from these countries to stay 18 months as industrial trainees or students learning the German language.

The fourth type of exemption is intended to fill a shortage of personnel in the information technology (IT) sector. For this purpose, in 2000 the government introduced the Green Card system ("Green-Card-Verordnung"). Foreigners with a Green Card can initially stay up to 5 years. Obtaining a Green Card requires a university degree in the IT sector and proof of annual income of at least 51,000 euros.

5.4 Comparison of Citizenship Between Korea and Germany

There are a number of similarities between the immigration policies of Germany and Korea. In both cases, foreigners must have a visa, residence permit or work permit. While each county actively encourages foreign professionals to stay, they have a 'return-home policy' for unskilled workers in the manufacturing sector.

Table 5.9 Number of naturalized citizens in Germany and Korea (1996–2005)

Year	Naturalized citizens		Percentage of naturalized foreigners	
	Germany	Korea	Germany	Korea
1996	86,356	1,439	1.2	1.0
1997	82,913	2,069	1.1	1.2
1998	106,790	1,409	1.4	1.0
1999	142,670	1,076	2.0	0.6
2000	186,688	646	2.5	0.3
2001	178,098	1,650	2.4	0.7
2002	154,547	3,883	2.1	1.5
2003	140,731	7,734	1.9	1.8
2004	127,153	9,262	1.9	2.0
2005	117,241	16,974	1.6	3.5

Source: Seol (2007: 402)
Note: The percentage of naturalized foreigners was calculated by dividing registered foreigners by those who received citizenship

Neither country discriminates against foreign workers on account of nationality (Seol 2007: 392), nor do they place any restrictions on emigration.

There are also several important differences between the two countries. Whereas Germany offers citizenship to ethnic Germans and welcomes their return, Korea has a visit-cum-employment system for ethnic Koreans who do not hold Korean citizenship. Ethnic Koreans who get visas can stay and work for up to 3 years.

The two countries also have different policies with respect to unskilled laborers in the manufacturing sector. Nationals of the European Union can enter and work freely in Germany, but other foreigners can work in Germany only after getting work permits. Unlike Germany, Korea admits foreign workers only from countries with which it has a formal agreement.

In 1999 it became much easier for foreigners living in Germany to obtain German citizenship. Children born in Germany to foreign parents now have dual citizenship. However, dual citizenship is not permitted for adults, and those having dual citizenship must choose to maintain citizenship in just one country within 5 years of reaching the age of 18. There are some exceptions to this rule for ethnic Germans.

Despite the more liberal citizenship policy introduced in 1999, the number of naturalized citizens is very small (1.6 % of foreign workers in 2005), and most foreign workers maintain their original nationality. The same is true in Korea, although the percentage of foreign workers granted citizenship has risen in recent years (3.5 % in 2005) (Table 5.9).

Germany and Korea have guaranteed basic human rights for immigrant laborers since they joined the International Covenants on Civil and Political Rights. That is, they have guaranteed civil liberties institutionally. However, a change of place of employment by immigrant laborers requires permission of the government. Regarding social rights, foreigners in Germany share the same benefits of the social security system as citizens, and the German government is actively executing its policy to assimilate foreign immigrants into German society. In 2007, the Korean government set up a legal framework to support foreigners by approving "Basic Laws of Treatment of Foreigners in Korea". However, it has rarely applied a system of public aid to foreigners due to higher priorities in the budget.

In Korea and Germany, suffrage is not granted to foreign workers. Based on the "Public Office Election Law", "Law of Resident Vote", and "Law regarding Resident Summons" the Korean government grants the right of resident vote and the right of resident summons to foreign residents possessing certain qualifications. To resolve problems regarding illegal aliens, the Korean government has taken several steps towards temporarily legalizing illegal aliens. By contrast, the German government has taken no such measures.

5.5 Suggestions for Applying Germany's Policy of Foreign Immigrant Assimilation to Korea

Statistics suggest that the educational standards of immigrants in Germany were lower compared to non-immigrants. Approximately 10 % of all immigrants did not graduate from general schools, whereas only 1.5 % of the entire population failed to graduate from general schools. Likewise, whereas only 27 % of Germans have not received vocational education, the figure among immigrants is 51 % (Bundesamt für Migration und Flüchtlinge (ed.) 2005).

Approximately 48 % of immigrants are considered to be laborers, compared to 26 % of non-immigrants. Around 64 % of immigrants work in service sector jobs, compared to 50 % of non-immigrants. The difference between immigrants and non-immigrants is even greater among office workers and public employees.

Germany has recently modified its immigration law to try to attract immigrants that are likely to benefit the country. Since 1 January 2005, laws have been enacted to attract non-EU immigrants. Businessmen and those who are self-employed are granted residency if they establish a business in Germany or meet a particular economic demand. They are considered to satisfy these conditions if they invest more than one million euros and employ more than 10 people. They are initially granted permission to reside in Germany for 3 years, but later they can be granted permanent residence. Experts, scholars and high officials are also granted residence if their employment in Germany is ensured.

The newly revised immigration law has become effective since 28 August 2007. Germany not only satisfies the EU's 11 guidelines regarding residence permission and asylum laws, but also supplements articles of the 2004 revised law. This revised law includes articles to prevent *Scheinehe* (false marriage) or *Zwangsehe* (forced marriage), enforcement of public order, establishment of a business, simplification of immigration procedure, immigrants' successful adaptation to German society, and others. In addition to modifying its immigration laws, the German government has also contributed to the assimilation of foreigners through direct funding of

Table 5.10 Foreign laborers who are obligatory members of the social insurance scheme

Year	Total	German laborers	Foreign laborers	Percentage of foreign laborers
1997	27,280	25,235	2,044	7.5
1998	27,208	25,178	2,030	7.5
1999	27,483	25,558	1,925	7.0
2000	27,826	25,862	1,964	7.1
2001	27,817	25,809	2,008	7.2
2002	27,571	25,611	1,960	7.1
2003	26,955	25,081	1,874	7.0
2004	26,524	24,719	1,805	6.8
2005	26,178	24,423	1,755	6.7

Source: Bundesamt für Migration und Flüchtlinge (Ed.) (2005: 105)

Table 5.11 The total unemployment rate and foreigners' unemployment rate in Germany (Unit: Person, %, 31 December 2005)

year	Total unemployed	Total unemployment rate	Foreign unemployed	Percentage of foreign unemployment rate
1997	4,384,456	12.7	547,816	20.9
1998	4,280,630	12.3	534,698	20.3
1999	4,100,499	11.7	510,168	19.2
2000	3,889,695	10.7	470,994	17.3
2001	3,852,564	10.3	464,739	17.4
2002	4,061,345	10.8	499,433	18.8
2003	4,376,795	11.6	542,966	20.2
2004	4,381,281	11.7	545,080	20.3
2005	4,860.685	13.0	672,903	25.2

Source: Bundesamt für Migration und Flüchtlinge (Ed.) (2005: 106)

language courses and 'assimilation education' for immigrants. Both proficiency in German and education in German culture are considered preconditions for immigration. According to the law revised January 2005, immigrants are to receive 630 h of assimilation education.

In addition to language education, vocational education for foreigners plays a key role in their successful assimilation. In particular, vocational education for foreign adolescents and women is very prevalent. Thus the federal government is making a large effort to promote vocational education for foreigners through various projects and to create employment for them. According to 2005 statistics, 79.5 % of foreigners who reside in Germany were born in foreign countries, making assimilation though education particularly important. Only 1.38 million (20.5 %) out of 6.7 million foreigners were born in Germany. These are second or third generation immigrants.

Foreigners' social assimilation is an assignment for the whole society which German residents and immigrants should fulfil together. In particular, the government is investing a large budget into socially integrating foreigners by means of education in democratic citizenship.

Table 5.12 Positions and wages of the West Germany area's immigrants (unit: %, Euro, 2004)

		German people	Immigrants			
			Turkish	Middle and Western Europe (till 2003)	Former Yugoslavia	German returnees
Position	Laborer	12 %	46 %	31 %	42 %	36 %
	Technician or artisan	14 %	20 %	33 %	18 %	25 %
	Simple office job	5 %	3 %	6 %	5 %	4 %
	General office job	23 %	24 %	20 %	25 %	29 %
	High-ranking position or Administrative position	8 %	0 %	4 %	1 %	1 %
	Self-employed	23 %	24 %	20 %	25 %	29 %
Wage	Average wage	1,560 euros	1,350 euros	1,470 euros	1,230 euros	1,200 euros
	Low earners (Less than 50 % of average wage)	23 %	24 %	20 %	25 %	29 %
	High earners (more than 200 % of average wage)	8 %	0 %	4 %	1 %	1 %
Society acknowledgement level of job (High: 100, Low: 0)		72 (Higher)	45 (Lower than moderate)	50 (Moderate)	49 (Moderate)	58 (Higher than moderate)

Source: Statistisches Bundesamt (Ed.) (2006: 570)

Note: These statistics focus on the West German area, because many immigrants live in this area

In spite of these various policies of social integration, there are significant differences in labor type, wage, position and other factors between foreign and German workers. The number of foreign laborers receiving social insurance is gradually decreasing as the number of foreigners in a permanent position is declining. The unemployment rate for foreigners has tended to increase; in 2005 the unemployment rate among foreigners was twice that of the general unemployment rate in Germany. In 2001, foreign workers in Germany made up approximately 8.3 % of all the workers in Germany, but the number of foreign laborers who were obligatory members of the social insurance scheme was 7.2 % of the whole. In general, the percentage of foreign laborers who are obligatory members of the social insurance scheme decreased gradually from 7.6 in 1996 to 6.7 % in 2005 (Table 5.10).

According to statistics, in 1997 approximately 0.54 million foreigners were unemployed and the foreigners' unemployment rate (20.9 %) was much higher than the total unemployment rate (12.7 %) in Germany. The number of unemployed foreigners decreased slightly during the period of economic recovery (1998–2001), but since then the number has increased. In 2005, the unemployment rate among foreigners was approximately twice that of the total unemployment rate (Table 5.11).

The following table provides information on types of employment and wages for Germans and various groups of foreigners. It is clear from this that the quality of jobs and wages is lower for foreigners than for native Germans.

The average wage among these foreign groups is about 1,250 euros per month, whereas the average among native Germans is 1,500 euros (Table 5.12).

As examined above, job segregation still seems to be apparent between German people and foreigners, although German society is operating with various social assimilation programs. In addition, foreigners are mainly low wage earners and their unemployment rate is twice as high compared to that of German people. Germany's efforts to integrate foreigners into society could serve as a useful example to Korea as it imports more and more foreign workers.

5.6 Conclusions

The number of foreign workers has increased in both Korea and Germany as part of globalization, and there has been a liberalization of the concept of citizenship. Both countries actively provide incentives to attract foreign professionals, while the "return home" policy towards unskilled workers is closer to exploitation. Both countries also have a similar policy prohibiting discrimination against foreign residents. Korea gives priority to the employment of Koreans, and Germany does so for citizens of the European Union. In this respect they are similar, with each country importing a minimum number of foreign workers based on the principle of complementarity in the labor market.

Germany offers citizenship to ethnic Germans and welcomes their return, whereas Korea has a visit-cum-employment system for ethnic Koreans of foreign citizenship. Germany allows foreign workers only if they have a work visa, whereas Korea has an employment permit system. Despite changes in citizenship policy, resulting from globalization, most foreign workers in the two countries keep their original nationality rather than becoming naturalized citizens. Thus, for unskilled migrant workers, globalization appears to have provided the opportunity to cross borders, but not to become full members of the countries in which they live and work.

In spite of the various policies of social integration in Germany, educational standards among immigrants in Germany are still low, compared to non-immigrants, and there are significant differences with regard to labor type, wage, position and other factors between foreign and German workers.

Endnotes

[1]They are Bosnia-Herzegovina, Bulgaria, Croatia, Latvia, Macedonia, Poland, Romania, Serbia, Montenegro, Slovakia, Slovenia, Czech Republic, Hungary.
[2]These countries include The Czech Republic, Estonia, Latvia, Lithuania, Hungary, Poland, Slovenia and Slovakia, all of which joined the EU in May 2004, and Romania and Bulgaria, which joined in 2007.

References

Brubaker, R. 1992. *Citizenship and Nationhood in France and Germany*. Cambridge, MA: Harvard University Press.
Brubaker, R. 1994. "Rethinking Nationhood: Nation as institutionalized form, practical category, contingent event". *Contention* 4 (1), 3–14.
Bundesanstalt für Arbeit (ed.). 2002. *Jahresbericht 2002: Die berufliche Situation von jugendlichen und erwachsenen Migranten in Deutschland*. Nürnberg: Bundesanstalt für Arbeit.
Bundesamt für Migration und Flüchtlinge (ed.). 2005. *Migration, Asyl und Integration in Zahlen*. Bonn: Das Druckhaus Bernd Brümmer.
Bundesagentur für Arbeit (ed.). 2006. Arbeitsmarkt 2006. *Amtliche Nachrichten der Bundesagentur für Arbeit* 55 (1).
Bundesamt für Migration und Flüchtlinge (ed.). 2008. *Ausländerzahlen 2008*. Nürnberg: Bundesamt für Migration und Flüchtlinge.
Choe, H. 2006. "Hankuk sitichŭn shwip: 1987 nŏn ihu siminkwŏn chedo pyŏnhwa wa simin ŭisik" (South Korean citizenship: the institutional changes since 1987 and their effects on citizen's consciousness). *Min chuchu ŭi wa inkwŏn (Democracy and Human Rights)* 4, 172–205.
Hollifield, J. F. 1992. *Immigration, Markets, and States: the political economy of postwar Europe*. Cambridge, MA: Harvard University Press.
Jacobson, D. 1997. *Right across Borders: Immigration and the Decline of Citizenship*. Baltimore: The Johns Hopkins University Press.
Joppke, C.H. 1998. *Challenge to the Nation-State. Immigration in Western Europe and the United States*. Oxford/New York: Oxford University Press.

Klusmeyer, D. 2001. "Introduction". In *Citizenship Today: global perspectives and practices*, Eds. T. A. Aleinikoff and D. B. Klusmeyer. Washington D.C.: Carnegie Endowment for International Peace.

Kymlicka, W., and W. Norman. 1995. "Return of the citizen: a survey of recent work on citizenship theory". In *Theorizing Citizenship*, Ed. R. Beiner. Albany: State University of New York Press.

Oltmer, J. 2005. Deutsche Migrationsgeschichte seit 1871. In Bundeszentrale für politische Bildung (Ed.), *Migration und Integration in Deutschland*. Bonn: Bundeszentrale für politische Bildung.

Seol, D.-H. 2007. "Kukche nodongnyŏk idong kwa oekukin nodongcha ŭi siminkwŏn e daehan yŏn gu" (International labor migration and the citizenship of migrant workers: a comparison of German, Japan and Korea). *Minchuchuŭi wa inkwŏn* (Democracy and human rights) 7 (2), 369–419.

Soysal, Y. N. 1994. *Limits of Citizenship: Migrant and Postnational Membership in Europe*. Chicago: University of Chicago Press.

Statistisches Bundesamt (ed.). 2006. *Datenreport*. Wiesbaden: Statistisches Bundesamt.

Yoo, K. S. and K.-Y. Lee, et al. 2004. *Chesukryŏn oekuk inryŏ nodong chichang punsŏk (Analyses of unskilled foreign labour market)*. Seoul: KLI.

http://www.auslaender-statistik.de/bund/gast_1.htm (accessed 20 January 2010).

http://www.immigration.go.kr (accessed 23 January 2010).

Chapter 6
Recent Status of Marriage-Based Immigrants and Their Families in Korea

Sung-Nam Cho

Abstract Foreign wives were never a visible social group in Korea until recently. Korean society has experienced a fast-growth in international cross-border marriage during the past few decades. Marriage migration across borders has come to be pervasive in Asia and other regions. A large group of young women from Southeast Asian countries, who reside in Korea as workers and brides, have also received increasing attention from scholars and policy-makers because marriage immigrants have emerged as an important social issue in contemporary Korean society. From the 1990s, a steady increase in the visibility of immigrant foreign spouses and immigrant laborers in Korea has had an unsettling effect on the long-held image of the perceived homogeneity of Korean society. This study tries to analyze important phenomena current in the upsurge of international marriages in South Korea. First, it examines the recent trend in the state of marriage-based immigrants and their families. Second, the study seeks to delineate their basic socio-cultural needs by analyzing data collected by a nationwide sample survey conducted in 2006 by three sociologists, Drs. Seol, D.H., Lee, H.K. and Cho, S.N. under a grant from the Ministry of Gender Equalities in South Korea. The study thus tries to capture actual living conditions of marriage-based immigrants and their families in Korea, focusing on those factors deemed to be a prerequisite for long-term policy measures towards their successful social integration.

S.-N. Cho (✉)
Department of Sociology, Ewha Womans University, 11-1 Daihyun-dong, Seodaimun-gu, Seoul 120-750, Korea

#201, Hyundai Village, 1-56, BookAhyun-dong, Seoul 120-190, Korea
e-mail: sncho@ewha.ac.kr

M. Pohlmann et al. (eds.), *Citizenship and Migration in the Era of Globalization*,
Transcultural Research – Heidelberg Studies on Asia and Europe in a Global Context,
DOI 10.1007/978-3-642-19739-0_6, © Springer-Verlag Berlin Heidelberg 2013

6.1   Introduction

With globalization, twenty-first century Korean society is undergoing rapid change and is forced to deal with diverse social issues that this is bringing about. One of these issues concerns the growth of immigrants stemming from international marriages and refugees escaping from North Korea.

According to the Korean National Statistics Office in 2007, the total number of foreign laborers working in Korea was 410,181 and the number of international marriages 332,752. The ethnic, cultural, and socio-economic backgrounds of these immigrants and their offspring are making Korean society more diverse than ever before (KNSO 2007).

Not long ago, marrying a foreigner in Korea was a rare thing - an option mostly available to those who had scarce foreign exposure. As a result, foreign wives have never been a visibly important social group in Korea until recently. However, Korean society has witnessed a fast growth in international or cross-border marriage during the past decade (see Fig. 6.1).

International marriages through the 1980s largely consisted of Korean women marrying foreign husbands and leaving the country. However, from the 1990s on have immigrant foreign spouses settled down in Korea and, together with a large group of immigrant laborers, challenged the long-held perception that Korean society is a homogeneous one.

Marriage migration across borders has been pervasive in Asia, as in other regions. An influx of young women from Southeast Asian countries, as well as their roles as workers and brides in Korea, have received increasing attention from scholars and policy makers (Kim 2008), turning marriage immigrants into an important social issue in contemporary Korean society (see Fig. 6.2).

Due to the recent upsurge in international marriages, the problems of socio-cultural adjustment as well as the need for reinforcement of family stability, along with the successful integration of multicultural families, have now become major social issues.

This study attempts to analyze major issues arising from this upsurge in international marriage, first, by examining the recent trend and the state of marriage-based immigrants and their families, and second, by accessing their basic socio-cultural needs through the use of the data set collected in the 2006 nation-wide research conducted by three sociologists, Drs. Seol D.H., Lee H.K. Lee, and Cho, S.N. (Lee et al. 2006) under a ROK Ministry of Gender Equalities grant. The study tries to delineate the actual conditions of marriage-based immigrants in South Korea to facilitate their successful social integration through a long term policy measure.

Since Korea is fast becoming a complex society made up by various ethnic groups with different national backgrounds, a study such as this is needed to develop long-term policy measures and bring about the social integration of the marriage-based immigrants and their families into Korean society.

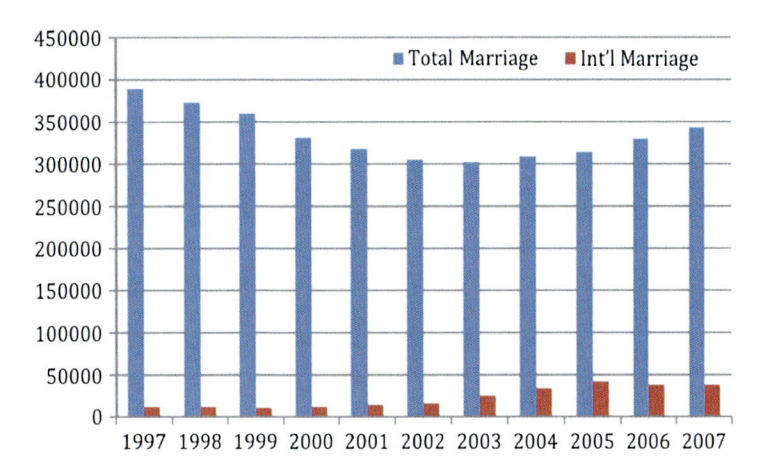

Fig. 6.1 Trends in international marriage (Source: South Korea National Statistics Office Population Trend 2007)

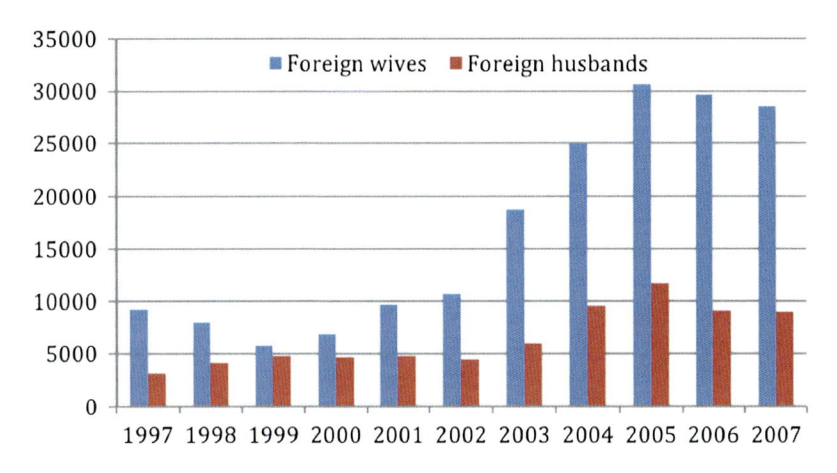

Fig. 6.2 Trends in international marriage (Foreign husbands/foreign wives)

6.2 Recent Trend in International Marriages and Their Social Background in Korea

According to the statistics given by the Immigration Office of the Ministry of Justice, the number of foreigners in Korea in 2008 was in excess of 1.16 million, accounting for 2.2 % of the total population. This marks a 135 % increase in 10 years. Among them, international marriages numbered 113,000, which is more than a threefold increase in 6 years.

To better grasp the characteristics of the marriage-based immigrants, an analysis of the "international marriage statistics" released by the National Statistical Office

Table 6.1 Number of international marriages in Korea, 1990–2005

(Unit: N, %)

Year	Total marriages	Int'l marriage		Foreign brides		Foreign husbands	
		Cases	%	Cases	%	Cases	%
1990	399,312	4,710	1.2	619	0.2	4,091	1.0
1991	416,872	5,012	1.2	663	0.2	4,349	1.0
1992	419,774	5,534	1.3	2,057	0.5	3,477	0.8
1993	402,593	6,545	1.6	3,109	0.8	3,436	0.9
1994	393,121	6,616	1.7	3,072	0.8	3,544	0.9
1995	398,484	13,494	3.4	10,365	2.6	3,129	0.8
1996	434,911	15,946	3.7	12,647	2.9	3,299	0.8
1997	388,591	12,448	3.2	9,266	2.4	3,182	0.8
1998	375,616	12,188	3.2	8,054	2.1	4,134	1.1
1999	362,673	10,570	2.9	5,775	1.6	4,795	1.3
2000	334,030	12,319	3.7	7,304	2.2	5,015	1.5
2001	320,063	15,234	4.8	10,006	3.1	5,228	1.6
2002	306,573	15,913	5.2	11,017	3.6	4,896	1.6
2003	304,932	25,658	8.4	19,214	6.3	6,444	2.1
2004	310,944	35,447	11.4	25,594	8.2	9,853	3.2
2005	316,375	43,121	13.6	31,180	9.9	11,941	3.8
1990–2005	5,884,864	240,755	4.1	159,942	2.7	80,813	1.4

Data: National Statistics Office, population dynamics (marriage, divorce). http://kosis.nso.go.kr

and of the statistics of marriage-based immigrants residing in Korea presented by the Ministry of Justice is in order.

This drastic increase in international marriage is observable inasmuch as by 2005, 13.6 % of all South Korean marriages involved a foreign spouse. Likewise, the marriage between Korean men and foreign females is also on the rise. Between 1990 and 2005, in the total 240,755 cases of international marriages, 159,942 female foreigners were married to Korean men while 80,813 male foreigners were married to Korean women (see Table 6.1).

A greater increase in international marriage took place in particular during the 4-year period beginning with the year 2000, resulting in 2004 in no less than 11.4 % of the total of marriages (KNSO 2005). In this year Korean men marrying foreign wives accounted for 8.2 % of the total marriages, and Korean women marrying foreign husbands for 3.2 %. In rural areas, one out of every four newly wedded couples was an international or cross-border marriage. Among these, the great majority of cases were those of Korean men marrying foreign women (see Table 6.1).

Moreover, according to the 2008 statistics issued by the Ministry of Justice, foreigners living in Korea came from 197 different countries, and those who married Koreans, from 127 countries. Among them, the majority came from China, followed by Southeast Asian countries including Vietnam and the Philippines, and then Japan (Ministry of Justice 2008).

Since the late 1990s, Korea has witnessed a surge of marriage-based female immigrants from China and Southeast Asia. Chinese wives comprised the vast majority

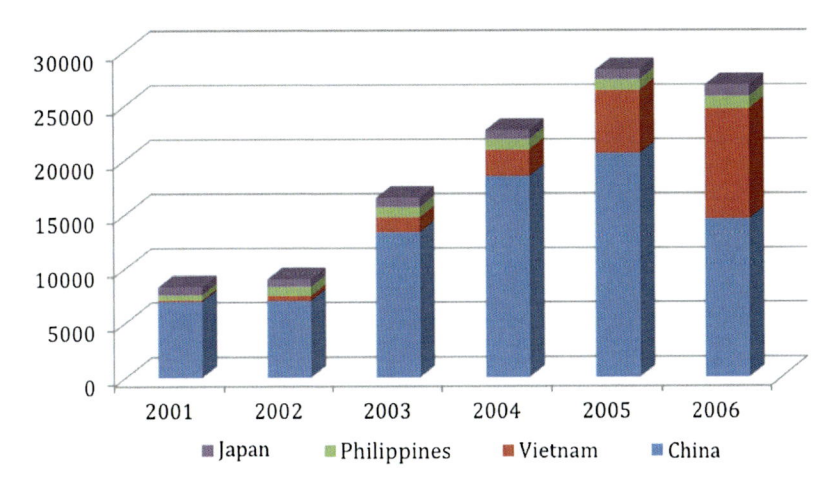

Fig. 6.3 Foreign wives by country background

of all foreign wives. The percentage of Vietnamese wives, in particular, increased rapidly, from 1 % in 2001 to 10 % in 2004. Meanwhile, the proportions of Filipino and Thai wives have slightly decreased. In 2006, 48.4 % (14,608 cases) were from China, 33.5 % (10,131cases) were from Vietnam, and 4.9 % (1,484 cases) were from Japan, and the number of marriages with Vietnamese women, in particular, sharply increased to 74 % in 1 year period, compared with its number in 2005 (see Fig. 6.3).

The two most conspicuous groups of Koreans who marry internationally were rural never-married men who could not find a bride locally, and divorced middle-aged men living in urban areas (Lee and Seol 2007).

In the 1960s and 1970s in Korea, with its rapid industrialization, many young rural women migrated to urban areas mostly as factory workers. A marriage squeeze for young rural men resulting from young women's massive outward migration for urban jobs has been one of the continuing social issues caused by urbanization since the 1970s. Even while the service sector expanded in the 1980s, gender-selective rural–urban migration continued, resulting in a serious gender imbalance in rural areas (Seol et al. 2005).

However, marriages between rural bachelors and foreign wives have increased since the beginning of the twenty-first century, reflecting the broad social changes that may be conveniently summarized as the globalization of Korean people (Lee, Seol and Cho 2006). In 2004, about one in four (27 %) marriages in rural areas was that of a Korean man marrying a foreign woman –accounting for about 7 % of the total marriages in Korea.

Lee, Seol, and Cho (2006) point out that that male surplus among young rural adults may worsen as those born in the 1980s and 1990s reach marriageable ages. While reproduction declined rapidly, falling below the replacement level in the mid-1980s, sex-selective abortions increased. The sex ratio at birth went beyond 110 in the mid-1980s and reached a peak of 116.5 in 1990 in favor of males. Since then it has steadily fallen but was still at 110-in 2002, only reaching 108 by 2004 (KNSO 2005). Thus, a female shortage among marriageable ages may occur even in some urban areas in the coming years.

Another reason why Korean men are involved in an increasing number of international marriages is the prevalence of remarriages by divorced middle-age men (41 % among men in 2004). In Korea, divorce rates increased drastically during the past few decades, and many divorced men tended to remarry internationally (Lee, Seol and Cho 2006).

The crude divorce rate (number of divorces per 1,000 population) was only 1.1 in 1990, but it reached 3.5 by 2003, following closely the United States' 4.1, which is among the highest in the world. As negative social perception on divorce weakens, high divorce rates may continue for the time being (Lee, Seol and Cho 2006). Statistics in 2004 show that a majority of male divorcees divorce in their thirties (46 % in 2004) whereas female divorcees are largely distributed across the 20s (34 %) and 30s (41 %) (KNSO 2005).

The percentage of divorced Korean men who remarry internationally has increased substantially over the 5 years from the year 2000. In 2004, second marriages comprised 45 % of all international marriages involving Korean males, consisting of former divorcees (41 %) and former widowers (4 %) (KNSO 2005).

For Korean men's international marriages, Chinese wives comprised 63 % of first marriages and 82 % of second marriages. Among all Chinese women marrying Korean men in 2004, for example, 53 % married previously married men. That percentage was in fact the highest in all ethnic groups, and the analogous numbers were much smaller among Southeast Asians, 24–28 % in 2004 (Lee, Seol and Cho 2006).

Also the age difference between spouses tended to be much larger among international couples than among other Korean couples (Seol et al. 2005). The age at marriage for the majority of the foreign wives was in their 20s and 30s, whereas the Korean husbands were in their 30s and 40s. Especially in rural areas, at marriage more than 80 % of the Vietnamese women, in particular, were in their early 20s or even in their teens. The average age difference between husband and wife was more than 10 years. Such age gaps and/or power imbalances between spouses may be a source of possible marital conflicts.

Marriage immigrants often experience difficulties regarding communication and cultural differences, and/or discrimination by other Koreans (Park 1982). These difficulties may cause conflicts in the family, resulting sometimes in family violence and eventually even in divorce. The divorce rate of the internationally married couples in recent years also has increased more rapidly than that of other Korean couples (see Fig. 6.4). Statistics show that the divorce cases among international marriage were 583 in year 2003, and 1,611 cases, 2,444 cases, 4,010 cases, and 5,794 cases in every consecutive year up until 2007. This was a more than four-fold increase in 3 years from 2004 to 2006 (KNSO 2008).

Many Koreans who married foreigners were often from low income classes, and hence they were the main recipients of welfare services provided by the government (Seol et al. 2005).

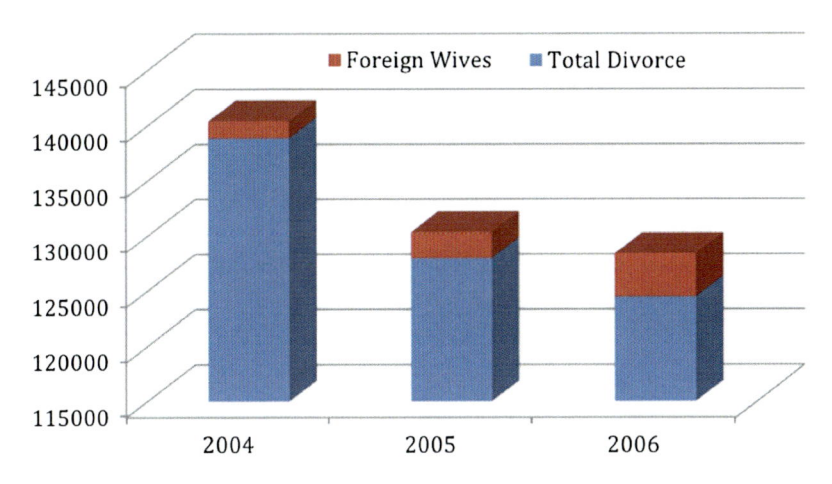

Fig. 6.4   Divorce rate in international marriages

When the residence of marriage-based immigrants was analyzed for 2006, 76.5 % lived in urban areas, and 23.5 %, in rural areas. For urban residence, 45.1 % were located in metropolitan areas, while 31.4 % lived in medium-sized cities. Based on their gender, marriage-based female immigrants lived predominantly in rural areas, and male marriage-based immigrants in urban areas.

Looking at the regions, in 2006 Seoul (26.5 %) and Gyeonggi (26.2 %) were the main residential areas for marriage-based immigrants, followed by Incheon (6.5 %), Gyeongnam (4.7 %), and Busan (4.7 %). Females resided most in the Gyeonggi area, while males lived mainly in Seoul.

6.3   Data and Research Method

As already noted, the data set used for this study was originally collected in 2006 by three sociologists, Drs. Seol D.H., Lee, H.K. and Cho, S.N., under a grant from the ROK Ministry of Gender Equalities. A nationwide sample survey as well as an in-depth interview were conducted from October 17, 2006 to November 30, 2006 (45 days) with marriage-based immigrants and their Korean spouse. The questionnaire was written in 11 different languages – Korean, English, Chinese, Japanese, Vietnamese, Tagalog, Thai, Mongolian, Russian, Uzbek, and Indonesian.

The standard unit used throughout this sample survey was a family consisting of marriage-based immigrants (the spouse being the target interviewees). Additionally, the sample was selected to reflect the distribution of the population. The database of "foreign spouses" and "naturalized citizens (Kwihwaja)" kept by the Ministry of Justice was used as the population for sampling (for example see Ministry Of Justice (MOJ), 2005, 2006).

From the database, a systematic sampling method within each quarter was used after setting the quotas relating to sex, nationality and residence. The target interviewees were marriage-based immigrants and her/his Korean spouse. The unit of analysis in this data set was the family. Although the goal was to collect a sample of 1,200 families, only a sample of 1,177 families, consisting of 1,063 foreign wives and 114 foreign husbands, was collected and analyzed.

Looking at the distribution of sex, nationality and domicile in the sample data, out of the 1,177 total samples, 822 female marriage-based immigrants (69.8 %) were residing in cities, while 241 female marriage-based immigrants (20.5 %) were residing in the countryside, but only 114 marriage-based male immigrants (9.7 %) were residing in cities.

Moreover, apart from the sample dataset, in-depth interviews were also conducted with 20 marriage-based immigrants. The in-depth interview was conducted in order to learn the interviewees' life stories. Instead of a brief nominal interview survey based on the questionnaire, an in-depth interview was chosen to build a rapport as well as a personal relationship with the marriage-based immigrants through regular meetings. The researchers interviewed repeatedly, meeting at least twice with immigrants and their family with time intervals between meetings.

6.4   Research Findings

6.4.1   Socio-demographics of Marriage-Based Immigrants

The average age of the marriage-based female and male immigrants in the dataset was 33 and 38, respectively. By comparison, the average age of a male Korean spouse in the same period was 42, about 9 years older than that of the marriage-based female immigrants in the dataset. Similarly, the average age of a female Korean spouse was 36, 2 years younger than that of the male immigrants. The age-gap was bigger between Korean husbands and foreign wives. Moreover, the average age difference between a Korean husband and a Vietnamese wife was almost 16 years (see Table 6.2).

In terms of the nationality of female marriage immigrants, Japanese women were the oldest, with an average age of 39, followed by the ethnic Korean Chinese *(Chosŏnjok)* and the Han Chinese with an average age of 34 and 35, respectively, while the average age of female marriage immigrants from the Philippines and other countries was about 32 and that of Vietnamese female marriage immigrants was the lowest at 24. The main reason behind these age differences among different countries was because of differences in their entry date (or in the duration of their stay in Korea), as well as whether their marriages were the first or second. In most cases, the Han Chinese and ethnic Korean Chinese *(Chosŏnjok)* were remarrying

Table 6.2 Mean age of internationally married couples

(Unit: each age)

Migrant survey			Age of Resp.	Age of spouse	Age difference
Total		(1,148)	33.6 (8.5)	41.4 (7.7)	−7.9 (7.6)
Sex	Female	(1,038)	33.1 (8.4)	42.0 (7.6)	−8.9 (7.0)
	Male	(110)	38.1 (7.9)	36.0 (6.9)	2.3 (5.9)
Sex and region	Fem-urban	(804)	33.7 (8.6)	42.4 (7.9)	−8.7 (7.0)
	Fem-rural	(234)	31.1 (7.5)	40.7 (6.0)	−9.8 (6.7)
	Male	(110)	38.1 (7.9)	36.0 (6.9)	2.3 (5.9)
Sex·and origin countries	F-Kor-Ch	(494)	35.1 (8.0)	43.4 (7.9)	−8.3 (5.2)
	F-Chinese	(109)	33.7 (7.8)	41.7 (8.0)	−7.9 (6.1)
	F-Viet.	(173)	24.3 (5.9)	40.0 (7.7)	−15.8 (8.8)
	F-Japanese	(100)	39.0 (5.5)	41.5 (5.9)	−2.6 (3.7)
	F-Filipino	(99)	32.2 (7.3)	41.1 (5.9)	−8.6 (5.5)
	F-other	(63)	32.4 (6.1)	39.9 (6.3)	−7.3 (6.3)
	M-Kor-Ch	(73)	39.4 (7.5)	36.7 (6.8)	2.9 (6.2)
	M-Chinese	(14)	32.6 (7.1)	34.9 (8.3)	−1.8 (5.7)
	M-other	(23)	37.3 (8.2)	34.8 (6.3)	3.1 (4.1)

while for the Vietnamese it was their first marriage and they had also come to Korea relatively recently.

The education of the marriage-based immigrants was mostly high school graduate level (39.6 %). In terms of gender, the educational level of marriage-based female immigrants was slightly lower than that of marriage-based male immigrants. Only 25 % of the former were college graduates whereas for males it was 34 %. In terms of the nationality of female marriage immigrants, the Japanese women's educational level was the highest, followed by the Filipinos, then Han Chinese, *Chosŏnjok,* and Vietnamese. The Vietnamese female marriage immigrants had the lowest educational level with 65 % having graduated from less than middle school.

6.4.2 Motives and Ways of International Marriage

International marriage in contemporary Korean society spread from rural areas. Even though the number was not large, the first influx occurred when Japanese females came as brides for the marriages arranged by the Unification Church. And then the *Chosŏnjok,* Han Chinese and Filipinos arrived in that order, while Vietnamese women have mostly only come to Korea since 2003 (KWDC 2003).

As for foreign males, they were of different nationalities, but came from early on, even though their number was small. By contrast, international marriages between Korean males and *Chosŏnjok* females have more recently become common and in large numbers.

Around 46 % of foreign male marriage immigrants reported that they met their Korean partners after they came to Korea for their jobs, and 45 % answered that

Table 6.3 Ways foreigners meet their Korean spouses

(Unit: N, %)

Migrant survey			Family/ friends	Myself	Mar. agency	Church	Local government	Other
Total		(1,117)	45.7	20.0	17.7	14.3	0.9	1.4
Sex	Female	(1,010)	45.7	17.2	19.5	15.4	1.0	1.1
	Male	(107)	44.9	45.8	0.9	3.7	0.0	4.7
Sex and region	F-urban	(778)	47.8	19.9	18.3	12.1	1.0	0.9
	F-rural	(232)	38.8	8.2	23.7	26.7	0.9	1.7
	Male	(107)	44.9	45.8	0.9	3.7	0.0	4.7
Sex and origin countries	F-Kor-Ch	(480)	68.8	18.1	10.2	1.7	0.8	0.4
	F-Chinese	(107)	46.7	37.4	9.3	4.7	0.9	0.9
	F-Vietnamese	(169)	21.3	5.9	69.2	0.6	3.0	0.0
	F-Japanese	(103)	1.9	9.7	0.0	87.4	0.0	1.0
	F-Filipino	(86)	18.6	12.8	18.6	45.3	0.0	4.7
	F-Other	(65)	43.1	24.6	7.7	20.0	0.0	4.6
	M-Kor-Ch	(71)	53.5	40.8	1.4	2.8	0.0	1.4
	M-Chinese	(14)	42.9	57.1	0.0	0.0	0.0	0.0
	M-Other	(22)	18.2	54.5	0.0	9.1	0.0	18.2

they met their partners on a blind date arranged by their friends. In the case of foreign female immigrants, however, their meeting varied depending on the countries of their origin. For example, most *Chosŏnjok* and Han Chinese who came to Korea for work met their partners through a blind date arranged by their family or friends. However, about 87 % of Japanese women and 45 % of Filipinos met their partners through the Unification Church, whereas around 70 % of Vietnamese women met their partners through matchmaking agencies, as was the case with 20 % of Filipinos and 10 % of *Chosŏnjok* and Han Chinese (see Table 6.3).

The rate of remarriage for both male and female was the highest (35 %) among the *Chosŏnjok,* followed by the Han Chinese (females 26 %, and males 13 %). Unlike the *Chosŏnjok* and Han Chinese, for most of other nationalities we find perseverance throughout their first marriage. However, we also find that Korean partners had more cases of remarriage than others, accounting for more than 40 % of Korean males and 20 % of females who married with foreigners.

Whether or not immigrants had the experience of inviting their families in their home countries to Korea depended on their times of entry (or duration in Korea) and their economic status. The shorter their duration in Korea and the worse their economic condition, the more difficulty they had in inviting their families to Korea. Accordingly, more than 2/3 of Japanese females as well as of the males from other nationalities, who had the longest period of stay in Korea, and who were better off in terms of their economic conditions, have been able to invite their families, while 61 % of the *Chosŏnjok* and 54 % of the Han Chinese have also been able to do. On the other hand, only 23 % of Filipinos and 14 % of Vietnamese females had the chance of inviting their families, largely due to their difficult economic situation as well as their relatively recent entry to Korea.

The reason why their families visited Korea was mostly to attend the wedding and/or just to see how they made their living in Korea. It should be also noted that the families of Filipinos and Vietnamese women have visited Korea less than the families of other marriage immigrants. Their most important reason for visiting Korea was to help deliver and nurse babies for their daughters. The *Chosŏnjok*, on the other hand, regardless of gender had their families visit Korea to look for jobs.

When Koreans were asked why they married foreigners, particularly with regard to their choices of certain nationalities as their partners, their answers varied in accordance with the gender of the respondents. The answer by 80 % of Korean women was: "because they loved their partners", while 38 % of Korean men answered "because they tend to be more submissive, and they may serve my parents well" (see Table 6.4). This shows a tendency among Korean males to prefer the traditional wife image and a patriarchal emphasis in marriage. However, they also wanted their foreign wife to conduct herself in a similar way to a Korean woman so that their international marriage would not look outlandish, and they especially hoped that their children would behave more like Korean children do.

The most important reason for Korean males marrying with Filipinos and Vietnamese was that they were perceived to be "more submissive and obedient to their parents". Therefore, those Korean males who married foreign females expected that females from Southeast Asian countries, such as the Philippines and Vietnam, were more likely to be submissive and good at serving their parents, when compared to women from China and Japan. On the other hand, Korean males who married *Chosŏnjok* and Vietnamese responded that they chose their spouse because "they look most similar to Korean females".

6.4.3 Family Life

Family life of marriage immigrants was examined by focusing on the members of their family including husband and wife relationship, relationship with children, and relationship with parents and relatives.

6.4.3.1 Living Arrangement

We found that international marriage families had somewhat higher rates of living together with the partner's parents, brothers, and sisters than other average Korean families.

Around 88.2 % of the respondents had a family of husband and wife while 56.4 % were couples living with children. An extended family that lived with his/ her spouse's parents came to 22.3 % while approximately 40.2 % of Vietnamese females, in particular, lived together with their husband's parents. Also it was shown that 37.3 % of women lived in rural areas.

Table 6.4 Reason of Koreans to marry foreign spouse

(Unit: N, %)

Korean spouse survey			Submissive/ obedience to my parents	Similar appearance to Koreans	Familiarity to the country	Persuaded by other internationally married couples	Persuaded by marriage agency	Love	Religious reason	Persuaded by parents/ families
Total		(1,017)	36.2	36.8	10.2	19.3	9.4	35.0	10.5	14.2
Sex and region	Female	(49)	10.2	32.7	6.1	8.2	0.0	79.6	6.1	6.1
	M-urban	(745)	36.9	38.0	10.6	21.1	8.7	35.6	8.5	14.0
	M-rural	(223)	39.5	33.6	9.9	15.7	13.9	23.3	18.4	16.6
Sex and origin countries	F-Kor-Ch	(36)	11.1	30.6	2.8	8.3	0.0	83.3	5.6	2.8
	F-Chinese	(9)	11.1	44.4	11.1	11.1	0.0	55.6	0.0	22.2
	F-other	(4)	0.0	25.0	25.0	0.0	0.0	100.0	25.0	0.0
	M- Kor-Ch	(458)	33.8	45.0	10.5	21.6	6.3	39.7	2.6	17.2
	M-Chinese	(94)	35.1	38.3	13.8	14.9	7.4	50.0	1.1	9.6
	M-Viet.	(170)	53.5	44.1	6.5	17.1	27.6	12.4	0.6	11.2
	M-Japanese	(94)	24.5	26.6	11.7	13.8	0.0	25.5	61.7	7.4
	M-Filipino	(92)	51.1	8.7	14.1	22.8	14.1	21.7	22.8	21.7
	M-other	(60)	23.3	13.3	8.3	26.7	0.0	38.3	18.3	11.7
(Multiple response)										

6.4.3.2 Conjugal Relations

People were very satisfied with conjugal relations in international marriages. However, the mean score of 4.13 point on a 5-point Likert scale for conjugal relations satisfaction among immigrants, ranging from 0 (very unsatisfied) to 5 (most satisfied), was lower than that of the Korean spouse (4.22 point).

When husbands and wives in international families had conflicts or disagreements, immigrants tended to rely on native friends (33.6 %) for help, followed by their own family or relatives (23.2 %), their spouse's family or relatives (23.2 %), and their spouse's friends (20.6 %).

Many international marriage couples seemed to have language difficulties. While most couples (96.3 %) answered that they used Korean when they communicate, Han Chinese and Japanese tended to communicate in Chinese and Japanese, respectively. More than one third of immigrants from the Philippines (31.6 %) spoke English with their Korean husbands

6.4.3.3 Children

About 52.8 % of the respondents gave birth to children from their current spouse. However, a relatively large proportion of Koreans (20.4 %) had children before their present marriage. About 16.4 % of the immigrants also replied that they had children before their current marriage. The rate of living together with Korean spouse's prior children was 48.2 %, but only 20.7 % lived with their immigrants spouse's prior children. As for women from Vietnam, this was mostly their first marriage and also their marriage being still relatively new, they had a fewer children than those of other national origin.

About 68.5 % of the respondents answered that the nursing their preschool children was taken care of either by themselves or by their partners. Moreover, only 23.7 % and 22.1 % of their children were taken to nurturing facilities and kindergartens, respectively. On the other hand, more than 38 % of the immigrants answered that their children were not given any outside care. This ratio was especially high among Vietnamese wives, showing that 70.9 % of their children were left without using any facilities for nursing care. Also, many marriage immigrant females residing in farm villages did not use outside nursing facilities largely because they could not find any – or none that they trusted.

According to the statistics furnished by the Ministry of Justice in 2007, approximately 10 % of the marriage immigrants pointed out that the lack of nursing facilities and/or having no person for child care was the most difficult problem for them.

The same statistics showed that the most difficult problems marriage immigrants faced in upbringing of their children was "children's education" (35 %), followed by the "high cost of education" (20 %), "studying at school" (20 %), and "alienation from friends" (15 %) (see Fig. 6.5).

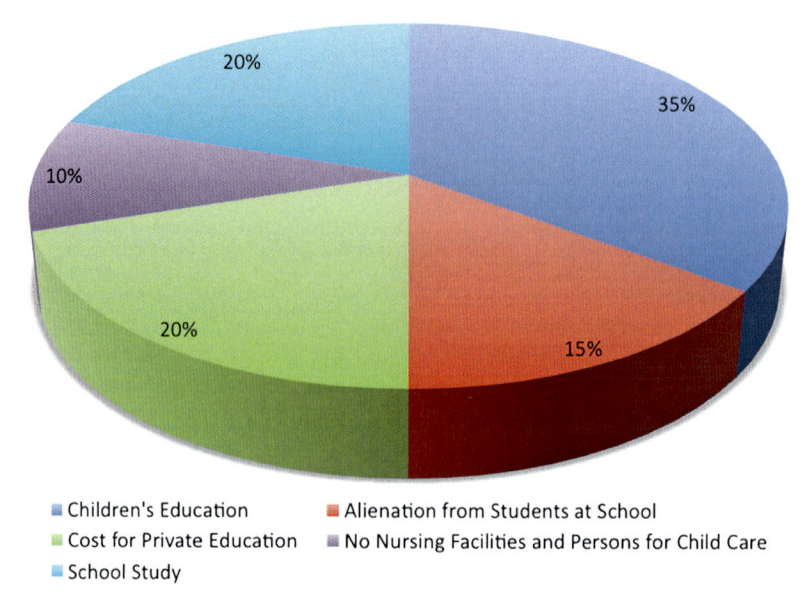

Fig. 6.5 Difficulties in children's education

The statistics also showed that the most worrying issues for children's school life were the relations with peer friends (35 %), study (23 %), too much homework (22 %), and parents' participation to school activities (20 %) (see Fig. 6.6).

In the dataset collected, 11.5 % of the immigrants specified in their response that their children were having difficulties in their school life, and 4.2 % responded that they were not satisfied with their children's teachers. They hoped mostly for "teacher's affectionate consideration of and care for their children", followed by the need for "multicultural education" (15.0 %) and for "affectionate concern and care from friends" (13.1 %). Families with Korean marriage partner picked "affectionate concern and care from friends" (20.5 %), followed by "extracurricular programs after school" (14.1 %) as the most wanted need for their children's school life.

6.4.3.4 Pregnant Women

The biggest difficulty for pregnant marriage immigrants was "longing for their homeland food" (53.1 %). Some answered "homesick for family" (15.6 %). The most difficult thing pregnant women faced when pregnant was "the lack of relevant education and information concerning pregnancy and child birth" (18.6 %), followed by the "post-natal nursing" (17.4 %) and "difficulty in communicating with medical staff" (14.5 %) (see Table 6.5).

However, when they were asked what they most desired when they gave a birth, only about 12.8 % gave their home country's food as the most desired.

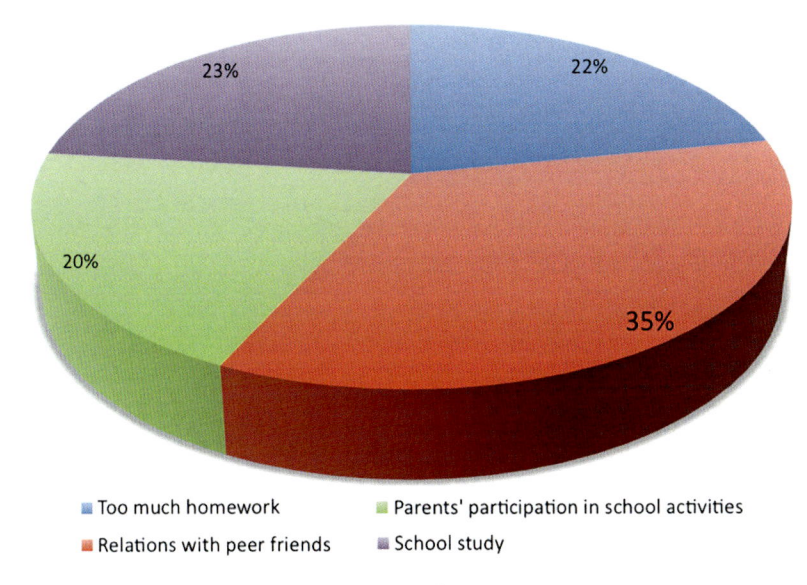

Fig. 6.6   Worrisome issues for children's school life

Others answered "the home country family's care" (19.8 %), the relevant "education on post-natal or baby care" (19.3 %) and "financial support" (14 %), while only around 9 % of the respondents indicated "health consultation after delivery" as the most needed help for them (see Table 6.6).

6.4.3.5   Relationship with Parents and Relatives

While satisfaction level with their spouse's parents and relatives was generally high, Vietnamese female marriage immigrants, in particular, showed the lowest level of satisfaction with this. About 27.8 % responded that they were in a difficult situation, showing that they usually had difficulty in dealing with their spouse's mother or sisters and brothers. In addition, 21.0 % of Filipinos indicated that they had problems with their partner's mother while 12.7 % of the Han Chinese females responded similarly (see Table 6.7).

6.4.3.6   Relationship with Friends and Neighbors

When asked, who were the closest persons for them, 48.9 % answered "neighbors", 36.3 % indicated "family, co-workers, association with like-minded people at church and other gatherings", and 26.4 % specifically pointed out "people at job and workplace". In order to deal with diverse problems arising from daily life, neighbors in general can be an important source for them to find the necessary social assistance. This also highlights the fact that a smooth relationship with

Table 6.5 Difficulties when giving birth in Korea

(Unit: N, %)

Migrant women survey			I don't have any difficulties	Lack of education and information about pregnancy and childbirth	Post-natal care	Difficulties in communicating with staff in the hospital	The burden of the cost of childbirth	Taking care of newborn baby	Not applicable
Total		(592)	22.0	18.6	17.4	14.5	10.1	7.8	9.6
Sex and region	F-urban	(422)	21.8	18.5	16.1	14.0	10.7	9.5	9.5
	F-rural	(170)	22.4	18.8	20.6	15.9	8.8	3.5	10.0
Sex and origin countries	F-Kor-Ch	(229)	25.3	17.9	20.1	3.5	16.6	8.3	8.3
	F-Chinese	(51)	27.5	13.7	11.8	15.7	11.8	7.8	11.8
	F-Vietnamese	(109)	25.7	14.7	7.3	28.4	3.7	4.6	15.6
	F-Japanese	(86)	12.8	25.6	25.6	12.8	5.8	9.3	8.1
	F-Filipino	(76)	10.5	28.9	17.1	23.7	6.6	9.2	3.9
	F-other	(41)	26.8	4.9	19.5	24.4	4.9	7.3	12.2

Table 6.6 Most necessary help when giving birth in Korea

(Unit: N, %)

Migrant women survey		(N)	My home country family's care of me	Education about post-natal or baby care	Financial support	My country's food	A health consultation for me after delivery	I don't need any help	Other
Total		(601)	19.8	19.3	14.0	12.8	9.0	9.3	15.8
Sex and region	F-urban	(427)	20.6	16.6	15.7	13.3	8.9	8.4	16.4
	F-rural	(174)	17.8	25.9	9.8	11.5	9.2	11.5	14.4
Sex and origin countries	F-Kor-Ch	(224)	18.3	17.4	22.3	9.4	9.4	10.3	12.9
	F-Chinese	(52)	19.2	21.2	13.5	19.2	7.7	13.5	5.8
	F-Vietnamese	(117)	23.9	14.5	5.1	20.5	5.1	10.3	20.5
	F-Japanese	(87)	6.9	31.0	10.3	9.2	11.5	5.7	25.3
	F-Filipino	(76)	28.9	18.4	7.9	14.5	14.5	2.6	13.2
	F-other	(45)	26.7	17.8	13.3	6.7	4.4	15.6	15.6

Table 6.7 The most difficult person in relationship

(Unit: N, %)

Migrant survey			Nobody	Mother-in-law	Spouse	Brother/ sister-in-law	Other family of spouse	Father-in-law	Children	Other
Total		(1,177)	72.2	8.2	4.1	3.7	1.4	0.8	0.8	8.9
Sex and region	F-urban	(822)	70.9	9.6	4.1	3.9	1.5	1.0	0.7	8.3
	F-rural	(241)	75.5	7.5	3.7	3.3	1.2	0.0	1.2	7.5
	Male	(114)	74.6	0.0	4.4	2.6	0.9	0.9	0.0	16.7
Sex and origin countries	F-Kor-Ch	(496)	73.4	8.1	3.2	4.4	1.4	0.6	0.8	8.1
	F-Chinese	(110)	66.4	12.7	7.3	1.8	1.8	0.9	0.0	9.1
	F-Vietnamese	(184)	73.9	7.1	3.3	1.1	1.1	0.0	2.2	11.4
	F-Japanese	(104)	74.0	5.8	6.7	7.7	1.0	0.0	1.0	3.8
	F-Filipino	(100)	55.0	21.0	4.0	5.0	3.0	4.0	0.0	8.0
	F-Other	(69)	87.0	4.3	2.9	1.4	0.0	0.0	0.0	4.3
	M-Kor-Ch	(75)	77.3	0.0	1.3	1.3	1.3	0.0	0.0	18.7
	M-Chinese	(15)	66.7	0.0	6.7	6.7	0.0	6.7	0.0	13.3
	M-other	(24)	70.8	0.0	12.5	4.2	0.0	0.0	0.0	12.5

neighbors was significant for getting personal assistance and the desired protection. With regard to friends with whom they can open their minds to, approximately 70.6 % of marriage immigrants answered "friends from the same homeland", while 47.8 % answered "Korean friends" and 14.8 %, "friends from a third country".

6.5 Ordinary Daily Lives and Social Attitude

Concerning female status and gender discrimination, 43.6 % of foreigners surveyed believed that women's status was actually lower compared to what Korean females believed. In particular, the Japanese, the Han Chinese and the Korean Chinese females rated the social status of Korean females as low. Concerning gender discrimination, 1/3 of the respondents answered that female discrimination was serious, and that females in farm villages faced more serious discrimination.

Many difficulties arose from cultural differences within international marriages in the couples' daily lives. It was shown that the most difficult issues, while living in Korea after their marriage, was "loneliness" (22.3 %), followed by "cultural differences" (14.6 %), "children issues" (13.8 %), "economic difficulties" (12.1 %), "language difficulties" (11.5 %), "family problems" (3.5 %), "being conscious of others' attention" (3.1 %), and "food and climate" (3.0 %). These findings suggested that the most urgent issue was overcoming socio-psychological loneliness and isolation while living in a different culture, especially in a country like Korea that for a long time took pride in its homogeneous culture (see Table 6.8).

Despite the increasing number of international marriages and the global environment that is making society more multicultural, Korean family culture is still centered on blood relations, manifesting a strong sense of intolerance or even hostility toward different cultures. Approximately 30.2 % of the respondents experienced varying degrees of social discrimination against international marriage couples. At the same time the extent of discrimination seems to differ in accordance with the nationalities and socio-economic levels of the immigrants' respective countries.

Considering that Korean society is more accustomed to its homogeneous culture, it is not surprising that prejudice and social discrimination against racial mixture still exist today, despite its rapid change, which has brought about a marked shift toward multicultural society through diverse contacts with foreigners.

Although the ethnic and cultural backgrounds of the marriage immigrants in Korea are becoming more complex, different groups seemed to experience, in varying degree, various difficulties in adjusting to the conditions of Korean society (Lee 2005). Moreover, it may be concluded from the above findings that new and diverse programs and policies of adjustment that would take into consideration the difference in the nationalities, together with that in the genders of foreign marriage partners, should be worked out for implementation as soon as possible.

Table 6.8 Most difficult thing, while living in Korea?

(Unit: N, %)

Migrant survey			Loneliness	Cultural difference	Childcare/ education problem	Financial problem (poverty)	Language problem	Troubles with family	Other people's attitude	Food, temperature
Total		(1,156)	22.3	14.6	13.8	12.1	11.5	3.5	3.1	3.0
Sex and region	F-urban	(805)	23.9	14.5	13.5	11.7	11.3	4.1	2.7	2.4
	F-rural	(239)	20.9	16.7	18.4	10.5	13.4	2.5	2.1	5.0
	Male	(112)	14.3	10.7	5.4	18.8	8.9	0.9	8.0	3.6
	F-Kor-Ch	(484)	27.9	15.1	13.6	14.7	3.1	4.8	4.1	2.1
	F-Chinese	(109)	20.2	11.0	14.7	11.9	24.8	4.6	0.9	2.8
	F-Vietnamese	(184)	19.0	10.3	14.7	6.5	18.5	1.6	2.2	5.4
	F-Japanese	(99)	11.1	18.2	30.3	10.1	16.2	6.1	0.0	2.0
	F-Filipino	(100)	30.0	21.0	4.0	8.0	17.0	2.0	1.0	5.0
	F-other	(68)	13.2	20.6	14.7	7.4	20.6	0.0	1.5	1.5
	M-Kor-Ch	(74)	14.9	9.5	5.4	23.0	4.1	0.0	8.1	4.1
	M-Chinese	(15)	20.0	6.7	0.0	20.0	20.0	0.0	0.0	0.0
	M-other	(23)	8.7	17.4	8.7	4.3	17.4	4.3	13.0	4.3

6.6 Economic Life

Regardless of whether an immigrant or a native, about 92 % of males in South Korea were employed in 2006; as shown in this dataset. On the other hand, 64 % of Korean females who are married internationally were employed, as opposed to only 34 % of foreign females who were employed. This clearly shows that while the employment rate of marriage-based female immigrants was considerably lower than that of Korean males, it was still much higher than that of all foreign females residing in Korea. A survey conducted by the Ministry of Health and Welfare in 2005, however, reported that 43 % of female marriage migrants had jobs (Seol et al. 2005), which is 9 % higher than the 34 % employment in 2006 that this study showed. The reason for this, in part at least, may have been that the employed marriage immigrants did not happen to be at home during the day when the survey was conducted, and thus not included in the survey. At any event, it is interesting to note that both surveys showed that the *Chosŏnjok* and Han Chinese registered the highest employment rate among female immigrants whereas the Vietnamese females had the lowest rate (see Table 6.9 below).

It is true that married immigrants also had already a relatively high rate of employment in their home country. Over 90 % of male immigrants and 3/4 of female immigrants have been employed before they came to Korea. The least employed female groups were Vietnamese females and Filipinas, of whom 44 % and 31 % respectively have had no experience of being employed in their home country. The jobs they held varied according to their nationality. Among male immigrants, those from the US, Europe and other advanced nations were mostly engaged in professional fields, as, for example, instructors in educational institutions. However, the *Chosŏnjok*, particularly its female immigrants, as well as those of the Han Chinese mostly worked in the catering and service sectors, while female workers from the Philippines and Vietnam mainly worked in factories, doing a manual labor job.

On the other hand, Korean husbands who married foreign females were mostly engaged in self-employed business, even though there were others who held a manual labor job. Also in rural areas, only 1/4 of them worked in the field of agriculture and fishing, while more than half of them were in manual labor. In the cases where Korean husbands had office jobs, we find approximately 26 % of their foreign wives were also employed. Among the respondents, whose Korean husbands had self-employed businesses or were not employed at all, about 40 % of their wives had jobs. These findings showed that the employment rate of female marriage immigrants varied according to their nationalities. The lower their husbands'economic status, the more foreign wives worked in order to sustain their living standard. When asked to pinpoint difficulties they felt most while working as a foreigner, male immigrants pointed out "low pay" and "long working hours," while female immigrants mentioned "financial burden in raising children" and "low pay."

Table 6.9 Employment status of internationally married couples

(Unit: N, %)

Migrants		Migrants	Worked in origin C.	Work in Korea	Korean spouse	
		N	%	%	N	%
Total		(1,170)	76.9	39.7	(1,098)	90.9
Sex	Female	(1,060)	75.4	34.2	(1,042)	92.3
	Male	(110)	92.2	91.8	(56)	64.3
Sex and region	F-urban	(819)	75.3	35.2	(806)	91.3
	F-rural	(241)	75.8	31.1	(236)	95.8
	Male	(110)	92.2	91.8	(56)	64.3
Sex and origin countries	F-Kor-Ch	(493)	76.8	43.4	(486)	92.0
	F-Chinese	(110)	84.2	44.5	(107)	94.4
	F-Vietnamese	(184)	55.6	17.9	(181)	92.8
	F-Japanese	(104)	86.1	21.2	(102)	94.1
	F-Fiilpino	(100)	69.3	28.0	(98)	89.8
	F-other	(69)	85.2	24.6	(68)	91.2
	M-Kor-Ch	(72)	96.6	94.4	(42)	66.7
	M-Chinese	(15)	83.3	86.7	(9)	55.6
	M-other	(23)	84.2	87.0	(5)	60.0

When asked who held the economic power and managed their living expenses, the responses unveiled the influence of the length of their stay in Korea as well as by gender. In other words, in the case of a couple with a foreign male and a Korean wife, it was the wife who managed both her own and husbands' incomes. In the case of Korean husband and foreign wife, on the other hand, the wife controlled her own income; even though there were a few cases where the husband managed his wife's income (see Table 6.10).

Furthermore, even in the cases of foreign wives and Korean husbands, many *Chosŏnjok*, Han Chinese, and Japanese wives managed their husband's income, even though this was relatively rare for the females from the Philippines and Vietnam. This is particularly true of Vietnamese wives who have had a shorter stay in Korea. However, because the Han Chinese and *Chosŏnjok* females had a higher ratio in managing their husbands' incomes than the Japanese females, despite the latter's longer period of living in Korea, one can conclude that cultural differences in the family's financial management do continue to influence internationally married couples.

As far as employment itself is concerned, the fact that men were mostly employed, in contrast to many women who were unemployed, mainly due to their 'child nursing', was more evident in rural areas than in urban areas. While there were more preschool children in rural areas than in urban areas, rural areas lacked institutional facilities or neighbors who can help immigrants take care of their children. Accordingly, 82 % of those unemployed female immigrants were willing

Table 6.10 Person who manages income (migrants' responses)

(Unit: N, %)							
Migrant survey			Myself	Both	Spouse	Parents-in-law	Other
Total		(338)	50.6	30.8	17.2	0.9	0.6
Sex	Female	(251)	61.8	29.5	6.8	1.2	0.8
	Male	(87)	18.4	34.5	47.1	0.0	0.0
Sex and region	F-urban	(209)	61.7	29.2	6.7	1.4	1.0
	F-rural	(42)	61.9	31.0	7.1	0.0	0.0
	Male	(87)	18.4	34.5	47.1	0.0	0.0
	F-Kor-Ch	(160)	65.6	27.5	5.6	1.3	0.0
	F-Chinese	(37)	59.5	27.0	8.1	0.0	5.4
Sex and origin countries	F-Vietnamese	(16)	43.8	37.5	12.5	6.3	0.0
	F-Japanese	(16)	62.5	31.3	6.3	0.0	0.0
	F-Filipino	(14)	64.3	21.4	14.3	0.0	0.0
	F-other	(8)	a	a	a	a	a
	M-Kor-Ch	(61)	14.8	34.4	50.8	0.0	0.0
	M-Chinese	(8)	a	a	a	a	a
	M-other	(18)	33.3	33.3	33.3	0.0	0.0

[a]% not shown due to small number of cases

to work if there was a chance, but they preferred jobs that would not affect their child nursing and education.

The main source of income in internationally married couples was "oneself, or spouse's income producing labor". According to our dataset for this study, in 2006, those who received government assistance accounted for 4 % only. It also showed that the *Chosŏnjok* male family (13 %) and Filipino family (8 %) received more government assistance because they had the lowest monthly income and experienced more financial difficulties.

It should also be noted that more than half of internationally married couples had the experience of remitting money to their families in their home country, sending about 1.5 million Korean Won (approximately US $1,500) on an average of three times a year, and that over 60 % of the Vietnamese and Filipino female marriage immigrants were sending money. Korean husbands, especially, those whose wives who were from the Philippines and Vietnam, believed that their foreign wives were sending money to their families more frequently than they themselves were aware of.

One can generally find out who has the economic power in a family by looking at their practices, such as how often marriage-based immigrants received an allowance and/or their family living expenses from their spouse, and who had direct access to a bank account or controlled their family's living expenses. Using these criteria, we found out that, among female marriage immigrants, those who had a certain economic power were the *Chosŏnjok*, Han Chinese, and Japanese wives, while those who had relatively low or no economic power were the Filipinos and Vietnamese wives (see Table 6.11).

Table 6.11 Ways of getting living costs from spouse

(Unit: N, %)

Migrant survey			Every time I need	Once a month	Draw some from my account	I manage living costs
Total		(585)	35.9	20.9	12.0	31.3
Sex	Female	(550)	34.0	21.1	11.6	33.3
	Male	(35)	65.7	17.1	17.1	0.0
Sex·region	F-urban	(412)	31.6	21.8	11.4	35.2
	F-rural	(138)	41.3	18.8	12.3	27.5
	Male	(35)	65.7	17.1	17.1	0.0
Sex·origin countries	F-Kor-Ch	(233)	20.6	18.9	14.2	46.4
	F-Chinese	(54)	18.5	24.1	18.5	38.9
	F-Vietnamese	(88)	65.9	23.9	3.4	6.8
	F-Japanese	(63)	28.6	15.9	12.7	42.9
	F-Filipino	(62)	58.1	22.6	9.7	9.7
	F-other	(50)	34.0	28.0	8.0	30.0
	M-Kor-Ch	(23)	73.9	17.4	8.7	0.0
	M-Chinese	(6)	33.3	33.3	33.3	0.0
	M-other	(6)	66.7	0.0	33.3	0.0

When asked to give a subjective evaluation of the status of their economic life in South Korea, spouses of married immigrants gave 3.8 point out of 10 (the 11 point scale ranging from 0 (the lowest) to 10 (the highest)). Presumably this indicates that they considered their economic status to be close to that of the poor. However, a more objective index showed that the *Chosŏnjok* wives believed that they were poorer than their Filipino counterparts, who were in fact more underprivileged.

In terms of their subjective life standard evaluations, the *Chosŏnjok* evaluated their status to be low, regardless of their gender, reflecting that their life in Korea was difficult, and that they were dissatisfied with the realities of their life there. The gap between their expectations and the reality may be bigger than that of other groups.

The marriage-based immigrants thus believed that while their families in their home country lived as a middle income family, they now enjoyed a relatively lower status in Korea, particularly when compared with the average Korean family. Only the Vietnamese women believed that their living standard in Korea had improved compared to that of their families in their home land.

6.7 Needs for Social Policy

During the last few years since 2006, the central and local governments have launched publicity campaigns announcing various policies supporting marriage-based immigrants in South Korea. As a result, many immigrants seemed to have become increasingly aware of the existence of the government's support systems and service programs. The survey data for this study also shows that about half of all marriage immigrants were aware of these services including the "child-care service for the poor and infants" and the "financial assistance for the poor". It also reveals that, in general, female immigrants were more aware of services provided for infants and women, while male immigrants were relatively more aware of services related to employment.

Even though most of these services have only been in existence since 2006, by the time our survey was conducted in October of 2006, one fifth of female marriage immigrants had already taken advantage of the Korean culture-related services such as Korean language education and Korean cuisine lessons. In particular, more women in rural communities than in urban cities have had more chances to experience such educational programs. This was particularly the case for the Japanese women and Filipinos, who tended to benefit more from these programs. The group that participated least in such immigrant social integration programs was the *Chosŏnjok*, who already spoke fluent Korean and were employed, and thus lacked free time.

The marriage-based immigrants thought that the Korean language education program was the most helpful service of all among the ones they have actually taken advantage of. When asked to pick their first and second most needed programs from a list of the ten programs, "Korean Language Education" was their most urgently needed program, followed by "Employment Education and Training" and "Computer and Information Technology (IT) Education". When asked how urgent each of these programs was for them, their response was that the "Computer and IT Education" and the "Employment Education and Training" as well as "Korean Language Education" were more urgent and essential.

Thus it appears that "Korean Language Education" was the most desired program by the marriage-based immigrants, except the *Chosŏnjok*, in their adjustment to the Korean society. However, it is also important to recognize that high demands for other programs such as "Employment Education and Training" and "Computer and IT Education" also existed, reflecting the immigrants'great desire to be employed as well as to meet their needs for practical and concrete programs that can actually help their real life experiences.

Moreover, significantly the male immigrants preferred a more "convenient time to attend" in order to take advantage of such social integration services, while the women immigrants, on the other hand, mostly wanted "support and assistance from one's partner and family", as well as more "convenient time to attend" in addition to "childcare service for their children". In this respect, it is also of great importance for those programs that are targeted at female married immigrants that more effective measures should also be instituted to help them receive the more urgently needed support and assistance from their Korean partners and families. Also, it is essential that these programs should be offered during hours that are convenient and easy for them to attend, and that they be accompanied by a child caring program while they attend these programs.

References

Kim, D.S. (2008). *Cross-Border Marriage: Process and Dynamics.* Seoul, Han yang University.

Korea National Statistics Office (KNSO) (2005/2007/2008). *Population Registration Statistics* (in Korean). <http://www.kosis.go.kr>. Accessed: October 2005 – April 2006.

Kwangju Women's Development Center (KWDC) (2003). *A Survey of Foreign Wives* (in Korean). Kwangju: KWDC.

Lee, H.K. (2005). "Marriage immigration and problems of coping among international marriage families" (in Korean). *Korean Journal of Population Studies* 28(1): 73–106.

Lee, Y.J., D.H. Seol, & Cho, S.N. (2006) "International marriages in South Korea: The Significance of nationality and ethnicity", *Journal of Population Research*, Vol. 23, No. 2, 165–182.

Ministry of Justice (MOJ). (2008). http://www.moj.go.kr/. *Annual Report of Statistics on Legal Migrants.*

Ministry of Justice (MOJ). (2006). http://www.moj.go.kr/. Accessed: 18 April 2006.

Park, J.S. (1982). "Communication problems between spouses in Korean–American international marriage" (in Korean). *Sungjŏn University Research Journal* 12: 99–136.

Seol, D.H, Kim, Y.T., Kim, H.M., et al. (2005). *Foreign Wives' Life in Korea: Focusing on the Policy of Welfare and Health* (in Korean). Kwachŏn: Ministry of Health and Welfare.

Seol, D.H., Lee, H.K, & Cho, S.N. (2007). "Marriage-based Immigrants and Their Families in Korea: Current Status and Policy Measures", Presented at the International Conference on Global Migration and the Household in East Asia, Seoul, 2–3 February 2007

Part III

Chapter 7
The Perception of Citizenship in Korea: Its Social and Political Variations

Jonghoe Yang

Abstract The purpose of this paper is to investigate how Koreans perceive citizenship and how their perceptions vary by some of their social and political characteristics. Analyses of 2004 KGSS data reveal that the citizenship, for the Koreans, consists of five components, that is, loyalty to the state, loyalty to the community, citizenship rights, political efficacy and political knowledge. But the concept is not uniform and bounded. People with different backgrounds conceptualize citizenship differently based on diverse grounds such as sex, age, political orientation, religion, and region of residence. Thus citizenship perceived by Koreans cannot be neatly characterized to be either the republican or the liberal, either the left or the right. Rather there are a variety of mixed forms, which reflect Korea's turbulent history of democratic development and recent changes including the neo-liberal reform after the 1997 economic crisis and the accelerated pace of globalization. Finally, a concept of culture-specific, but liberal, citizenship is proposed as a viable alternative in this conflicting situation.

7.1 Introduction

The purpose of this paper is to investigate how Koreans perceive citizenship, and how their perceptions vary in connection with some of their social and political characteristics, by analyzing a set of survey data collected on a national sample.

The concept citizenship can be traced back to the ancient Greek city states, but its modern use is closely related to the formation of the modern democratic nation-state in the eighteenth century (Oliver and Heater 1994, pp. 11–16). In democracy,

J. Yang (✉)
Department of Sociology, Sungkyunkwan University, 53 Myungryun-dong, Jongro-gu, Seoul 110-745, Korea

#1104 Lotte Castle Forest, Seocho-gu, Bangbae 4-dong, Seoul 137-836, Korea
e-mail: jhyang@skku.edu

M. Pohlmann et al. (eds.), *Citizenship and Migration in the Era of Globalization*, Transcultural Research – Heidelberg Studies on Asia and Europe in a Global Context, DOI 10.1007/978-3-642-19739-0_7, © Springer-Verlag Berlin Heidelberg 2013

every member of a state is guaranteed a set of basic rights claimable to the state, and is expected to perform certain duties required by the state. In other words, citizenship is a concept that defines the relationship between a citizen and the state and that delineates basic requisites prescribed for a member of a democratic society. Thus it is often noted that without the adequate development of citizenship, democracy cannot be truly consolidated (Isin and Turner 2007; Seligman 1992).

Democracy in Korea[1] has had a relatively short and turbulent history. A democratic government was first established after the American model by the US military government in 1948, followed by three decades of dictatorship and military rule. It was only after 1987 that the Korean polity and society were truly democratized. Prior to 1987, some of the basic rights of citizens were curtailed and dissidents were harshly persecuted by the ruling political elites, who claimed that Korean society was not ready yet for Western-style liberal democracy and that Asian values are different to those of a Western democracy.[2] There may be a certain truth in these claims; Koreans had long been accustomed to the monarchical form of government, then to colonial rule. They were only exposed to the democratic ideology after the establishment of the modern government about 60 years ago. During this short period of modern political experiment, however, Koreans have learned the value of democracy, fought for it, and won it.

Still, democracy in Korea cannot be said to be a uniform concept; it has different meanings to different people. And the same applies to citizenship; not only different political parties but also different groups of people may have different ideas about it. Some would demand a more egalitarian and republican form of citizenship; others a more liberal type. Politically progressive citizens may prefer active citizenship, while conservatives may refer to a more passive form. Due to the short history of democracy and the rapid social changes that occurred in recent years in Korea, we expect that the concept citizenship varies widely across different groups of people. In addition, the recent pace of globalization that is rapidly breaking down national borders poses an important challenge to the traditional concept of citizenship.

Research on citizenship has mostly been centred on its legal or institutional aspects. Very few empirical studies, both in Korea and worldwide, have focused on the experiences of ordinary people (Choe 2006; Lister 2003; Miller-Idriss 2006; Theiss-Morse 1993). However, as cases in many developing countries attest, democracy cannot succeed by legal provisions and institutional arrangements alone; the understanding, competence, and active participation of ordinary citizens are essential. This paper attempts to fill at least in part the lacuna created by the paucity of empirical studies on this subject and to contribute to the understanding of Korean people's ideas on citizenship.

7.2 Theoretical Arguments and Empirical Studies

7.2.1 The Concept of Citizenship

The concept of citizenship has a long history; consequently it has diverse meanings and definitions depending on ideological inclinations and political visions. The classical Greco-Roman idea of "civic virtues" or of being a "good citizen" is probably the first approach to citizenship, which is now known as the civic republican or communitarian view. In the seventeenth century the liberal version of citizenship emerged in England when Englishmen demanded and won a set of fundamental legal and political rights that could not be overridden by the monarch (Oliver and Heater 1994, pp. 11–16). In addition to these citizens' duties and rights, political identities and loyalty to the state and to the community have been associated with citizenship in the modern nation state. Democracy also requires active citizens who know about, and participate actively in, public and political life.

The concept of citizenship basically involves the freedom and equality of the individual members of a state. However, depending on what freedom and which equality are guaranteed, and on whether the issues of identity and competence are considered, there are a variety of definitions and models of citizenship. For example, Oliver and Heater (1994, pp. 206–212) introduce four models of citizenship: Robert N. Bellah et al.'s model of modern citizenship, which includes three distinct types, the politics of community, the politics of interest, and the politics of the nations; Bryan Turner's historical model, which distinguishes four different types of citizenship by two criteria, rights either handed down from above or extracted from below, and the emphasis on either public space or private space; Derek Heater's model of citizenship which consists of five essential elements; finally A.E. Porter's model which includes three components of citizenship.

These models are basically similar, but Heater's model (Heater 1990) seems to provide a comprehensive picture of citizenship with the relationships among the essential elements. The model contains five elements, that is, civil, political, and social rights and duties, plus civic virtue and identity. The first three elements flow from citizenship as status, which are adopted from T. H. Marshall's influential definition. According to Marshall, "the civil element is composed of the rights necessary for individual freedom – liberty of person, freedom of speech, thought and faith, the right to own property and to conclude valid contracts, and the right to justice (that is) the right to defend and assert all one's rights and terms of equality with others and by due process of law". The political element includes "the right to participate in the exercise of political power as a member of the body invested with political authority or as an elector of the members of such a body". The social element consists of "the right to a modicum of economic welfare and security (and the) right to share to the full in the social heritage and to live the life of civilized being according to the standards prevailing in society" (Marshall 1973, pp. 71–72).

The fourth component of Heater's model is "civic virtue" which denotes the attitudes and behavior of a "good citizen", who is loyal to the state and to the

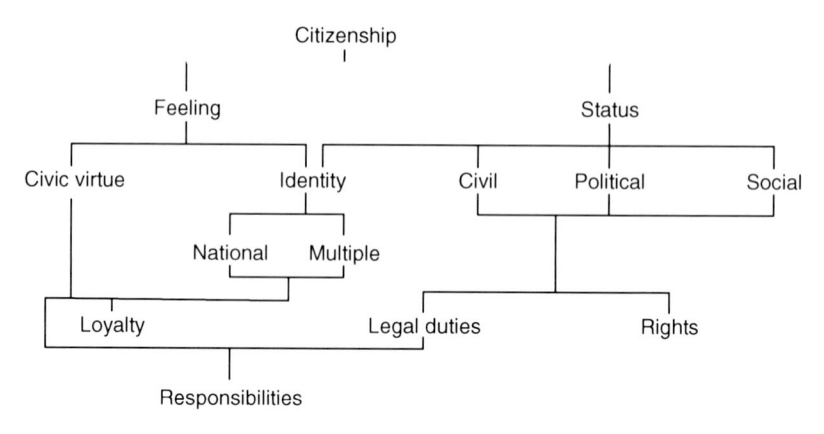

Fig. 7.1 Heater's model of citizenship (Source: Oliver and Heater (1994, p. 210))

community. Together with legal duties, it expresses itself as a sense of responsibility. Finally, identity refers both to legal status as a member of a state, and to a feeling or a sense of belonging to a nation (see Fig. 7.1).

Porter proposes a similar but more simplified model of citizenship (Porter 1993). According to his model, citizenship consists of three components, that is, status, volition and competence. Citizenship as status refers to the relationship of the citizen to the state, more precisely the citizens' legal, political and social position in relation to the state. This component is often defined as a set of rights and duties, and includes legal identity. Volition is equivalent to feeling in Heater's model. It is defined in the form of attitudes and behavior in relation to others in the community. It also includes identity in the sense of fraternity, and loyalty in the sense of honor and pride. Up to this point, Porter's model is almost exactly the same as Heater's. However, Porter's model has one more component, competence. Competence involves a citizen's knowledge and efficacy, that is, "understanding of the political, legal and social systems, skills for participation, and a predisposition to respect democratic modes of procedure" (Oliver and Heater 1994, pp. 209–212). By combining these two models, we can come up with a comprehensive model of citizenship, consisting of status (or rights), civic virtue (or responsibilities), identity and competence. In this study I consider three components of citizenship, namely, status (civil, political and social rights), civic virtue, and competence, leaving out the identity element due to the lack of information in the data to be analyzed.

In approaching the concept of citizenship, there are two ways or aspects: legal or institutional, and empirical or experiential. Many studies testify that these two aspects of citizenship diverge considerably. In other words, the emphasis on its legal and institutional aspects tends to mislead people into regarding the concept as fairly uniform and static. But "a nation-state's legal policies for citizenship and naturalization cannot be automatically extrapolated to the understanding of citizenship among ordinary citizens in their everyday lives. Citizenship is a concept whose meaning can shift for individuals and vary across populations, rather than acting as a bounded, unified or essential identity shared by all members of the same national or ethnic groups" (Miller-Idriss 2006, pp. 541–542). In short, individuals and groups within a country may conceptualize citizenship differently. So the questions are: What (factors) makes the concept vary? Which individuals or groups extract which meanings from the concept? Let me first examine some theoretical issues and review some of the existing empirical studies on these questions before analyzing empirical data.

7.2.2 Theoretical Issues and Empirical Studies

Such recent changes as the accelerated pace of globalization, the advent of postmodernism, and the onslaught of economic liberalism that are observed in most of the advanced societies have provoked renewed controversies about the meaning of citizenship. Especially the rise of global market forces has eroded the state's autonomy, weakening the citizens' bond with the state (Falk 2000). Thus Andrew Vandenberg states that citizenship is "not just controversial but essentially controversial" (Vandenberg 2000, p. 3). There are basically two contested theoretical issues surrounding citizenship. One is the tension or antagonism between the republican or communitarian emphasis on duties and obligations, and the liberalists' stress on rights. The other is the dichotomy between freedom, which is essential for capitalist free market, and equality, which is the principal impetus for the welfare or socialist state. This section examines not only these basic theoretical issues and related empirical studies, but also some of the newly-emerging issues and studies.

The first issue is the tension between the republican and the liberal views on citizenship. The republican idea of citizenship is a traditional one emphasizing civic virtues or the citizen's duties. An ideal citizen in old city-states was a good citizen who was loyal to the state as well as to the community. The republican idea is often regarded as synonymous with the communitarian one that emphasizes common traditions and understandings shared with neighbors. In contrast to the communitarian view, the liberal view is a recent one, developed chiefly in the United States. The core of the view is individualism, assuming that individuals are autonomous and that as citizens they have rights or privileges unencumbered by the state (Oliver and Heater 1994, pp. 115–122).

In their comparative study, Pamela Johnson Conover and others attempted to test the hypothesis that Americans have the liberal conception of citizenship while the British the communitarian, due to their particular histories and political traditions, by analyzing a set of empirical data on citizens' notions of rights, duties and identities. They found that Americans mostly concentrate on civil rights while the British give primacy to social rights, thus confirming the hypothesis. However, they also found substantial cases which contradict the typical patterns in both countries, suggesting that the two countries are not homogeneous in terms of people's views on citizenship (Conover et al. 1991, p. 803).

In a study of young British people, Ruth Lister and her colleagues (2003) draw a similar conclusion to that of Conover et al. by indicating that young British citizens are more likely to subscribe to the communitarian model than the liberal one.

According to the authors, the young British have a relatively clear idea of a good citizen, one who has a "considerate and caring attitude toward others and a constructive approach towards and active participation in the community" (Lister et al. 2003, p. 244). But they understand citizenship in fluid terms drawing on diverse theoretical categories.

On the other hand, others try to find out how citizens conceptualize "a good citizen". For example, Elizabeth Theiss-Morse (1993) defines a good citizen as a politically active and informed citizen, and devises a scale consisting of ten items to measure how citizens themselves conceptualize a good citizen. The ten items include: (1) control own lives, (2) participate politically, (3) vote regularly, (4) choose a good leader, (5) civil disobedience, (6) leave government officials alone, (7) make efforts to find out about candidates and issues, (8) do not waste time participating, (9) need not be involved in politics, (10) let the government know their opinions. Using a factor analysis, she identifies four perspectives on citizenship which turn out to be useful in predicting behavior.

In a similar vein, Russell J. Dalton defines "citizenship as a set of norms of what people think people should do as good citizens" (Dalton 2008, p. 78), and constructs a scale of 9 items to measure citizenship norms. They are: (1) vote in elections, (2) be active in voluntary organizations, (3) be active in politics, (4) form his or her opinion independently of others, (5) serve on a jury when called, (6) always obey laws, (7) serve in the army when required, (8) report a crime, (9) support people. Using factor analytic techniques, Dalton extracts two dimensions from these 9 items, which are: citizen duty and engaged citizenship. The concept of engaged citizenship is associated with what Ronald Inglehart calls postmaterial values. Dalton finds in an American sample that these two sets of norms are not contradictory, but "reflect contrasting emphases in the role of a democratic citizen" and generational differences indicating a shift from duty-based citizenship to engaged citizenship (Dalton 2008, p. 83).

German citizenship is a little different from either the American or British cases, according to the study by Cynthia Miller-Idriss (2006). Her analysis of interviews with young German students about conceptions of citizenship and belonging shows that citizenship and national identity are closely intertwined with each other, and that young Germans understand citizenship as being based primarily on cultural criteria. A good citizen is one "who helps others, who are a part of society, pay their taxes, have or raise children, try to do good and don't engage in criminal activity" (Miller-Idriss 2006, p. 554).

From this review of previous empirical studies, it seems clear that the notions of citizenship perceived by the people in one country tend to differ from those in other countries, depending on their political histories and cultural traditions. These studies also suggest that perceptions of citizenship within a society are not uniform but vary.

The second theoretical issue concerns whether an emphasis should be placed on freedom or equality in citizenship. Marshall's idea of the tripartite rights of citizens, that is, civil, political, and social rights, addresses this issue, reflecting not only the history of their emergence but also the relationship between citizenship and capitalism (Marshall 1973). Capitalism is said to contribute to the consolidation of civic rights because freedom includes economic freedom, but is antithetical to social rights which involve the government's intervention in the economy and in private property in its effort to level off economic inequality among citizens. This is one of the principal issues that divide the socialists or social democrats and the new right. The leftists give higher priority to welfare than to the property right, which is regarded as sacrosanct by the rightists. Thus there is an ideological divide in the citizenship components, the left stressing social rights in contrast to the civic rights emphasized by the right. Recently Isin and Turner (2007) have observed that there is a tendency toward the erosion of welfare economies and social rights because of neo-conservative or neo-liberal economic policies by modern democratic states.

Chack Kie Wong and Ka Ying Wong investigate Chinese perceptions of citizenship and explore whether social rights and responsibilities are unified at both ideal and practical levels. From their analyses of a sample of Hong Kong citizens, the authors find that contrary to conventional wisdom, the Chinese have a strong belief in social citizenship. According to the results of their analyses, the Chinese have a high expectation of the universal ideals of social citizenship, and at the practical level, the Chinese generally have a "right deficit", referring to their recognition of more responsibilities than rights (Wong and Wong 2004).

A third issue confronting the citizenship theory is "hierarchical citizenship". A significant feature of citizenship is egalitarianism. But in reality, many groups, especially women and minority groups, are often deprived of their basic rights or discriminated against, and feel that they are "second-class citizens" (Oliver and Heater 1994, p. 40). Race, ethnicity and religion are among the most often found grounds for deprivation and discrimination. Sometimes, less-educated, less well-to-do and certain members of a subculture such as homosexuals are also regarded, albeit implicitly, to be inferior citizens. Thus they may demand more rights and protection than others and have different ideas on citizenship to the "first-class citizens". Indeed, according to Evelyn Glenn, the history of citizenship is a history of "struggle by those excluded to gain the rights of citizens" (Glenn 2000, p. 1). Even in the era of globalization when the ties between citizenship and a particular nation-state significantly diminish, "new forms of race, class and gender inequality" emerge (Glenn 2000, p. 16).

In fact, many empirical studies reveal differing degrees of variation in the notion of citizenship according to individuals' demographic and socio-economic characteristics. For example, Wong and Wong (2004) find that gender, age, educational level, housing type, occupation, household income and subjective social position of their Chinese sample are correlated with components of social rights. In general, the respondents with a middle-class background are more idealistic about the social rights and responsibilities of citizenship. Lonnie R. Sherrod's study (2008) also reveals the significant relationships between young people's views of citizenship rights and the individual variables of age, parental education, ethnicity, and aspects of political self-concept. Russell J. Dalton (2008) shows strong generational differences between patterns of citizenship, and interprets these results as reflecting the recent shift of citizen values in advanced industrial democracies. But Theiss-Morse's study (1993) on American citizens does not find any strong relationship between citizenship perspectives and respondents' background variables, except for age and education.

Fourthly, citizenship must be learned and cultivated. In other words, education is required for acquiring citizenship. Citizens should know about the state and politics, perform duties, enjoy rights, and be loyal and responsible to the state and the community. Thus, knowledge and efficacy are regarded as among the essential components of citizenship.

Fifth is the issue of coherence or incoherence among the components of citizenship. As in the case of the contrasting emphasis between civil and political rights on the one hand, and social rights on the other, the patterns of relationship among the components of citizenship are expected to differ among countries with different democratic histories and social and political cultures. For example, Marie-Hélène Chastenay and her colleagues (2004) tried to distinguish dimensions of Canadian and Belgian citizenship, and to correlate the dimensions with one another. Results reveal that three dimensions of citizenship, namely national identity, social equality and norms, and participation are identified in both countries, and that the relationships among the dimensions and variables vary across sub-samples, with the exception of a possible link between aspects of identity and participation.

Other important issues brought up by scholars include the relationship between human rights and the rights of citizenship, and the issue of global versus cosmopolitan citizenship (Isin and Turner 2007).

From the above discussion it seems clear that the meaning of citizenship may differ according to a society's or an individual's historical, ideological, and socio-economic backgrounds. Indeed empirical studies reveal divergent conceptualizations of citizenship by different societies and by people with different characteristics. In the next section, a brief review of the history of Korean citizenship and empirical works is presented.

7.3 Citizenship in Korea: A Brief Review of Its History and Existing Studies

Traditionally the Koreans have had a strong sense of ethnic identity. The notion of nationalistic and exclusive national identity has been reinforced by the Koreans' historical experiences such as the centralized monarchical regimes until the end of nineteenth century, Japanese colonial rule (1910–1945), and the division of the country into the communist North and the liberal South since 1945. During the colonial period, nationalist leaders emphasized Korea's long, unbroken history and ethnic homogeneity. The military government (1961–1992) not only stressed ethnic nationalism in its efforts for economic development, but also greatly curtailed many of the citizenship rights (Choe 2003).

It was the Great Struggle for Democracy in 1987 that provided decisive momentum for the consolidation of democracy and citizenship. As a result of the 1987 Struggle, the Constitution was amended to expand people's political rights, to better protect citizens' bodies and lives, to guarantee more fully the freedom of expression, and to include the citizen's right to resist unjust government actions. Subsequent civilian and progressive governments have added to these constitutional provisions the legal and institutional frameworks to protect and expand citizenship rights (Choe 2006).

Recent democratic reform, particularly the neo-liberal reform after the 1997 IMF bailout, has almost uprooted the lingering traditional (Confucian) values such as collectivism, harmony, cooperation and community (Yang 2003). As a consequence, individual rights and private interests have taken precedence over communal concerns and public interests. In terms of citizenship and national identity, these recent changes imply that communitarian citizenship and ethnic national identity recede, whereas liberal citizenship and more flexible identity are brought forward, especially amongst the well-to-do (Kim 2007, p. 458).

However, these institutional and structural changes have not necessarily been accompanied by corresponding changes in the public understanding of citizenship and nationality. In fact Koreans do not usually distinguish between nationality and citizenship (Lee 2008, p. 247). Nor do they have a clear concept of citizenship, especially among the older Koreans. Probably reflecting this historical experience, there are very few empirical studies on citizenship in Korea. It is only within the last few years that a few empirical works have appeared on citizenship and nationality. Among these, Hyun Choe's works are almost singular. He has presented a number of empirical studies on citizenship since the turn of the century.

In his 2005 paper, Choe (2005) compared public understanding of citizenship between Korea and Japan by analyzing, in light of Bryan Turner's model of citizenship, the 2004 Korean General Social Survey (KGSS) data, which contain the 2004 International Social Survey Program (ISSP) citizenship module. His study finds both similarities and differences between the two countries; they are similar in that the citizens in both countries have strong political concerns with the orientation more toward public space, but Koreans are more active than their Japanese counterparts in public activities. According to Turner's scheme, the Korean concept of citizenship resembles the French model while the Japanese concept shares many characteristics with the British model.

Choe's 2006 paper reports the results of an analysis of the same 2004 KGSS data. A major purpose of his study was to see how the recent consolidation of democracy and expansion of citizenship on the institutional level affected civil consciousness among average Koreans. One of the findings is that the younger generation educated after 1987 tends to place more emphasis on individual human rights than the older generation. But the younger citizens' egalitarianism and solidarity are relatively weak (Choe 2006).

In a different paper Choe (2007) investigates how Koreans conceptualize national identity and multicultural citizenship by analyzing a set of survey data. According to his findings, Koreans do not have a strong national identity based on kinship. Instead they seem to support a kind of political national identity by placing a great emphasis on political-economic contribution, communication, and the feeling of belonging as the criteria of citizenship. This study also finds that Koreans are not yet ready for multicultural citizenship by showing biased attitudes toward foreign immigrants, favoring the American and European immigrants in contrast to their unfavorable attitudes toward East and South Asian ones.

On the other hand, Kiseon Chung (2004) analyzes the 2003 KGSS data to compare Koreans' conception of national identity with those of other countries. Some of her findings are as follows. First, Koreans tend to emphasize civic factors more than ethnic factors among the constituents of national identity. Second, a comparison with 24 other countries reveals that Korea is placed about in the middle among the countries considered on the inclusiveness-exclusiveness scale of national identity. Third, the better-educated and the younger have more inclusive and open ideas of national identity than those of their less-educated and older counterparts.

Though these studies have made some significant contributions to the nascent area of the public's perceptions of citizenship in Korea, many issues still remain unanswered.

7.4 Data, Measurement of Variables and Methods of Analysis

7.4.1 The Data

The data to be analyzed in this study is from the Korean General Social Survey (KGSS) conducted in 2004 by the Survey Research Center, Sungkyunkwan University. The survey was conducted on a national sample of 2,500 respondents, but the response rate was 66 %, or 1,312 cases. The data include the 2004 ISSP citizenship module which contains a set of items about civic virtues (responsibilities), citizenship rights, civic tolerance, political and social participation, and political competence. Among these items, those representing civic virtues, citizenship rights and political competence have been utilized in this study.

7.4.2 Measurement of Variables

The variable, civic virtues, consist of ten items, to each of which respondents were asked to answer on a seven-point scale of importance. The items are (1) to vote in public elections, (2) never to try to evade taxes, (3) always to obey laws and regulations, (4) to keep watch on the actions of government, (5) to subject your own opinion to critical examination, (6) to be active in social or political associations, (7) to choose products which are good for society or nature even if they cost a bit more, (8) to help those people in Korea who are worse off than oneself, (9) to help those people in the rest of the world who are worse off than oneself, (10) to be willing to serve in the military at a time of need.

Citizenship rights contain six items, each of which was to be answered on a ten-point scale of importance. They are: (1) all citizens have an adequate standard of living; (2) the government authorities respect and protect the rights of minorities; (3) the government authorities treat everybody equally regardless of their position in society; (4) politicians take into account the views of citizens before making decisions; (5) people be given more opportunities to participate in public decision-making; (6) citizens may engage in acts of civil disobedience when they oppose government actions.

Political competence includes four items, two measuring political efficacy, two representing political knowledge. These items were designed to be answered on a five-point scale from "strongly agree" to "strongly disagree". The items read as follows: (1) people like me don't have any say in what the government does, (2) I don't think the government cares much what people like me think, (3) I feel I have a pretty good understanding of the important political issues facing our country, (4) I think most people are better informed than I am about the important political issues we are facing.

An independent variable, political ideology, was measured by the answers to the following question on a five-point scale from "strongly progressive" to "strongly conservative". The question is: to what extent do you think you are politically progressive or conservative? Another variable that measures political ideology was types of political party supported. Respondents were asked to answer which political party they favor most among the existing five major parties. These parties were grouped into the three types, that is, conservative, progressive and radical depending on their ideological orientations.

Other independent and control variables include respondents' gender, age, education, occupation, household income, religion (Buddhism, Protestantism, Catholic, Other religions and No religion), region of residence (four broad regions of Korea, that is, Seoul, Yeoungnam, Honam and Others), subjective stratification (six point scale), class (Hong Doo-Seung's class scheme 1983).

7.4.3 Methods of Analysis

First, the three kinds of dependent variables that measure Korean citizenship were analyzed using factor analysis to find the components that constitute the Korean understanding of citizenship.

Second, these components of Korean citizenship were correlated with each other to investigate the internal relationships among them.

Third, in order to decide whether political ideology distinguishes between the liberal and the communitarian citizenship, measures of political ideology were correlated with the components of citizenship.

Fourth, to find out the possible variations in the People's concepts of citizenship, respondents' demographic and socio-economic characteristics were correlated with the components of citizenship. To measure relative importance of the independent variables in their effects on the dependent variables, a series of multiple regression analyses was conducted.

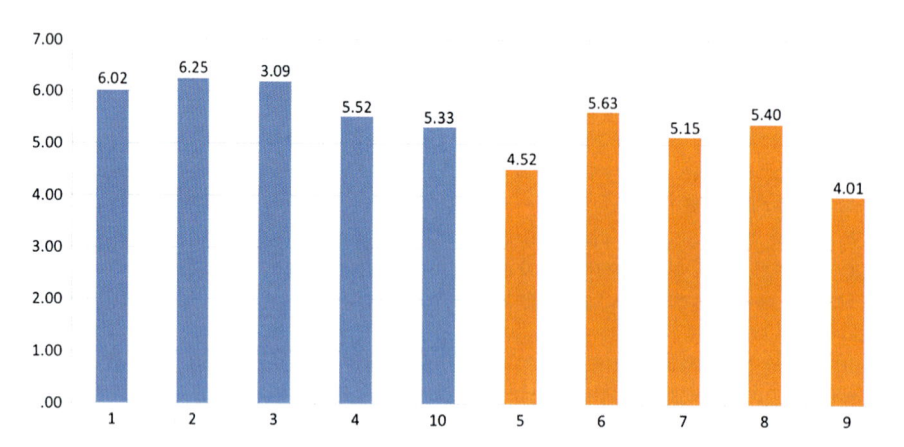

Fig. 7.2 Average scores of the ten items of civic virtues
Note: The first five items represent citizens' loyalty to the state, and the next five citizens' loyalty to the community. The wording of each item appears on page 128.

7.5 Components of Citizenship and Their Internal Relationships

The items of civic virtues that we aimed to measure were what the respondents thought to be important for being a good citizen, and which are traditionally regarded as the core of citizenship. They are basically the responsibilities that a good citizen is supposed to fulfill faithfully. According to the traditional conceptualization, a good citizen should be loyal both to the state and to the community. In other words, a good citizen must have a good relationship with, and commitment to, not only the state, but also fellow citizens.

Indeed a factor analysis extracts two factors from the ten items (see Appendix A.1 for the results of the factor analysis). One factor consists of five items from (1) to (4) and (10), which represent a citizen's loyalty (or duties) to the state. The other five items, from (5) to (9), constitute another factor indicating one's loyalty (or duties) to the community. As Fig. 7.2 shows, the Korean citizens regard loyalty to the state as slightly more important than loyalty to the community. Among the ten items, paying taxes and obeying laws, both in loyalty to the state, attain the highest average points, implying that average Koreans still maintain a state-oriented concept of citizenship.

In terms of citizenship rights, the six items turn out to represent a single factor according to a factor analysis (see Appendix A.2). As seen in the Fig. 7.3, however, there are significant internal variations. In general the political rights represented by items (3)–(5) are regarded to be more important than the economic and social rights, which support at least in part Marshall's theory of a historical development of citizenship rights. In other words, the Korean concept of citizen's rights is still in the process of developing, unlike the case of Western democracies. The right of disobedience and the minority right are the least important items. This result seems to reflect the distinct Korean situation that Korea has few minority problems and that civil disobedience is a relatively new concept to many of the Koreans.

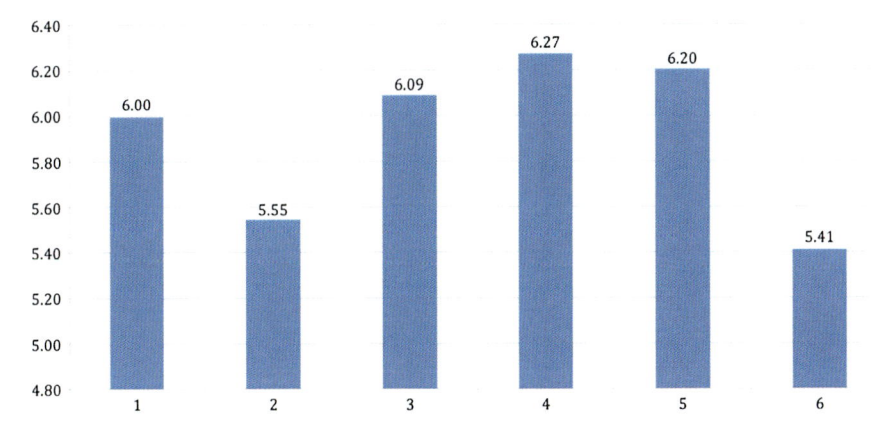

Fig. 7.3 Average scores of the six items of citizenship rights
Note: The wording of each items appears on page 128.

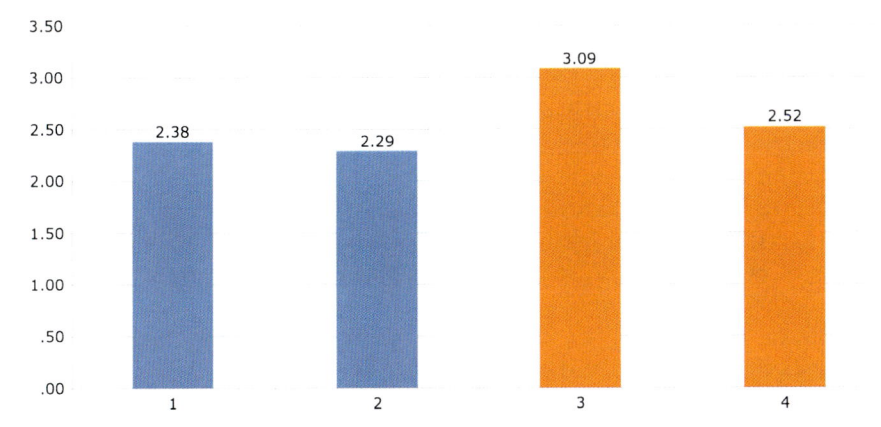

Fig. 7.4 Average scores of the four items of political competence
Note: The first two items represent political efficacy, and the next two measure political knowledge. The wording of each items appears on page 128–129.

The political competence items are divided into two factors. The first factor consisting of the two items (1) and (2) measures political efficacy, and the second factor comprising the items (3) and (4) represents political knowledge. In general Korean citizens have slightly more political knowledge than political efficacy, as seen in Fig. 7.4.

Among these five components of citizenship to be considered here, the three components representing civic virtues and citizenship rights are closely related with each other, as the results of Pearson's correlation analyses between the factors show. The coefficients are above .400 (Table 7.1). In other words, those who think that civic virtues are important also regard citizenship rights to be important, and vice versa. On the other hand, the two components of political competence do not uniformly correlate with civic virtues and rights. Political efficacy has a significant

Table 7.1 Correlation among the five components of citizenship

	L-state	L-comm	C-right	P-effic	P-know
1-state	1.000	0.514[***]	0.477[***]	−0.002	0.018
1-comm		1.000	0.407[***]	0.084[***]	0.54
c-right			1.000	−0.018	0.059[*]
p-effic				1.000	0.158[***]

L-state loyal to the state, *L-comm* loyal to the community, *C-right* citizenship rights, *P_effic* political efficacy, *P-know* political knowledge
[*]$p < 0.05$, [**]$p < 0.01$, [***]$p < 0.001$

relationship with loyalty to the community, and political knowledge with civic rights. However, the Pearson's coefficients for the relationships are rather small, .084 and .059 respectively. Thus, in the average Korean's mind, citizenship consists mainly of civic virtue and rights. Political competence may be a slightly distant component of citizenship to many of the Koreans.

7.6   Political Ideology and Perception of Citizenship

One of the most important theoretical issues on citizenship is the tension between the liberal and the republican or communitarian conception of citizenship, as discussed in the previous section. The liberal model emphasizes individual rights more than responsibilities, and among the rights, civic and political rights more than social rights. On the other hand, the communitarian model prioritizes communal aspects of civic virtue, and regards social rights more important than civic or political rights. These contrasting views on citizenship are closely related to differing political orientations. The left or the socialists are basically communitarian, while the conservatives or the right generally support the liberal view of citizenship.

Classes also have a bearing on social rights. According to Marshall, securing rights erodes class differences and enhances egalitarianism, which implies a threat to class privileges on the part of capitalist class. Thus the economically well-to-do class would oppose the extension of social rights, while lower or working classes are likely to support it (Oliver and Heater 1994, p. 34).

Tables 7.2, 7.3, and 7.4 show the results of correlation and regression analyses between each of the five components of citizenship and four independent variables, namely, political orientation, ideological type of the political party supported, class (Hong Doo-Seung's class scheme), and subjective class position. According to the results, political orientation is negatively correlated with both measures of political competence, indicating that the more politically conservative a person is, the less politically competent they are liable to be (Table 7.2). Similarly, the more one supports the conservative party, the less politically efficacious, as seen in Table 7.3. On the other hand, the findings show that the upper classes tend to be more politically competent than lower classes, regardless of whether they are objectively or subjectively perceived classes (Tables 7.2 and 7.4). In sum, the progressive upper class members turn out to be politically more competent than others. The variable, subjective class is also significantly, but negatively, related to loyalty to the state,

Table 7.2 Correlation coefficients for the relationships between components of citizenship and respondents' political orientation and subjective class position

	L-state	L-comm	C-right	P-effic	P-know
Political orientation	−.002	−.029	−.041	−.111***	−.145***
Subjective class	−0.66*	.002	−.003	.128***	.218***

Note: *p < 0.05, **P < 0.01, ***P < 0.001

Table 7.3 Regression results for the relationships between components of citizenship and types of party supported

	Dependent variables								
	L-state			L-comm			C-rights		
Party dummy	B	SE	ß	B	SE	ß	B	SE	ß
Conservative	.143*	.062	.075	.051	.073	.023	.063	.058	.036
Radical	−.109	.074	−.048	.013	.087	.005	.081	.068	.039
Constant	5.834***			4.908***			5.891***		
R square	.011			.000			.002		
N	1,083			1,088			1,081		

	Dependent variables					
	P-efficiency			P-knowledge		
Party dummy	B	SE	ß	B	SE	ß
Conservative	−.133*	.064	−.068	−.083	.046	−.060
Radical	.014	.076	.006	.042	.054	.025
Constant	2.391***			2.851***		
R square	.005			.005		
N	1,102			1,106		

Note: *p < 0.05, **P < 0.01, ***P < 0.001

meaning that the higher one's subjective class position, the less important he or she regards loyalty to the state as a condition of being a good citizen. Conservative party supporters also consider loyalty to the state an important component of citizenship. Thus, the conservative (subjective) lower class members seem to regard loyalty to the state more important than other class members do.

However, none of the independent variables considered here is significantly related with citizenship rights as a whole. In order to see whether citizenship rights are divided into civic and political rights on the one hand, and social rights on the other, according to class position and political orientation as Marshall argues, regression analyses were conducted between each of the six items of citizenship rights and the four class and political orientation variables. Among the six items, the first one measures citizen's social right in the sense of Marshall's scheme. The results of statistical analyses show that working class and old-middle class members consider it less important as an essential right of a citizen, contrary to Marshall's theory. Instead, the working class along with the new-middle class and the politically progressive regard civil disobedience an important citizenship right. Some politically radical respondents also think that equal treatment by the government is an important citizen's right (Table 7.5). These findings probably reflect the democratic history of modern Korea, or the experiences of great struggles against harsh dictatorship in the

Table 7.4 Regression results for the relationships between components of citizenship and class

| | Dependent Variables | | | | | | | | |
| | L-state | | | L-comm | | | C-rights | | |
Class Dummy	B	SE	ß	b	SE	ß	B	SE	ß
Working Class	−.093	.109	−.042	.083	.122	.034	.014	.099	.007
Old-Middle	−.142	.112	−.061	.160	.125	.061	−.036	.102	−.017
New-Middle	−.145	.105	−.072	.198	.118	.087	.050	.096	.027
Uper Class	−.023	.122	−.008	.138	.137	.043	−.010	.111	−.004
Constant	5.975***			4.806***			5.918***		
R square	.003			.003			.002		
N	1,123			1,133			1,132		

| | Dependent Variables | | | | | |
| | P-efficiency | | | P-knowledge | | |
Class Dummy	B	SE	ß	B	SE	ß
Working Class	−.022	.107	−.010	−.005	.075	−.003
Old-Middle	.096	.109	.041	.088	.077	.052
New-Middle	.220*	.103	.108	.239**	.073	.163
Upper Class	.266*	.121	.092	.473***	.085	.227
Constant	2.227***			2.677***		
R square	.013			.052		
N	1,153			1,152		

Note: $^*p < 0.05$, $^{**}P < 0.01$, $^{***}P < 0.001$

latter half of the twentieth century, especially on the part of the working class and the politically progressive, later joined by the new-middle class (Choe 2006).

The above findings do not seem to constitute a set of evidence for Marshall's idea of the contradictory relationship between citizenship and capitalism. Nor does political orientation clearly distinguish between the liberal and the communitarian concept of citizenship in the Korean context, though there are some indications in this direction. Instead, citizenship in many of the Koreans' minds means primarily citizens' relationship with the state, be it citizens' duties to the state or their rights from it. This probably reflects not only the Confucian idea of the state as a family held for long by Koreans (Kim 2007), but also recent intense and successful, popular struggles against dictatorial regimes for democracy.

7.7 Demographic and Socio-economic Variations of Perception of Citizenship

It is assumed that the concept of citizenship is not uniform, but varies according to diverse demographic and socio-economic characteristics, as many previous studies demonstrate. The reasons for the variations include historical exclusion of certain populations or groups from full citizenship, and explicit and implicit discrimination based on gender, ethnicity, race, property etc. Socio-cultural changes such as economic and cultural globalization, changes toward postmodern or post-material

Table 7.5 Regression of each item of citizenship rights on the class and the political orientation variables

	Citizenship rights								
	Adequate living			Minority rights			Equal treatment		
Independent variables	B	SE	ß	B	SE	ß	B	SE	ß
Sub. class	.023	.040	.019	.003	.050	.002	−.038	.044	−.030
Political orientation	.024	.041	.021	−.064	.051	−.044	.005	.044	.004
Party, conservative	.115	.089	.048	.070	.110	.024	.120	.096	.047
Radical	−.066	.098	−.024	−.048	.122	−.014	.213*	.107	.072
Class, working	−.315*	.151	−.118	.164	.187	.050	−.104	.163	−.036
Old-middle	−.413**	.153	−.149	.044	.190	.013	−.029	.165	−.010
New-middle	−.279	.148	−.115	.110	.183	.037	−.150	.160	−.057
Upper	−319	.169	−.092	.032	.210	.007	−.158	.183	−.042
Constant	6.158***	.208		5.655***	.257		6.215***	.225	
R square	.013			.003			.008		
N	942			942			942		

	Citizenship rights								
	Citizen's view			Participation			Civil Disobedience		
Independent variables	B	SE	ß	B	SE	ß	B	SE	ß
Sub. class	.057	.038	.051	.018	.035	.018	.013	.049	.009
Political orientation	−.037	.038	−.034	−.069	.036	−.067	−.110*	.050	.077
Party, conservative	.098	.083	.044	.145	.078	.070	.076	.109	.026
Radical	.107	.092	.042	.063	.086	.026	.235*	.120	.070
Class, working	−.016	.141	−.006	−.115	.132	−.050	.403*	.183	.125
Old-middle	−.136	.143	−.053	−.120	.134	−.050	.223	.186	.066
New-middle	−.055	.138	−.024	−.091	.129	−.043	.380*	.179	.128
Upper	−.069	.158	−.021	.004	.148	.001	.353	.206	.083
Constant	6.236***	.194		6.400***	.182		5.362***	.253	
R square	.008			.009			.018		
N	940			939			936		

Note: $^{*}p < 0.05$, $^{**}P < 0.01$, $^{***}P < 0.001$

value, neo-liberal structural reform after the economic crisis, and IT revolution, all profoundly affect people's relationship with the state and the nation, and consequently their ideas of national identity and citizenship.

Table 7.6 gives the results of Pearson's correlation analyses of the relationships between each of the five components of citizenship and various demographic and socio-economic variables. First of all, demographic variables turn out to be significant predictors for variations of citizenship, as demonstrated in previous studies. Women more than men emphasize the importance of loyalty to the state and of citizenship rights as necessary conditions for a good citizen, but men are more politically competent than women. On the other hand, older respondents rather than younger ones regard both loyalty to the state and to the community as important for citizenship, but younger citizens have more knowledge than their older citizens. Similarly the less-educated are more concerned about the duties to the state, but the more educated are more politically competent than the less educated. In the case of

Table 7.6 Correlation among the components of citizenship and socio-economic background

Independent variables	Dependent variables				
	L-state	L-comm	C-right	P-efficacy	P-knowledge
Sex	−.046	−.070[*]	−.079[**]	.060[*]	.248[***]
Age	.254[***]	.111[***]	−.027	−.039	−.110[***]
Education	−.136[***]	−.046	−.001	.118[***]	.321[***]
Occupation	−.012	.040	.029	.109[***]	.235[***]
H-income	−.051	−.021	.013	.097[***]	.225[***]

Note: [*]$p < 0.05$, [**]$P < 0.01$, [***]$P < 0.001$

respondents' occupation, higher-status occupation holders tend to be politically more competent than their lower status counterparts.

These findings support the hypothesis that citizenship is likely to be conceptualized differently by the privileged and by the discriminated, and by the advantaged and the deprived. As is the case in most other countries, the women, the older, the less-educated, and the less well-to-do are the minorities in the Korean context. They are politically less competent, need more protection for their basic rights, and want stronger ties with the state and the community.

Two more variables were considered as possible dividers in the perceptions of citizenship. Religion is increasingly gaining prominence in the political and social fields in Korea. Especially Christianity has played an important political role since Japanese colonial rule. During the popular protest against the military dictatorship in the 1970s, and 1980s, not only have churches provided sanctuaries for the dissidents, but also some of the clergies have actively participated in the protest movements (Chang 1998; Kang 2007). Thus Korean Christians are supposed to be more politically alert, and more concerned with human rights than others. In fact, our data support this claim. According to Table 7.7, Protestants and Catholics, and Buddhists to a lesser extent, all regard loyalty to the state to be an important component of a good citizen. But only Protestants consider loyalty to the community important, while Catholics emphasize citizenship rights more than others do. These findings also suggest that Korean Protestants are more community-oriented, while Catholics are more concerned about human rights.

Since it has not only been acknowledged by many experts in this field, but also believed by the general public that regional gaps in terms of social, economic and cultural conditions are serious and that there is widespread discrimination, albeit implicit and subtle, based on the place of birth (KSA 1989; Na 2005), regional variations in the perception of citizenship was hypothesized. Table 7.8 gives the regression analyses.

As is expected, respondents from the Yeoungnam and the Honam regions distinguish themselves in their perceptions of citizenship rights from those of other regions. But, contrary to our expectations, they consider citizenship rights less important than people from other regions do. The Yeoungnam dwellers also place less emphasis than those from other regions on loyalty to the state as an important condition for a good citizen. These results may point to the parochial character of Korean politics. In other words, Korean citizens may be concerned more with regional interests than national interests. However, this interpretation begs further evidence that cannot be provided by the data analyzed here.

Table 7.7 Regression of components of citizenship on religion

Religion	Dependent variables								
	L-state			L-comm			C-rights		
	B	SE	ß	B	SE	ß	B	SE	ß
Buddhism	.153[*]	.066	.073	.098	.075	.041	.044	.060	.023
Protestant	.235[***]	.068	.108	.187	.077[*]	.076	.031	.062	.016
Catholic	.273[***]	.097	.084	.195	.108	.054	.237[**]	.087	.082
Constant	5.739[***]			4.846[***]			5.877[***]		
R square	.013			.006			.006		
N	1,255			1,265			1,259		

Religion	Dependent variables					
	P-efficacy			P-knowledge		
	B	SE	ß	B	SE	ß
Buddhism	−.041	.066	−.019	−.023	.048	−.015
Protestant	.010	.069	.004	.013	.050	.008
Catholic	.104	.096	.032	−.029	.070	−.012
Constant	2.336[***]			2.813[***]		
R square	.002			.000		
N	1,288			1,290		

Note: [*]p < 0.05, [**]P < 0.01, [***]P < 0.001

Table 7.8 Regression of the components of citizenship on place of residence

Region dummy	Dependent variables								
	L-state			L-comm			C-rights		
	B	SE	ß	B	SE	ß	B	SE	ß
Seoul	−.045	.073	−.019	−.051	.083	−.019	−.073	.067	−.034
Youngnam	−.145[*]	.067	−.069	−.040	.075	−.017	−.16[**]	.061	−.086
Honam	−.101	.088	−.035	.084	.098	.026	−.172[*]	.080	−.066
Constant	5.917[***]			4.946[***]			5.998[***]		
R square	.004			.002			.008		
N	1,221			1,231			1,226		

Region dummy	Dependent variables					
	P-efficacy			P-knowledge		
	B	SE	ß	B	SE	ß
Seoul	.040	.073	.017	.039	.054	.023
Youngnam	.108	.067	.051	.006	.049	.004
Honam	.106	.087	.037	−.029	.064	−.014
Constant	2.284[***]			2.802[***]		
R square	.003			.001		
N	1,225			1,256		

Note: [*]p < 0.05, [**]P < 0.01, [***]P < 0.001

Finally, the relative importance of independent variables in their effects on the components of citizenship was established by multiple regression analyses (Table 7.9). For loyalty to the state, age, the Protestant, the Catholic and the Yeoungnam region turn out to be significant variables. That is, older Christians

Table 7.9 Multiple regressions of each components of citizenship on background variables

Independent variables	Loyal to the state			Loyal to community			Citizenship rights		
	b	S.E.	ß	b	S.E.	ß	B	S.E.	ß
Sex	−.101	(.066)	−.056	−.172 [*]	(.081)	−.080	−.177 [**]	(.065)	−.104
Age	.186 [***]	(.030)	.268	.137 [***]	(.036)	.167	−.021	(.029)	−.031
Education	−.085	(.058)	−.068	.005	(.071)	.003	−.075	(.057)	−.063
H. income	.038	(.023)	.067	−.009	(.028)	−.013	−.003	(.022)	−.006
Sub. class	−.015	(.035)	−.016	.005	(.043)	.004	.017	(.034)	.019
Pol. orientation	−.037	(.033)	−.040	−.088 [*]	(.040)	−.080	−.047	(.032)	−.054
Relig. Buddhism	.089	(.077)	.043	.100	(.094)	.041	.016	(.076)	.008
Protestantism	.222 [**]	(.075)	.107	.236 [*]	(.092)	.096	.018	(.074)	.009
Catholicism	.221 [*]	(.108)	.071	.216	(.130)	.060	.206 [*]	(.105)	.072
Reg. Soeul	−.057	(.080)	−.026	−.081	(.099)	−.031	−.055	(.079)	−.027
Yeongnam	−.171 [*]	(.075)	−.085	−.040	(.092)	−.017	−.116	(.074)	−.061
Honam	.018	(.099)	.006	.120	(.120)	.037	−.084	(.096)	−.033
Party conservative	.098	(.075)	.052	.056	(.092)	.025	.125	(.074)	.070
Radical	.024	(.078)	.011	.095	(.095)	.037	.111	(.076)	.055
Manual worker	−.090	(.095)	−.047	−.172	(.116)	−.075	−.050	(.093)	−.028
Clerical, semi-prof.	−.194	(.109)	−.094	−.041	(.132)	−.017	−.030	(.107)	−.015
Manager, prof.	.044	(.165)	.019	−.164	(.202)	−.058	.018	(.162)	.008
Working class	−.045	(.124)	−.021	−.014	(.152)	−.006	−.043	(.121)	−.022
Old-middle class	−.116	(.129)	−.053	−.046	(.159)	−.018	−.079	(.128)	−.038
New-middle class	.070	(.159)	.037	.059	(.194)	.026	−.072	(.156)	−.040
Upper class	−.067	(.220)	−.024	.034	(.271)	.010	−.036	(.217)	−.014
(Constant)	5.654 [***]	(.254)		4.862 [***]	(.312)		6.409 [***]	(.250)	
R-square	.110			.047			.028		
N	891			897			896		

Independent Variables	Political efficacy				Political knowledge			
	B		S.E.	ß	B		S.E.	ß
Sex	.156	*	(.070)	.083	.246	***	(.046)	.188
Age	−.005		(.032)	−.008	.055	**	(.021)	.110
Education	.077		(.061)	.059	.189	***	(.040)	.208
H. income	.026		(.024)	.044	.039	*	(.016)	.094
Sub. class	.055		(.037)	.056	.034		(.024)	.049
Pol. orientation	−.083	*	(.034)	−.086	−.078	***	(.023)	−.115
Relig. Buddhism	.096		(.082)	.045	.084		(.054)	.057
Protestantism	.050		(.080)	.023	.078		(.053)	.052
Catholicism	.080		(.113)	.025	−.013		(.074)	−.006
Reg. Seoul	.046		(.085)	.020	−.066		(.056)	−.041
Yeongnam	.180	*	(.080)	.086	.026		(.052)	.018
Honam	.153		(.104)	.054	.014		(.068)	.007
Party conservative	−.032		(.079)	−.016	−.028		(.052)	−.021
Radical	−.058		(.082)	−.026	−.042		(.054)	−.027
Manual worker	.010		(.100)	.005	.037		(.066)	.026
Clerical, semi-prof.	−.074		(.115)	−.035	.063		(.075)	.042
Manager, prof.	.039		(.175)	.016	.094		(.115)	.055
Working class	−.011		(.131)	−.005	−.041		(.086)	−.027
Old-middle class	.133		(.137)	.058	−.007		(.090)	−.005
New-middle class	.274		(.168)	.138	.101		(.110)	.073
Upper class	.108		(.234)	.038	.056		(.154)	.028
(Constant)	1.888	***	(.269)		2.056	***	(.178)	
R-square	.057				.164			
N	907				906			

Note: ***$P < 0.001$, **$P < 0.01$, *$P < 0.05$
Note: *$P < 0.05$, **$P < 0.01$, ***$P < 0.00$

residing in regions others than Yeoungnam are more likely to emphasize loyalty to the state than others. Among the variables, age is the most important followed by Protestantism and the Yeoungnam region. Similarly, sex, age, political orientation and Protestantism are significantly associated with loyalty to the community. Women, older people, the politically progressive and the Protestant seem to consider loyalty to the community more important for a good citizen than others do. Among the variables, age again turns out to be the most important factor. For citizenship rights, however, only two variables, sex and Catholicism have statistically significant relationships with the dependent variable. Women and Catholics are more concerned with citizen's rights than any others are. And sex is more important than religion in this relationship. Political efficacy is only weakly related to three independent variables. In general, those who are male, politically progressive and residing in Yeoungnam tend to be more politically effective than others.

Finally, sex, age, education, household income and political orientation turn out to be better predictors of political knowledge than other variables. Those who are male, older, more educated, politically progressive, and have a higher household income are likely to be more politically knowledgeable. Among the independent variables, education is most important followed by sex and political orientation. It should be noted that if we control other variables, the effects of occupation and of subjective and objective class position disappear altogether. Class variable, once a very effective variable for explaining many social phenomena, seems no longer to exert much influence, at least in the Korean context. Rapid social change, fluidity of social structure and high mobility rates all seem to contribute to the decreasing importance of the class factor. Instead of class, such cultural variables as religion, values and cultural tastes become paramount in the everyday lives of many Koreans.

7.8　Summary and Conclusion

As a core element of democracy, citizenship is important in Korea because Korea has a turbulent history of democratic development, and because it was the people's power and struggle that proved crucial for the final attainment of a truly democratic state and society. Citizenship can be approached from the legal or institutional point of view, as many researches have done. However, people's lived experiences of citizenship are more important in the Korean context. Unlike the legal or institutional aspects of citizenship, which are however fairly uniform and static, ordinary citizens' conceptions can shift and vary widely. Taking the latter approach, this study aimed to investigate how Koreans perceive citizenship and how their perceptions vary by what factors.

In order to achieve these goals, the 2004 KGSS data, which contains the ISSP module of citizenship, was analyzed on the basis of Heater's conceptual framework and of the theories proposed by Marshall, Turner, Oliver and others. Some of the major findings are as follows.

First, factor analyses of the data reveal that civic virtues or a set of duties for a good citizen are divided into two factors, which may be called loyalty (or duties) to the state and loyalty (or duties) to the community. Citizenship rights – which include civic, political and social rights in Marshall's sense – constitute a single factor, while political competence is divided into political efficacy and political knowledge.

Second, there are fairly close relationships between the two factors of civic virtues and citizenship rights, but the two aspects of political competence have weak and scant relationships with other components of citizenship.

Third, as expected by the major theories, conservative and the lower class members regard loyalty to the state as more important for being a good citizen than others do. Also, the progressive and the upper and middle class members are more efficacious and knowledgeable politically than the conservatives and people in the lower classes.

Fourth, contrary to Marshall's theory of social rights, the working class and the old middle class members consider social rights less important in terms of being essential for a citizen. Instead, the working class along with the new middle class and the politically progressive regard civil disobedience very highly as a condition for being a good citizen. These results probably reflect the recent experiences of democratic struggles against harsh dictatorship on the part of ordinary citizens. Citizenship for average Koreans is primarily defined by their relationship with the state.

Fifth, as shown in many previous studies, demographic variables as well as socioeconomic ones turn out to be significant predictors for variations in the citizenship concept in Korea. Women are more concerned than men with loyalty to the community and citizenship rights, while older people consider both loyalty to the state and to the community to be important elements of a good citizen. However, men and younger people are more politically competent than women and elderly people. Similarly, the less educated are more concerned about loyalty to the state. But the more–educated and the higher-status occupation holders are more competent politically. These results seem to support the "second-class citizen" thesis.

Sixth, religious differences and regions of residence turn out to be important dividers in the perceptions of citizenship among Koreans. Christians, and to a lesser extent Buddhists, consider loyalty to the state important for a good citizenship. Protestants also regard loyalty to the community important, while Catholics show a strong concern with citizenship rights. This seems to reflect the important political role played by Christians during the recent democratic struggles.

Seventh, the regional gap has been an important, albeit controversial, issue in Korea. Especially the Yeungnam and the Honam regions have long been the seats of two opposing political parties. But, contrary to our expectations, residents of both regions consider citizenship rights less important, and the Yeungnam residents regard loyalty to the state less important than dwellers in other regions do.

Finally, multiple regression results show that after controlling for other variables, the effects of occupation disappear, as do the effects of subjective and objective class positions. Class, once a strong predictor of social behavior and social phenomena, seems to be losing its effect due to recent changes which make social structures fluid and mobile. But such demographic variables as sex and age, political orientation, religion, and region of residence remain significant in affecting the perception of citizenship.

These findings once again prove that the citizenship concept is not uniform and unbounded. People with different backgrounds conceptualize citizenship differently based on diverse grounds, including demographic differences, differing socio-economic status, sometimes different political experiences and orientations, and certain cultural factors such as religion. Thus citizenship perceived by Koreans cannot be neatly characterized to be either republican or liberal, either left or right. Rather there are a variety of mixed forms, which is understandable in view of the traditional Confucian culture that does not distinguish between state and nation. Also Korea's turbulent history of democratic development, and recent changes such as the neo-liberal reforms after the 1997 economic crisis and the accelerated pace of globalization, have all contributed to the diversity of the conception of citizenship.

In this changing context, a pluralistic concept of citizenship seems to be becoming a norm, even suggesting a cross-border nationality and citizenship. Also the rapidity of recent social change makes generational differences in the conception of citizenship more acute and inevitable, while class and economic status seem to give way to political and cultural variables in accounting for the variation in the perception of citizenship. As a result, there could be conflicts between the liberals and the progressives, between the young and the old, and between the modernists and the postmodernists, regarding the concept of citizenship and the form of democracy. Thus, a conception of culture-specific, but liberal, citizenship, such as the liberal nationalistic concept of citizenship proposed by Kim (2007) after Y. Tamir's concept of liberal nationalism, should be not only a possibility, but also a viable option for democratic consolidation in Korea.

Endnotes

[1]Korea refers to South Korea in this article, unless noted otherwise.
[2]See, for example, Jeon (2000) and Yang and Lim (2007).

Appendix. Results of Factor Analysis

Civic Virtues: Rotated Component Coefficient Matrix

	Factor 1	Factor 2
(1) To vote in public elections	−.117	.342
(2) Never to try to evade taxes	−.181	.416
(3) Always to obey laws and regulations	−.086	.350
(4) To keep watch on the actions of government	.037	.208
(5) To subject your own opinion to critical examination	.318	−.099
(6) To be active in social or political associations	.179	.068
(7) To choose products which are good for society or nature even if they cost a bit more	.252	−.039
(8) To help those people in Korea who are worse off than oneself	.300	−.037
(9) To help those people in the rest of the world who are worse off than oneself	.408	−.210
(10) To be willing to serve in the military at a time of need	.066	.145

Note: principal component analysis. Rotation: Varimax with Kaiser normalization

Citizenship Rights: Component Coefficient Matrix

	Factor 1
(1) All citizens have an adequate standard of living	.221
(2) The government authorities respect and protect the rights of minorities	.227
(3) The government authorities treat everybody equally, regardless of their position in society	.224
(4) Politicians take into account the views of citizens before making decisions	.260
(5) People are given more opportunities to participate in public decision-making	.264
(6) Citizens may engage in acts of civil disobedience when they oppose government actions	.193

Note: Principal component analysis

References

Chang, Y.-S. (1998). "The progressive Christian church and democracy in South Korea". *Journal of Church and State*, 40(2), 437–465.

Chastenay, M.-H., Pagé, M., Phalet, K., Swyngedouw, M., & Jean-Claude Lasry, J.-C. (2004). "Identity, equality and participation: Testing the dimensions of citizenship in Canada and Belgium". *Canadian Ethnic Studies*, 36(3), 84–112.

Choe, H. (2003). "Taehanmin'guk kwa chunghwainmin'gonghwaguk ŭi kungmin chŏngch'esŏng kwa simin'gwŏn chedo" (National identity and citizenship in the PRC and the ROK) *Han'guksahoehak (Korean Journal of Sociology)*, 37(4), 143–173.

Choe, H. (2005). "Han'il sit'ichŭnship pigyo: simin'ŭisik ŭi kongjŏk yŏngyŏk chihyang kwa nŭngdongsŏng ŭl chungsim ŭiro" (Comparison of citizenship between Korean and Japan: Focusing on citizens' public space orientation and positivity). Paper Presented at Che ihoe Han'guk chonghap sahoejosa simposium (the 2nd KGSS Symposium on Koreans' Economic and Civil Consciousness and Social Networks: International Comparison). May 19, 2005. Seoul, Korea.

Choe, H. (2006). "Han'guk sit'ichŭnship: 1987nyŏn ihu simin'gwŏn chedo ŭi pyŏnhwa wa siminŭisik" (South Korean citizenship: The institutional changes since 1987 and their effects on citizens' consciousness). *Minjujuŭi wa in'gwŏn* (Democracy and Human Rights), 6(1), 171–205.

Choe, H. (2007). "Han'gukin ŭi damunhwa sit'ichŭnship: damunhwa ŭisik ŭl chungsim ŭiro" (National identity and multicultural citizenship in South Korea). *Siminsahoe wa NGO* (Civil Society and NGO), 5(2), 147–227.

Conover, P. J., Crewe, I. M., & Searling, D. D. (1991). "The nature of citizenship in the United States and Great Britain: Empirical comments on theoretical themes". *Journal of Politics*, 53 (3), 800–832.

Chung, K. (2004). "Han'gugin ŭi kukka chŏngch'esŏng kugje pigyo" (International comparison of Koreans' national identity: Focusing on evaluation of membership requirements). Paper Presented at Che ilhoe Hanguk chonghapsahoejosa symposium (the 1st KGSS Symposium on Koreans' value Orientations: International Comparison). June 2, 2004. Seoul, Korea.

Dalton, R. J. (2008). "Citizenship norms and the expansion of political participation". *Political Studies*, 56, 76–98.

Falk, R. (2000). "The decline of citizenship in an era of globalization". *Citizenship Studies*, 4(1), 5–13.

Glenn, E. (2000). "Citizenship and inequality: historical and global perspectives". *Social Problems*, 47(1), 1–20.

Heater, D. (1990). *Citizenship: The civic ideal in world history, politics and education*. London: Longman.

Hong, D.-S. (1983). "Chigŏp punsŏk ŭl t'onghan kyech'ŭng yŏngu: Hanguk p'yojun chigŏp punryu rŭl chungsim ŭro" (A study of stratification through the analysis of occupations: focusing on Korean Standard Occupational Classification. (In Korean) *Sahoe kwahak kwa chŏngch'aek yŏngu* (Social Science and Policy Studies), 5(3), 69–87.

Isin, E. F. & Turner, B. S. (2007). "Investigating citizenship: An agenda for citizenship studies". *Citizenship Studies*, 11(1), 5–17.

Jeon, J. (2000). *Park Chung Hee, the reactionary modernist*. (In Korean) Seoul: Chaeksesang.

Kang, I.-C. (2007). "Pak chŏng-hi chŏnggwŏn kwa kaesin'gyo kyohoe" (Park Chung-Hee regime and the Protestant Church). *Chonggyo wa munhwa yŏn'gu* (Studies in Religious Culture), 9, 83–118.

Kim, S. (2007). "Liberal nationalism and responsible citizenship in South Korea". *Citizenship Studies*, 11(5), 449–463.

Korean Sociological Association. (1989). *Regionalism and regional conflicts in Korea*. (In Korean) Seoul: Seongwon-Sa

Lee, C. (2008). "Nation-state v. nation-state: The transformation of citizenship and the state-nation nexus in South Korea". Paper presented at the Symposium on Globalization of South Korea: Its Impact and Opportunities. Dec. 17–18, Seoul Korea.

Lister, R., Smith, N., Middleton, S., & Cox, L. (2003). "Young people talk about citizenship: Empirical perspectives on theoretical and political debates". *Citizenship Studies*, 7(2), 235–253.

Lonnie, R. S., & Bogard, K. L. (2008). "Citizenship attitudes and allegiances in diverse youth". *Cultural Diversity and Ethnic Minority Psychology*, 14(4), 286–296.

Marshall, T. H. (1973). *Class, citizenship and social development*. Westport, Conn.: Greenwood Press.

Miller-Idriss, C. (2006). "Everyday understanding of citizenship in Germany". *Citizenship Studies*, 10(5), 541–570.

Na, E. Y. (2005). "Chiyŏk pulgyunhyŏng kwa chiyŏk kaldŭng" (Regional gaps and regional conflict). In Hyunho Seok et al. *Hanguksahoe ŭi pulpyŏngdŭng kwa kongjŏngsŏng* (Changes in perspectives on inequality and justice in Korean society). (pp. 263–288). Seoul: Sungkyunkwan University Press.

Oliver, D., & Heater, D. (1994). *The Foundations of Citizenship*. New York: Harvester Wheatsheaf.

Porter, A. E. (1993). "Impoverished concepts of citizenship in the debate on the National Curriculum". In J. Gundara and A. Porter (Ed.). *Diversity, citizenship and the National Curriculum Debate*. London: Institute of Education.

Seligman, A. B. (1992). *The Idea of Civil Society*. New York: Ontario Macmillan Press.

Theiss-Morse, E. (1993). "Conceptualization of good citizenship and political participation". *Political behavior*, 15(4), 355–380.

Vandenberg, A. 2000. "Contesting Citizenship and Democracy in a Global Era". In Andrew Vandenberg (Ed.). *Citizenship and Democracy in a Global Era*, (pp. 3–17). London: Macmillan.

Wong, C. K., & Wong, K. Y. (2004). "Universal Ideals and Particular Constraints of Social Citizenship: The Chinese Experience of Unifying Rights and responsibilities". *International Journal of Social Welfare*, 13, 103–111.

Yang, Jonghoe. "Globalization and Value Change in Korea: With a Special Emphasis on the Impact of the Recent Economic Crisis and Neoliberali Reform on the Confucian Value System". *Korean Social Science Journal*, XXX(2), 1–23.

Yang, Jonghoe., & Hyun-Chin, Lim. (2007). "Asian Values in Capitalist Development Revisited", In Kyong-Dong Kim and Hyun-Chin Lim (Eds.), *East Meets West: Civilizational Encounters and the Spirit of Capitalism in East Asia*, Leiden, Neth: Brill, pp.121–36.

Chapter 8
Attitudes of Local Workers Towards Civil Rights of Migrant Workers in Korea

Jungwhan Lee

Abstract This study examines the attitudes of Korean workers towards the civil rights of migrant workers, and predictors of their attitudes. Main questions addressed in the study are as follows: how do Korean workers think about conferring civil rights on migrant workers? What factors affect Korean workers' attitudes towards the civil rights of migrant workers? The findings reveal that Korean workers, on the one hand, are largely in favor of conferring migrant workers the same labor rights as Korean workers and of allowing them to bring their family members into Korea, but on the other hand, they are somewhat in disfavor of granting residence or citizenship status to migrant workers. The most important determinant of attitudes towards the civil rights of migrant workers is the perception of multiculturalism: the greater their awareness of multiculturalism, the more likely Korean workers are to express favor and to recognize migrant workers' civil rights.

8.1 Introduction

Although people have always moved, globalization has radically changed the scale and mode of migration.[1] With increasing globalization, mobility and migration are becoming an increasingly necessary and natural part of the lives of millions of people; more people are moving across international borders, the reasons for their mobility are becoming increasingly more diverse, and the demographic make-up of these mobile populations is less uniform. It is estimated that there are approximately 200 million people, or about 3 % of the world's population, currently living temporarily or permanently outside their countries of origin (IOM 2005). Although

J. Lee (✉)
Department of Sociology, Cheongju University, Daeseong-ro 298, Sangdang-gu Cheongju Chungbuk, 360-764, Korea

242-44 Nonhyun-dong, Gangnam-gu, Seoul 135-010, Korea
e-mail: jungwlee@cju.ac.kr

M. Pohlmann et al. (eds.), *Citizenship and Migration in the Era of Globalization*, 145
Transcultural Research – Heidelberg Studies on Asia and Europe in a Global Context,
DOI 10.1007/978-3-642-19739-0_8, © Springer-Verlag Berlin Heidelberg 2013

the forces driving migration are many and complex, it is generally recognized that the pursuit of economic opportunities such as gainful employment and decent work is a major factor explaining contemporary international migration (Martin and Widgren 2002). Among the mobile population, there are over 80 million migrant workers,[2] as well as some 10–15 million undocumented migrants (ILO 2004).

In this global trend, South Korea (hereafter referred to as "Korea") is no exception. Currently, more than one million migrants reside and about a half of them work 'legally' or 'illegally' in Korea (MOJ various years). It is widely expected that the influx of migrant workers will continue to increase in the country due to the avoidance of manufacturing jobs by natives, the competition for low-end products, and the continuation of demographic transition involving low birth rate[3] and increasingly aging population.

The growing number of migrant workers and the extension of their stay have resulted in an expansion of their residential areas, more frequent contacts with local Koreans, and widespread and various social relations in many spheres. As the impact of migrants spreads out into the base of society, the volume of academic research and discussions about them have risen rapidly, paralleling the growing attention and support by local and central governments, media, and other social organizations (Lee and Lee 2007). Nevertheless, the continuation of social problems, such as racial discrimination, overdue and unpaid wages, illegal migrant workers and inferior labor conditions, still require more research and a deeper understanding of migrant workers and their families.

Most studies on migrants in Korea up till now are based on interviews and surveys. It is essential to know their status, living conditions and feelings through their own experiences and views to gain a better understanding and to improve their lives. Attitudes and responses of local people towards migrants, however, also implicate their social status and overall adaptation in a host society. Despite their increasing visibility and their social networks, migrants represent a vulnerable minority group whose social acceptance depends a great deal on the attitudes and perceptions of native Koreans (Ward and Kennedy 1999; Massey et al. 2005; Castles and Miller 2009). In addition, opinions of local residents and workers are far more likely to shape migrant worker policies than the voices of migrants. For these reasons, it is necessary to identify the attitudes and responses of local people towards migrant workers in order to facilitate their integration into the local community and to enhance their social status.

Although it is possible to survey the general public concerning perceptions of the migrant population, this study focuses on Korean workers who work with migrant workers at the same workplace, because people who interact with migrants closely and directly can provide more realistic and valid information than the people who only know migrants vaguely and indirectly. The main questions addressed in this study are as follows: how do Korean workers think about conferring civil rights on migrant workers? What factors affect the Korean workers' attitudes towards the civil rights of migrant workers?

Korea is one of the few countries to have changed its status from a labor exporting to a labor-importing country in a very short period of time. Just before the middle 1980s, Korea fostered emigration of its citizens in order to earn foreign exchange, but in less than 5 years, Korea started to import migrant workers. For a country that has maintained a homogeneous existence for centuries, a sudden massive influx of migrant workers was quite a new experience and has brought about various and complicated situations and circumstances to the society. Korea thus offers to provide a more comprehensive understanding of the matrix of global migration.

8.2 Influx of Migrant Workers

With its poor natural endowment but abundant labor, historically Korea has been a country of emigration. In the early 1900s, Koreans immigrated to Hawaii to be employed as sugar cane workers. During the Japanese colonization period between 1910 and 1945, there was a mass movement to northeast China in order to escape the harsh rule of the Japanese. The ethnic Koreans from China currently residing in Korea represents the descendants of people who moved to the area in that period. In the 1960s and the early 1970s, Koreans again left in large numbers for Germany as miners and nurses and to South Vietnam as workers and soldiers. Simultaneously, in the 1970s and the early 1980s, many construction workers moved to the Middle East.

The government's initiation of the rapid industrialization plans in the 1960s fundamentally transformed the country from a poor agrarian nation to a newly industrializing country poised to join the ranks of advanced capitalist countries. The average annual increase in gross domestic product (GDP) was 8.5 % from 1961 to 1973 and continued to grow at an average rate of 8.1 % from 1973 to 1985 and 7 % from 1986 to 2002, despite the oil shocks of the 1970s, the domestic political turmoil of the early 1980s, and the financial crisis in 1997. Along with economic growth, Gross National Income (GNI) per capita rose more than 8 times from $1,600 in 1980 to $12,700 in 2003, and the average wages increased 13 times in the same period. With the rapid economic development and the steep increase of wages, Korea began to suffer a serious labor shortage in the mid-1980s, especially in the manufacturing sector. The rates of labor shortage for manufacturing were 4.35 % in 1987, 4.15 % in 1989 and 7.02 % in 1991, while the rates for whole industry were 3.29 % in 1987, 3.21 % in 1989 and 5.48 % in 1991 (MOL each year). Confronted with these labor shortages, Korean companies began to search for alternative sources of labor. A large number of migrant workers started to flow into Korea after 1988 when Korea hosted the 24th Olympic Games in Seoul that showcased Korea's economic development to the world and prompted the Korean government to relax restrictions on immigration.

The Korean Chinese, who share a similar culture and speak the Korean language, came in first, followed by the Filipinos, Pakistanis, Bangladeshis and Nepalese. The number of migrant workers increased from only a few thousand to 70,000 in just 4 years between 1988 and 1992. In 1991, the government officially launched the so-called Industrial Trainee System, allowing companies that have branches and factories abroad to bring in foreign workers as trainees. In 1994, the

Table 8.1 Number of migrant workers in Korea, 1991–2008 (%)[a]

	Documented migrant workers		Undocumented migrant workers	Total
	Professionals/skilled workers[b]	Industrial trainees/unskilled workers[c]		
1991	2,973 (6.5)	599 (1.3)	41,877 (92.1)	45,449 (100.0)
1992	3,395 (4.6)	4,945 (6.7)	65,528 (88.7)	73,868 (100.0)
1994	5,265 (6.4)	28,328 (34.6)	48,231 (58.9)	81,824 (100.0)
1997	15,900 (6.8)	69,052 (29.6)	148,048 (63.5)	233,000 (100.0)
1999	17,554 (7.6)	78,945 (34.1)	135,338 (58.4)	231,837 (100.0)
2001	18,511 (4.8)	110,028 (28.7)	255,206 (66.5)	383,745 (100.0)
2003	21,095 (4.7)	291,572 (64.7)	138,056 (30.6)	450,723 (100.0)
2004	26,267 (4.8)	310,706 (56.9)	209,073 (38.3)	546,046 (100.0)
2006	34,426 (5.4)	395,437 (61.6)	211,988 (33.0)	641,851 (100.0)
2007	39,369 (5.8)	412,349 (61.1)	223,464 (33.1)	675,182 (100.0)
2008	43,778 (6.0)	481,565 (66.4)	200,489 (27.6)	725,832 (100.0)

Sources: MOJ (various years)

[a] The number is as of 31 December for each year

[b] Professionals, skilled workers and semi-skilled workers such as managers, lawyers, professors, English teachers and technicians

[c] The numbers for the years before 2003 include only the people engaged in industrial trainee employment

Korea Federation of Small and Medium Business (KFSB) pressured the government to expand the trainee system. Since then, the number of migrant workers quickly increased and reached 250,000 by the end of 1997. This was just before Korea underwent a financial crisis which swept across most Southeast Asian countries, reducing the number to 140,000 by the middle of 1998. But the migrant population underwent a new upsurge as Korea recovered from the crisis. By the end of 2008, the total number of migrant workers was 725,832 (see Table 8.1). Currently, workers come from over 30 countries, including 15 countries[4] which signed a Memorandum of Understanding (MOU) with the Korean government.

The increase of migrant workers has been led by a low-skilled population. Since 1991, industrial trainees, non-professional workers and undocumented workers who are mostly engaged in low-skilled jobs, have comprised more than 90 % of the total migrant workers, while the proportion of professional, skilled and semi-skilled migrant workers has never exceeded 8 % of the total. There has, however, also been a steady increase in the number of professional, skilled and semi-skilled workers. The numbers of the population increased 13 times in the last 16 years from 2,973 in 1991 to 43,778 in 2008.

Since its inception, several changes have taken effect in the migration importation program. In the beginning, the Korean government allowed industrial trainees to stay for just 1 year. Two years later, the sojourn period was extended to 2 years and, again in 1996, the government lengthened the period to 3 years (2 years as trainees and 1 year as workers). In April 2002, the trainee system underwent another minor change that adjusted the migrants' status to a 1-year term as trainees and 2 years as workers, reversing the order from the previous system as a way of

Table 8.2 Number of low-skilled migrant workers by status and gender in 2008 (%)

		Male	Female	Total
Documented	Industrial trainees	13,160 (74.9)	4,403 (25.1)	17,563 (100.0)
	Employment permitted workers[a]	181,435 (87.4)	26,168 (12.6)	207,603 (100.0)
	Visit employment workers[b]	161,339 (53.9)	137,993 (46.1)	299,332 (100.0)
Undocumented		132,505 (66.1)	67,984 (33.9)	200,489 (100.0)

Sources: MOJ (2009)

[a]The number of employment permitted workers includes workers engaged in post-training employment

[b]Koreans and Korean descendants who reside abroad, such as in China and the former Soviet Union, and enter Korea through the Visit Employment System (former Employment Managed System), which allow them to visit and work freely in Korea for a maximum stay of 5 years

providing a greater measure of worker protection. Finally, in July of 2003, the Korean government decided to abolish the trainee system by replacing it with the Employment Permit System (EPS), which provides added protection from labor abuses and allows a longer working period of up to 5 years. The principal difference between the trainee system and the permit system is that in the latter, migrants are considered as workers and are protected by the Labor Standards Act, the Minimum Wages Act, and the Industrial Safety Health Act. A significant drawback of EPS, however, is that migrants are expected to return to their home country upon completion of the 3 years and that the employer has the authority to renew the contract for an additional 2 years.

Concerned about the possible social effects of settlement and structural dependence on migrant labor, the Korean government has maintained a strict social integration policy by limiting civil rights and discouraging permanent settlement. The current law under EPS also prohibits family reunion during the initial 3-year period. As and when they are permitted to return after a month-long departure, migrants could conceivably be separated from their family for the duration of 5 years. While some Asian labor-importing countries such as Taiwan, Hong Kong and Singapore have experienced a feminization of migration, Korea has yet to experience this (Castles 1998; Lim and Oishi 1996; Wong 1996). The proportion of female migrant workers never exceeded 35 % in the 1990s and the early 2000s (Lee 2003). Among EPS workers, males accounted for 87.4 % while females constituted 12.6 % of the total in 2008 (see Table 8.2). When the Korean government initiated the industrial trainee policy in the early 1990s, the intention was to meet labor shortage in the manufacturing sector. The sector consisted largely of small businesses and low-skilled jobs, such as operating metal pressing and shearing machines, moving heavy materials, and dealing with toxic chemicals in adverse working conditions. Therefore, companies preferred male workers to female workers. On the other hand, the government has restricted the employment of migrant workers in sectors other than the manufacturing and construction industries. Elsewhere in Asia, migrant women have found niches in domestic work, hotels and restaurants, and entertainment-related services (Lim and Oishi 1996).

Many jobs available and open to migrants are located in so-called 3D (dirty, dangerous and difficult) industries and require physically demanding labor. The specification of available jobs also draws particularly young, male workers. Most male migrant workers in Korea are in 20s and 30s, who account for 70 % of the total migrant workforce (Seok et al. 2003). In addition, most companies that hire migrant workers are generally small, and their main purpose of hiring migrant workers is to reduce production costs. Consequently, migrant workers are channeled into jobs with poor working conditions, long working hours, and low-pay status.

8.3 Theoretical Discussions on Majorities' Attitudes Towards Minorities

Increasingly, scholars and government entities have demonstrated an interest in understanding the public perception of migrants. The greater part of the literature on the topic suggests that members of the majority population hold negative views and express prejudice and discriminatory attitudes towards members of ethnic minorities. A number of studies in the U.S. and Europe affirm this basic dilemma where the target population is generally immigrants (Quillian 1995; Bobo and Hutchings 1996; Jackson et al. 2001; Sheepers et al. 2002; Raijman et al. 2003; EUMC 2005; Dixon 2006). In Korea, negative attitudes are mostly directed towards migrant workers and migrant spouses (Park and Chung 2006; Hwang et al. 2007; Song 2008).

The literature on the host society's attitudes towards migrants has consistently shown that the degree of anti-migrant sentiment is likely to vary with socioeconomic background, including social status, employment level and educational differences (Miller et al. 1984; Case et al. 1989; Ruefle et al. 1992; Espenshade and Hempstead 1996; Hello et al. 2002). In general, people of lower socioeconomic status are more likely to express antagonistic attitudes towards migrants and to support their exclusion from social, economic and political rights. In addition, ethnocentric views mobilize negative opinions towards out-group members, activate prejudice, and lead to discrimination against minority populations (Wimmer 1997; Fetzer 2000). These findings reflect a fear of the intrusion of values and practices that are perceived as both alien and potentially destructive of the national character and to the cultural homogeneity of society.

Recent studies have emphasized the role of threat and competition in predicting intergroup attitudes, and empirical research has borne out their negative consequences for attitudes towards ethnic minorities and migrants (Olzak 1992, 1995; Quillian 1995; Jackson et al. 2001). The competition model argues that attitudes towards migrants are shaped by group identifications and struggle between groups for scarce resources, particularly economic assets and employment opportunities and further cultural capital concerning differences in norms, beliefs, and values. The explanation based on the competition model suggests that discrimination towards out-group members is the response to external threat to the interests and privileges of the dominant group. The roots of anti-migrant sentiments are thus derived from perceptions of the detrimental impact of minorities and migrants on the well-being of nationals and on the welfare of the host country.

The concept of threat or fear of competition is rather complex and multidimensional (Finlay and Stephan 2000). It can be applied to an individual or the entire group; it can take place in the socio-cultural as well as in the economic arena; and it can be discussed in general terms or in specific 'zero-sum game' beliefs, that is, the notion that as more resources become available to migrant out-group, less is accessible to the native-born in-group (Blalock 1967; Bobo and Huthcings 1996; Taylor 1998; Esses et al. 2001; Scheepers et al. 2002). Although the concept of threat is used differently, the various theoretical models share a common view that fear of competition is the major determinant of anti-migrant sentiments and discriminatory attitudes.

The logic of this framework contends that fear and a sense of threat mediate the relationship between the socioeconomic position of individuals and the level of negative attitudes towards out-group populations. For example, citizens of low social and economic status are assumed to be more susceptible to fears that migrants will take jobs from native workers, contribute to higher unemployment, and reduce the wages and working conditions because low-skill and low-wage native workers have occupational characteristics similar to those of migrant workers (Simon and Alexander 1993; Borjas and Freman 1992; Quillian 1995; Castles 1998). Thus, it can also be expected that the perception of a threat may lead to objections against migrant workers obtaining equal access to social, economic and labor rights.

More general influences on attitudes toward migrants include both personal factors, such as general attitudes toward diversity, and situational experiences, including contact with migrants. Attitudes toward diversity have been mostly examined under the advocacy of multiculturalism and associated with a sense of economic and cultural security, as well as a greater acceptance of migrants (Schalk-Soekar et al. 2004; Berry 2006; Ward and Masgoret 2008). Multiculturalism generally refers to an acceptance of and, in some cases, active support for diverse cultures (Berry and Kalin 1995). The adoption of a multicultural ideology has two implications (Berry 2001); one, that cultural diversity is good for a society and its members; two, that diversity should be shared and accommodated in an equitable way. Accordingly, embracing multiculturalism may yield a positive evaluation of different groups.

Several studies have also established a correlation between intergroup contact and attitudes. Direct contact can lead to more positive attitudes and to less negative viewpoints. Contact experiences not only enable a better understanding of one another, but also produce such beneficial effects as a reduction in prejudice that allow the majority population to hold positive attitudes toward the minority (Brewer and Brown 1998; Pettigrew and Tropp 2000).

This study, therefore, uses indicators of perceived threat or fear of competition and degree of agreement with multiculturalism in order to examine their roles in shaping Korean workers' attitudes towards migrant workers. In addition, it identifies the extent to which socioeconomic characteristics, including contact with migrant workers, perception of threat, and degree of agreement with multiculturalism exert an influence on Korean workers' attitudes towards migrant workers, thus assessing the mediating roles of perception of threat and multiculturalism between socioeconomic variables with respect to the attitudes towards migrant workers.

8.4   Research Methods

8.4.1   Data

The data for this study derived from a survey conducted in July 2007 among Korean workers employed at the companies that also hire migrant workers. The survey site was Gyeonggi Province and Incheon Metropolitan City, where the majority of Korean firms employ migrant workers. Using multistage cluster sampling, we first selected six blocks (cities) based on the number of companies hiring migrant workers. In the second stage, we sampled 30 companies from each of the five selected blocks and 50 companies from the remaining one block, where the size is almost twice as big as the other five blocks. Finally, we sampled Korean workers from the selected companies. The resulting sample consisted of 500 workers, who filled out a structured questionnaire.

The sociodemographic characteristics of the respondents in the analysis are shown in Table 8.3. The mean age of the respondents is 32 years old, and the majority are male (75.8 %) and married (65.2 %). Their average years of formal schooling is 12.9 and their mean monthly wage is about 2,086 US dollars. With respect to their status in their current company, 32.0 % are general workers, 32.2 % supervisors, and 35.8 % manager-level or higher. The average period each has worked with migrant workers is about 34 months and the average number of migrant worker friends is much less than one at 0.47.

8.4.2   Variables

The background variables and individuals' characteristics included in the analysis are age (in years), sex, marital status, education (years of school attendance), wage (monthly), rank (in the current company), period of working with migrant workers (in months), and number of migrant worker friends.

In addition to socioeconomic and demographic items, the study measured their level of agreement with multiculturalism, the feeling of threat, and the attitudes concerning civil rights of migrant workers. Multiculturalism was assessed by a measure of attitudes toward diversity. This was composed of two items: "How much do you agree or disagree that it is better for a country if a variety of

Table 8.3 Sociodemographic characteristics of respondents

Variables		Mean or %
Age (in years)		32.0
Sex (%)	Male	75.8
	Female	24.2
Marital status (%)	Not married	34.8
	Married	65.2
Education (in years of school)		12.9
Monthly wage (USD)		2,086
Rank in the current company (%)	General worker	32.0
	Supervisor	32.2
	Manager or higher	35.8
Period of working with migrant workers (in months)		33.8
Number of migrant worker friends		0.47

ethnicities, religions and cultures coexist"; and "How much do you agree or disagree that diversity in a country in terms of ethnicity, religion and culture is helpful to the country's competitiveness". The items were adapted from various international surveys, including the Eurobarometer Survey 2000 and the European Social Survey (ESS) 2002–2003. Each item was rated using a five-point scale ranging from strongly disagree (1) to strongly agree (5). Higher scores indicate a stronger endorsement of cultural diversity.

Fear of competition or threat in relation to migrant workers was measured by the following three questions, also adapted from the European Social Survey (ESS) from the years 2002–2003 and other international instruments: "How much do you agree or disagree that wages in our country remain low due to migrant workers"; "How much do you agree or disagree that migrant workers take jobs from Korean people"; and "How much do you agree or disagree that migrant workers take more than they contribute to our economy". Each of the threat measures was assessed using a five-point agree-disagree scale with higher scores indicating stronger feelings of threat.

Attitudes towards civil rights of migrant workers were measured with three questions: "How much do you agree or disagree that legal migrant workers should be given the same labor rights as Korean workers"; "How much do you agree or disagree that legal migrant workers should be given the right to bring their family members to Korea"; and "How much do you agree or disagree that legal migrant workers should be able to get residence or citizenship status easily". The items were adapted from the Eurobarometer Survey 2000 and the European Social Survey (ESS) 2002–2003 and rated on five-point agree-disagree scales with higher scores indicating more positive attitudes toward migrant workers.

The data was analyzed in three steps: analyses of measurement scale, descriptive data on variables, and regression model of attitudes towards civil rights of migrant workers based on the socioeconomic and demographic variables, and factors of multiculturalism and feeling of threat.

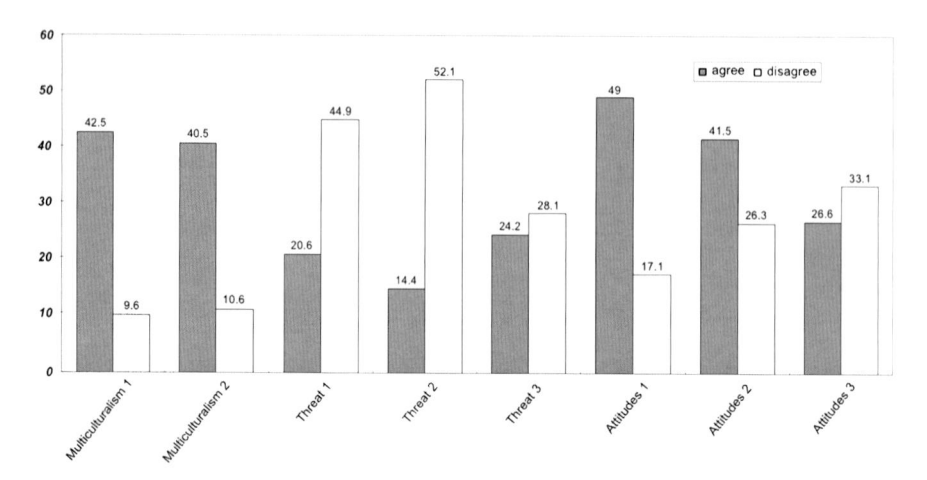

Fig. 8.1 Perception toward multiculturalism, feeling of threat, and attitudes towards civil rights of migrant workers, agreement in percent (%)

8.5 Results

First of all, the analyses of the measurement scales were conducted in order to assess internal consistencies in all multi-item measures. Cronbach alpha reliability for the scales assessing multiculturalism (2 items, $\alpha = .77$), feeling of threat (3 items, $\alpha = .71$), and attitudes towards migrant workers (3 items, $\alpha = .64$) demonstrated acceptable internal consistency considering the small number of items in each scale (Hair et al. 2006).

Figure 8.1 shows Korean workers' perception of multiculturalism, feeling of threat, and attitudes towards civil rights of migrant workers. Overall, Korean workers have positive views towards multiculturalism. More than 40 % of the respondents agree with the statements: one, it is better for a country if there is a variety of ethnicities, religions and cultures; two, diversity in a country, in terms of ethnicity, religion and culture, is helpful to the country's competitiveness. Only about 10 % disagree with each of the statements. The presence of migrant workers seems to pose little threat to Korean workers. For example, 20.6 % agree that wages in our country remain low due to migrant workers while 44.9 % disagree with the statement. Similarly, only 14.4 % agree and 52.1 % disagree that migrant workers take jobs from Korean people. Concerning the statement that migrant workers take more than they contribute to our economy, views of respondents are split with 24.2 % in agreement and 28.1 % in disagreement.

For the issue of conferring civil rights on migrant workers, Korean workers show different attitudes depending on the kinds of civil rights. Respondents are supportive of policies that grant migrant workers the same labor rights as Korean workers and that allow them to bring their family members into Korea, but they showed reluctance towards bestowing residence or citizenship status. More than 40 % of respondents agree with both statements that legal migrant workers should be given

Table 8.4 Means, standard deviations, and correlation coefficients for multiculturalism, feeling of threat and attitudes towards civil rights of migrant workers

Variables		Multiculturalism	Threat	Attitudes
Age[a]		−0.01	0.01	−0.09[*]
Sex[b]	Male	3.40 (0.76)[c]	2.64 (0.81)	3.11 (0.79)
	Female	3.29 (0.71)	2.67 (0.81)	3.23 (0.69)
Marital status	Not married	3.34 (0.77)	2.66 (0.75)	3.19 (0.76)
	Married	3.40 (0.73)	2.64 (0.84)	3.11 (0.77)
Education		0.09	−0.05	0.11[*]
Wage		0.14[**]	−0.14[**]	0.06
Rank	Workers	3.34 (0.69)	2.74 (0.73)	3.18 (0.74)
	Supervisor	3.33 (0.80)	2.64 (0.83)	3.09 (0.80)
	Manager	3.45 (0.74)	2.56 (0.84)	3.15 (0.78)
Period of working with migrant workers		0.02	0.00	0.08
Number of migrant worker friends		−0.06	0.03	−0.06
Multiculturalism		NA[d]	−0.20[***]	0.25[***]
Threat		NA	NA	−0.15[***]

[*]$p < .05$, [**]$p < .01$, [***]$p < .001$
[a]The numbers given under age, education, wage, and period of working with migrant workers, number of migrant worker friends, multiculturalism, and attitudes are correlation coefficients
[b]The numbers given for sex, marital status and rank are proportions
[c]The numbers in parenthesis are standard deviations
[d]Not applicable

the same labor rights as the Korean workers and that legal migrant workers should be given the right to bring their family members into Korea. The disapproval rates for the same statements are 17.1 % and 26.3 %, respectively. Concerning the statement that legal migrant workers should be able to gain residence or citizenship status, the results show more unfavorable views (33.1 %) than favorable ones (26.3 %).

Table 8.4 shows means and standard deviations concerning multiculturalism, feeling of threat and attitudes towards civil rights of migrant workers based on socioeconomic variables, and it demonstrates correlation coefficients between the scaled variables and numerical socioeconomic variables. Both age and education are moderately correlated only with attitudes towards civil rights of migrant workers, although the directions of their correlations are opposite; the correlation between age and the attitudes is negative while the one between education and the attitudes is positive. Wage is strongly correlated in a positive direction with multiculturalism but correlated in a negative direction with feeling of threat. Both variables, the period of working with migrant workers and the number of migrant worker friends, are not significantly correlated with any of the three scaled variables. Multiculturalism, feeling of threat and attitudes towards civil rights are strongly correlated with each other though the directions of their correlations are different; both correlations between multiculturalism and the threat and between the threat and the attitudes are negative, while the correlation between multicultur-alism and the attitudes is positive. There are no differences regarding

Table 8.5 Regression equation coefficients predicting universalism, threat and attitudes

	Multi-culturalism (model 1)	Threat (model 2)	Attitudes (model 3)	Attitudes (model 4)	Attitudes (model 5)	Attitudes (model 6)
Age	-0.116^+	0.067	-0.119^+	-0.090	-0.110^+	-0.086
Sex[a]	-0.018	-0.059	0.065	0.070	0.057	0.065
Marital status[b]	0.090	0.006	0.012	-0.011	0.013	-0.009
Education	0.079	0.009	0.110^*	0.090^+	0.111^*	0.092^+
Wage	0.154^*	-0.195^{**}	0.120^+	0.082	0.095	0.067
Rank[c] Supervisor	-0.073	-0.015	0.058	-0.040	-0.059	-0.043
Manager	-0.043	-0.038	-0.055	-0.045	-0.060	-0.049
Period of work	0.004	0.049	0.093^+	0.095^*	0.100^*	0.099^*
Number of migrant worker friends	-0.059	0.022	-0.066	-0.049	-0.064	-0.048
Multiculturalism				0.250^{***}		0.234^{***}
Threat					-0.129^{**}	-0.085^+
Constant	2.984	2.947	2.460	1.683	2.831	1.976
R^2	0.040	0.029	0.047	0.107	0.063	0.114
F	2.147^*	1.539	2.550^{**}	5.555^{***}	3.133^{***}	5.396^{***}

$^+p < .1, ^*p < .05, ^{**}p < .01, ^{***}p < .001$
[a]The criteria value is male
[b]The criteria value is not married
[c]The criteria value is ordinary worker

multiculturalism, feeling of threat and attitudes toward migrant workers between male and female, between married and not married, and among ranks.

A series of regression equations were estimated in order to determine whether or not socioeconomic status and experiences with migrant workers affect multiculturalism, feeling of threat, and attitudes toward migrant workers; and, to assess the extent to which multiculturalism and perceived threat mediate between the socioeconomic background characteristics and attitudes towards civil rights of migrant workers. In models 1, 2 and 3 shown in Table 8.5, we predicted that each of the factors, i.e. multiculturalism, feeling of threat and attitudes towards civil rights of migrant workers, would reflect the respondent's socioeconomic characteristics. In models 4, 5 and 6, we estimated attitudes towards civil rights of migrant workers as a function of respondent's socioeconomic characteristics and feeling of threat in order to examine whether and to what extent they intervene between all exogenous variables and the attitudes towards civil rights of migrant workers. These models also tell whether the differences in attitudes towards civil rights of migrant workers are a result of differences in multiculturalism or differences in feeling of threat or differences in socioeconomic attributes of respondents.

In model 1, in which only the socioeconomic variables are included to predict multiculturalism, we find that the increases in wage led to a positive effect on multiculturalism, while increases in age produced the opposite effect on multiculturalism. With the exception of the two variables mentioned, none of the socioeconomic variables are significant in the model. In model 2, only wage is strongly associated with feeling of threat, such that the lower wage is associated with higher levels of threat. In model 3, four of eight respondents' characteristics are significant predictors of attitudes towards civil rights of migrant workers. Education, wage and period of working with migrant workers are positively associated with attitudes towards civil rights of migrant workers, but age is once again negatively associated with attitudes towards civil rights of migrant workers.

The models 4, 5 and 6 test the hypothesis that multiculturalism and feeling of threat intervene between individual socioeconomic characteristics and their attitudes towards civil rights of migrant workers. In model 4, in which multiculturalism is added to the set of independent variables in model 3, attitudes towards civil rights of migrant workers are strongly associated with multiculturalism, moderately with period of working with migrant workers, and somewhat weakly with education. That is, positive attitudes towards civil rights of migrant workers tend to increase with education, period of working with migrant workers and acceptance of multiculturalism. With the addition of multiculturalism in the model, the effects of age and wage on attitudes towards civil rights of migrant workers shown in model 3 lost their significance. Importantly, multiculturalism accounts for a large degree of the variation, raising R^2 6 % from 4.7 % in model 3 to 10.7 % in model 4. In model 5, in which feeling of threat is added to model 3 as a predictor, the level of attitudes towards civil rights of migrant workers is likely to rise with education and working with migrant workers, but declines with age and feeling of threat.

Model 6 incorporates all the independent variables in the analysis. Among the variables, education, period of working with migrant workers, multiculturalism and feeling of threat are significantly associated with the dependent variable, attitudes towards civil rights of migrant workers. Attitudes towards civil rights of migrant workers are likely to increase with education, period of working with migrant workers and multiculturalism, but decreases with feeling of threat. Higher education, longer period of work experience with migrant workers, more retention of multiculturalism and less perception of threat from migrant workers tend, therefore, to lead Korean workers to have positive attitudes towards civil rights of migrant workers.

Of the variables, multiculturalism is the most salient variable in predicting attitudes towards civil rights of migrant workers, and the persistence of its strong effect on the attitudes indicates that the ideology of multiculturalism has a significant impact on people's attitudes towards civil rights of migrant workers, even when holding other variables constant. The result lends firm support to the hypothesis that multiculturalism affects attitudes towards civil rights of migrant workers. Education and period of working with migrant workers also maintain their positive effects on attitudes towards civil rights of migrant workers. In contrast, the effect of feeling of threat, which appeared very strongly in predicting attitudes towards civil rights of migrant workers in model 5, decreased significantly when multiculturalism is factored into the analysis. The positive effect of wage and the negative effect of age also lost their significance with an addition of multiculturalism in the analysis.

The effects of multiculturalism on the socioeconomic variables imply that whereas multiculturalism plays an important role in mediating the impact of age and wage on attitudes towards civil rights of migrant workers, it partially affects the relationship between education, period of working with migrant workers, and

Korean workers' support for policies that grant rights to migrant workers. That is, the results suggest that attitudes towards civil rights of migrant workers are influenced not only by multiculturalism but also by individuals' socioeconomic characteristics, such as education and period of working with migrant workers. The sharply decreased effect of feeling of threat on attitudes towards civil rights of migrant workers suggests a possibility that maybe what is much more important in influencing attitudes towards civil rights of migrant workers is multiculturalism.

8.6 Conclusions

The major purpose of this study is to gain a general overview of Korean workers' attitudes towards civil rights of migrant workers. The analysis focused on Korean workers who work with migrant workers at the same workplace in order to understand better the sources and mechanisms underlying their attitudes and to gather more realistic and valid data. The findings reveal that Korean workers show different attitudes towards migrant workers' rights, as there are varieties of civil, political, labor, and human rights. On the one hand, Korean workers are largely in favor of conferring migrant workers the same labor rights as Korean workers and to allow them to bring their family members to Korea, while on the other they are somewhat in disfavor of granting residence or citizenship status to migrant workers. Contrary to popular expectations, a considerable proportion of Korean workers do not view migrant workers as posing a threat to their wages and jobs, specifically, and to the economy of society, generally. To some extent, a positive view of multiculturalism is widely shared among Korean workers.

In predicting multiculturalism and the feeling of threat, the increase in wage leads to more acceptance of multiculturalism and to less feeling of threat. As discussed earlier, the negative effect of wage on the feeling of threat proves that the level of threat is more pronounced among the people with lower socioeconomic status. The data also indicate that the most important determinant of attitudes towards civil rights of migrant workers is the perception of multiculturalism. The greater the sense of multiculturalism the more likely Korean workers are to express favor and to recognize migrant workers' rights.

While multiculturalism is the most important determinant of attitudes towards civil rights of migrant workers, it only partially explains the correlation between individual characteristics and attitudes towards civil rights of migrant workers. When multiculturalism is included, the effects of age and wage on attitudes towards civil rights of migrant workers become insignificant, suggesting that the associations between age, wage and the attitudes could be spurious. Period of working experience with migrant workers and education, however, continue to affect directly the attitudes towards civil rights of migrant workers even after considering multiculturalism. Consistent with previous studies, attitudes towards civil rights of migrant workers tend to become positive with period of working experience with migrant workers and education. The longer the period of work experience with migrant workers and the more education, the more favorable the opinion Korean workers have towards migrant workers. The positive effects of period of work experience with migrant workers and education on attitudes towards civil rights of migrant workers indicate that attitudes towards civil rights of migrant workers would improve considerably if people were better informed about both migrant workers and multiculturalism.

Although perceived threat has an influence on attitudes toward civil rights of migrant workers, its effect decreases sharply when multiculturalism is taken into consideration. The relatively weak impact of perceived threat on attitudes towards civil rights of migrant workers, which differs substantially from the previous arguments and results, as well as low level of perceived threat among Korean workers can partially be explained by terms and conditions of employment for the migrant workers in Korea. The migrant workers' marginal status and precarious employment situation means they cannot compete with Korean counterparts and are not likely to prompt feelings of threat among Korean workers.

While this study has found an association between feeling of threat against migrant workers and multiculturalism, the causal relation between them is as yet unknown. In addition, little is explained about the relationship between the socio-economic and demographic characteristics such as age, wage and multiculturalism (Breugelmans and Vijver 2004). Future studies may explore these relationships further and provide a theoretical foundation. Finally, it goes without saying that this study is limited in extending its findings to a national setting. Since the study focuses on Korean workers who work closely with migrant workers, one should take caution in applying the results to other Korean workers or the general public.

Endnotes

[1]This paper is a newly revised version of the article published in *International Area Studies Review* 13(2), 2009.
[2]Migrant workers in this study are people who migrate across country borders, often called international migrant or foreign workers.
[3]The fertility rate has dropped from 1.45 in 1998 to 1.19 in 2008 (NSO 2009).
[4]Philippines, Thailand, Indonesia, Sri Lanka, Vietnam, Mongolia, Uzbekistan, Pakistan, Cambodia, China, Bangladeshi, Kyrgyzstan, Nepal, Myanmar and East Timor.

References

Berry, J. W. (2001). A Psychology of Immigration. *Journal of Social Issues*, 57, 115–631.
Berry, J. W. (2006). Mutual Attitudes among Immigrants and Ethnocultural Groups in Plural Societies. *International Journal of Intercultural Relations*, 30, 719–734.

Berry, J. W. & Kalin, R. (1995). Multicultural and Ethnic Attitudes in Canada: An Overview of the 1991 National Survey. *Canadian Journal of Behavioral Science*, 27, 301–320.

Blalock, H. (1967). *Toward a Theory of Minority-Group Relations*. New York: Wiley.

Bobo, L. & Hutchings, V. L. (1996). Perception of Racial Group Competition: Extending Blumer's Theory of Group Competition to Multiracial Social Context. *American Sociological Review*, 61, 951–972.

Borjas, G. J. & Freeman, R. B. (1992). *Immigration and the Work Force: Economic Consequences for the United States and Source Areas*. Chicago: The University of Chicago Press.

Breugelmans, S. & Vijver, F. (2004). Antecedents and Components of Majority Attitudes toward Multiculturalism in the Netherlands. *Applied Psychology: An International Review*, 53, 400–422.

Brewer, M. B. & Brown, R. J. (1998). Intergroup Relations. In D. T. Gilbert, S. T. Fiske, G. Lindzey (Eds.), *The Handbook of Social Psychology* (pp. 554–594). New York: McGraw-Hill.

Case, C., Greely, A., Fuchs, S. (1989). Social Determinants of Racial Prejudice. *Sociological Perspectives*, 32, 469–483.

Castles, S. (1998). New Migrations in the Asian-Pacific Region: A Force for Social and Political Change. *International Social Science Journal*, 50(2), 215–227.

Castles, S. & Miller, M. J. (2009). *The Age of Migration; International Population Movements in the Modern World*. New York: The Guilford Press.

Dixon, J. (2006). The Ties That Bind and Those That Don't: Toward Reconciling Group Threat and Contact Theories of Prejudice. *Social Forces*, 84, 2179–2204.

Esses, V. M., Dovidio, Jackson, J. F., L. M., Armstrong, T. L. (2001). The Immigration Dilemma: A Role of Perceived Group Competition, Ethnic Prejudice and National Identity. *Journal of Social Issues*, 57, 389–412.

Espenshade, T. & Hempstead, K. (1996). Contemporary American Attitudes toward US Immigration. *International Migration Review*, 30, 535–570.

EUMC (European Monitoring Centre on Racism and Xenophobia) (2005). *Majorities' Attitudes towards Minorities: Key findings from the Eurobarometer and the European Social Survey*. Vienna.

Fetzer, J. S. (2000). *Public Attitudes toward Immigration in the United States, France, and Germany*. New York: Cambridge University Press.

Finlay, K. A. & Stephan, W. G. (2000). Improving Intergroup Relations: The Effects of Empathy on Racial Attitudes. *Journal of Applied Social Psychology*, 8, 1720–1737.

Hair, J., Black, W., Babin, B., Anderson, R., Tatham, R. (2006). *Multivariate Data Analysis*. Upper Saddle River, NJ: Pearson Education.

Hello, E., Scheepers, P., Gijsberts, M. (2002). Education and Ethnic Prejudice in Europe: Explanations for Cross-national Variances in the Educational Effect on Ethnic Prejudice. *Scandinavian Journal of Educational Research*, 46, 5–24.

Hwang, J., Kim, I., Lee, M., Choi, H., Lee, D. (2007). *Hanguk sahoe'eui daminjok·damunhwa jihyangseong'e daehan josayeongu (A Research on Multiethnic and Multicultural Orientation in Korean Society)*. Seoul: Hanguk yeoseongjeongchaekyeonguwon (Korea Women's Development Institute).

ILO (International Labour Organization) (2004). *Towards a Fair Deal for Migrant Workers in the Global Economy*. Geneva.

IOM (International Organization for Migration) (2005). *World Migration Report*. Geneva.

Jackson, J. S., Brown, K. T., Marks, B. (2001). Contemporary Immigration Policy Orientations among Dominant Group Members in Western Europe. *Journal of Social Issues*, 57, 431–456.

Lee, H. (2003). Gender, Migration and Civil Activism in South Korea. *Asian and Pacific Migration Journal*, 12(1–2), 127–153.

Lee, J. & Lee, S. (2007). Oegukin nodongja'eui iju teukseong'gwa yeongudonghyang (Migrant Characteristics of Foreign Workers and Research in Korea). *Hangukinguhak (Korea Journal of Population Studies)*, 30(2), 147–168.

Lim, L. L. & Oishi, N. (1996). International Labor Migration of Asian Women. *Asian and Pacific Migration Journal*, 5(1), 85–116.

Martin, P. & Widgren, J. (2002). International Migration: Facing the Challenge. *Population Bulletin*, 57(1), 3–40.

Massey, D. S., Arango, J., Hugo, G., Kouaouci, A., Pellegrino., A., Taylor, J. E. (2005). *Worlds in Motion: Understanding International Migration at the End of the Millennium*. New York: Oxford University Press.

Miller, W., Polinard, J., Wrinkle, R. (1984). Attitudes toward Undocumented Workers: the Mexican American Perspective. *Social Science Quarterly*, 65, 482–494.

MOJ (Ministry of Justice) (various years). *Chulipguk tonggye yeongam (Annual Report on Emigration and Immigration)*. Seoul.

MOL (Ministry of Labor) (each year). *Nodong Suyo yeongam (Annual Report on Labor Demand)*. Seoul.

NSO (National Statistical Office) (2009). *2008 Chulsaeng tonggye jamjeong gyeolgwa (2008 Tentative Results on Birth Statistics)*. Daejeon.

Olzak, S. (1992). *The Dynamics of Ethnic Competition and Conflict*. Stanford: Stanford University Press.

Olzak, S. (1995). The Dynamics of Ethnic Competition and Conflict. *Ethnic and Racial Studies*, 18, 373–374.

Park, S., & Chung, K. (2006). Sahoejeok sosuja'e daehan pyeongyeonjeok taedo'e gwanhan yeongu (Study on Prejudice towards Minority Groups). *Yeoseongyeongu (The Women's Studies)*, 70(2), 5–26.

Pettigrew, T. & Tropp, L. (2000). Does Intergroup Contact Reduce Prejudice: Recent Meta-analytic Findings. In S. Oskamp (Ed.), *Reducing Prejudice and Discrimination* (pp. 93–114). NJ: Lawrence Erlbaum.

Quillian, L. (1995). Prejudice as a Response to Perceived Group Threat: Population Composition and Anti-immigrant and Racial Prejudice in Europe. *American Sociological Review*, 60, 586–611.

Raijman, R., Semyonov, M., & Schmidt, P. (2003). Do Migrants Deserve Rights? Determinants of Public Views towards Migrants in Germany and Israel. *European Sociological Review*, 19, 379–392.

Ruefle, W., Ross, W., & Mandell, D. (1992). Attitudes toward Southeast Asian Immigrants in a Wisconsin Community. *International Migration Review*, 26, 877–898.

Schalk-Soekar, S., Vijver, F., & Hoogsteder, M. (2004). Attitudes toward Multiculturalism of Immigrants and Majority Members in the Netherlands. *International Journal of Intercultural Relations*, 28, 533–550.

Scheepers, P., Gijsberts, M., & Coenders, M. (2002). Ethnic Exclusionism in European Countries: Public Opposition to Civil Rights for Legal Migrants as a Response to Perceived Ethnic Threat. *European Sociological Review*, 18, 17–34.

Seok, H., Chung, K., Lee, J., Lee, H., Kang, S. (2003). *Oegukin nodongja'eui ilteo'wa salm (Workplace and Life of Foreign Workers in Korea)*. Seoul: Jisikmadang.

Simon, R. & Alexander, S. H. (1993). *The Ambivalent Welcome: Print Media, Public Opinion and Immigration*. Westport, CT: Praeger.

Song, Y. (2008). Hanguk, Daeman, Ilbon'eui iminja'e daehan taedo (A Comparative Analysis of Individual Attitudes towards Immigrants in Korea, Taiwan, and Japan). *Hangukinguhak (Korea Journal of Population Studies)*, 31(2), 1–20.

Taylor, M. (1998). How White Attitudes Vary with the Racial Composition of Local Populations: Numbers Count. *American Sociological Review*, 63, 512–535.

Ward, C. & Kennedy, A. (1999). The Measurement of Sociocultural Adaptation. *International Journal of Intercultural Relations*, 23, 659–677.

Ward, C. & Masgoret, A. (2008). Attitudes toward Immigrants, Immigration, and Multiculturalism in New Zealand: A Sociopsychological Analysis. *International Migration Review*, 42, 227–248.

Wimmer, A. (1997). Explaining Xenophobia and Racism: A Critical Review of Current Research Approaches. *Ethnic and Racial Studies*, 20, 17–41.

Wong, D. (1996). Foreign Domestic Workers in Singapore. *Asian and Pacific Migration Journal*, 5(1), 117–138.

Chapter 9
Ethnic Chinese in South Korea: Interplay Between Ethnicity, Nationality, and Citizenship

Sang-Hui Nam

Abstract This paper aims to explore historical changes in the citizenship status of ethnic Chinese in South Korea. The first stage, from 1882 to 1948, was characterized by strong influences of Confucian familism. Koreans perceived ethnic Chinese immigrants simply as a different clan or family. Although both sides were strictly separated, they respected each other. The second stage, which lasted until the 1990s, could be described as an ongoing struggle for either inclusion or exclusion of the Chinese minority in the South Korean nation-state. The implementation of an ethnic-based nationality in South Korea legally excluded the ethnic Chinese from participation in the social, political, and economic life of South Korean society. In the third stage, the period since the 1990s, the impact of democratization and globalization took public discussions about a more comprehensive concept of citizenship and nationality beyond ethnicity. Based on historical analysis, this paper comes to the conclusion that the formation of the nation-state in the late 1940s and early 1950s represents a critical juncture for the ethnic Chinese community in South Korea. However, after the democratic regime change in 1987, the concept of citizenship profoundly changed. It appears that membership in the South Korean nation-state did not depend on a single principle; the discussion was, rather, characterized by a sometimes fierce competition between different concepts of citizenship and participation.

9.1 Introduction

This study deals with current changes in the citizenship status of Chinese residents who have lived for decades in South Korea.[1] Their forebears immigrated to Korea as part of Chinese military troops over a 100 years ago. They mostly resided in local

S.-H. Nam (✉)
Department of Sociology, Heidelberg University, Bergheimer Str. 58, Heidelberg 69115, Germany

Untere Seegasse 10, Heidelberg 69124, Germany
e-mail: sang-hui.nam@soziologie.uni-heidelberg.de

M. Pohlmann et al. (eds.), *Citizenship and Migration in the Era of Globalization*, Transcultural Research – Heidelberg Studies on Asia and Europe in a Global Context, DOI 10.1007/978-3-642-19739-0_9, © Springer-Verlag Berlin Heidelberg 2013

Chinese communities in several Korean cities. Since then, ethnic Chinese in Korea have been exposed to the same historical events and social conditions as indigenous Koreans. However, their inclusion in Korean society was neither taken into account nor explicitly mentioned in the South Korean nationality law prior to the 1990s. The improvement of their citizenship status was seriously considered for the first time in connection with a revision of the law around 2000. Choi states, "While the new (nationality) law is framed in a broader context, the immediate and significant beneficiaries are nevertheless the ethnic Chinese, the only ethnic minority group in Korea which has resided for generations as foreign nationals" (Choi 2008: 140). In this respect, the ethnic Chinese in South Korea – although their proportion of all Korean nationals is only approximately 0.3 % – have played an important role in recent changes in the definition of nationality and citizenship in Korea.

In the Korean Chosŏn dynasty (1392–1897), the network of clans and families was governed by the royal family of the *Lee* at the top of the social hierarchy. Thus, the Korean monarchy is often called Chosŏn of the *Lee* dynasty. According to this model, the relationship between Korea and China was considered to be hierarchical, like the relationship between younger and elder brothers. China, as the elder brother, had a "superior" status to Korea, as the younger brother. On the basis of this legitimation, the Korean government was obliged to pay respect (in form of tributes) and to be loyal to the Chinese Empire. The crowning ceremonies for the kings of the Chosŏn dynasty had to be less pompous and elaborate than those of the Chinese emperors. In return, the Chosŏn people were allowed to import China's technical achievements and economic products and to learn from its advanced civilization.

In the beginning of their immigration history, the status of ethnic Han Chinese depended almost exclusively on the influence of their homeland, China, on the host country, Korea. In addition to the Sino-Korean relationship based on the principles of brotherhood and authority, their status was embedded in the internal structure of the Korean Chosŏn dynasty. Individual membership of Chosŏn society was proved with genealogical documents of clans or families (Nam 2010).[2] Under these circumstances, the collective identity of the Korean people – the distinction between "us" and "them" – was inseparably linked to their family ties and bonds. Strangers were, principally, nothing but members of other family groups. These strangers were allowed to exist parallel to Korean families without any pressure to integrate themselves into the leading culture.

On the one hand, ethnic Chinese in Korea could, to some extent, benefit from the asymmetric relationship between the two countries. On the other hand, every change in this definition of the relationship between China and Korea immediately affected the social position of ethnic Chinese in Korea. As ethnic Chinese focused on trade and business activities, their social position in Korea relied heavily on the stability of the regional economic order (Schwinn 2001). Against this background, this study follows Marshall's approach by shifting the concept of citizenship to the center of sociological analysis (Crowley 1996, 1998; Marshall 1992). Accordingly, social integration begins and ends with the question of whether someone belongs to a community or not, and respectively, whether someone is one of "us" or "them".

This study conceives the current citizenship status of the Chinese minority in South Korea as the result of a path-dependent process. According to Mahoney (2001), path dependence occurs "when the choices of key actors at critical juncture points lead to the formation of institutions that have self-reproducing properties" (Mahoney 2001: 111). The first critical juncture of this process was the establishment of the constitution of the South Korean state after the end of Japanese colonial rule in 1948. In the preceding 70 years, the relationship between the ethnic Chinese minority and the Korean majority was defined solely in terms of ethnic identity: the first three decades were characterized by a peaceful co-existence between different "clan identities" under the cultural, economic, and military hegemony of China over Korea. In the next four decades, both ethnic identities were dominated by the imperial power of the Japanese colonial government in Korea. In this period, the citizenship status of both groups, ethnic Korean and ethnic Chinese, was highly constrained. In the 40 years following Japanese colonial rule, an ethnic-centered national identity constituted the core of the South Korean citizenship concept. All other ethnic groups, such as the Chinese, were more or less excluded from participation in and membership of the South Korea nation-state. The ethnic Chinese minority was classified as a group of foreign aliens. In the 1990s, after the end of the Cold War, increasing international exchange softened the strong connection between Korean ethnic identity and Korean nationality. In the 2000s, the citizenship status of the Chinese minority slowly improved.

9.2 Interplay Between Ethnicity, Nationality, and Citizenship

9.2.1 Ethnic Chinese as "Otherness" in Trade and Business

The first wave of immigration of ethnic Han Chinese to Korea took place in the final stage of the Korean Chosŏn dynasty in 1882. At this time, the country was shaken by the growing influence of foreign colonial powers. It was an age of rearrangement in the East Asian regional political order. China, allegedly the "elder brother" of the Chosŏn dynasty, was repeatedly defeated by Western countries such as the British Empire. Meanwhile, Japan emerged as a new military power in the region after a rapid process of modernization under the *Meiji* regime (1868–1889). Facing the breakdown of the Chinese Empire spurred by Western imperial powers, the Chosŏn dynasty searched for a new political and cultural orientation beyond the shadow of China.

In this context, the ruling dynasty of the *Lee* family established the Great Korean Empire (1897–1910), and the former King restyled himself as "Emperor". This Empire turned out to be a temporary solution in a time of political disorientation. The Great Korean Empire had no military power to keep its population and territory under control. Shortly after, the country was colonized by Japan (1910–1945). Against this backdrop, the transition from the nineteenth to the twentieth century is often described as a period in which the relationship between China and Korea fundamentally changed. As a consequence, the status of ethnic Chinese in Korea had to face new challenges. Choi speaks of a "reorientation of the two nations [i.e., China and Korea; S.-H. Nam] relationship to each other and, more broadly, to the world" (Choi 2008: 128).

Korean efforts to turn away from the long brotherly alliance with China reach back to the earlier regime change in China from the Ming dynasty (1368–1644) to the Qing dynasty (1644–1912). At that time, the authority of China over Chosŏn was undermined by the weak legitimation of the Chinese Qing dynasty. The ruling Confucian elites of Chosŏn Korea regarded the former Ming dynasty in China as the center of the world and as a role model for a true Confucian social order. By contrast, the Qing dynasty that succeeded the Ming dynasty was not fully appreciated by the leading Korean Confucian scholars. They regarded the Qing dynasty as Manchurian barbarians (Kim Haboush and Deuchler 1999). Therefore, the Korean Confucianists were still loyal to Ming China even after its downfall (Hulbert 1969). This circumstance sometimes favored an arrogant attitude toward the Chinese minority in Korea at the turn of the twentieth century.

When the first Chinese migrants arrived in Chosŏn in 1882, they were not welcomed by the Korean population because they accompanied Chinese troops. To counter the growing influence of Japan on the Korean peninsula, Qing China sent 3,000 troops to the western port city of Incheon under the pretext of helping Chosŏn Korea against Japanese intruders. The material support for the Chinese soldiers was organized by 40 Chinese merchants who initially came from the Shandong province in east China. From the beginning, the commercial activities of these immigrants were protected by unequal trade agreements that granted special privileges to Chinese merchants. Such regulations, based solely on military power, could not be regarded as legitimate by ordinary Chosŏn people, although they still respected the superiority of Chinese culture and civilization.

Furthermore, the activities of the Chinese in Korea were not particularly respected by the Chosŏn people. The Chinese merchants and laborers were engaged in exporting and importing groceries, miscellaneous goods, and seafood, as well as conducting predatory money lending. In the Confucian social order, mercantile activities were traditionally carried out by the most humble classes, who were generally despised.[3] Chinese restaurants provided cheap, customary food for Chinese laborers. By 1885, "Chinatowns" extended from Incheon to Seoul. Nevertheless, most Koreans regarded the Chinese merchants as ridiculous and greedy.

In this respect, the first wave of Chinese immigration to Korea was a crucial step in the process of constructing Chinese "otherness" in Korea. After the defeat of China in the first Sino-Japanese War (1894–1895), Chosŏn gradually emerged from the shadow of the cultural, economic, and political hegemony of China. The image of the Chinese minority as representatives of a great civilization was increasingly replaced by that of a "strange" social group with a strong negative connotation. Under these circumstances, it is not surprising that their economic success engendered contempt and envy among most Koreans.

With the annexation of Korea by Japan (1910), the social and political status of the Chinese minority in Korea changed yet again. After the establishment of the colonial regime, the formal host country for the ethnic Chinese was Japan. This historical event was less serious for the Chinese minority than for the Korean population. Primarily ethnic Koreans were now treated as second-class citizens (by comparison with ethnic Japanese): The Koreans were obliged to serve the Japanese Empire while having only limited political, economic, and cultural rights as compared with the ethnic Japanese population (Nam 2010). The policies of the Japanese colonial administration focused on strengthening its control, mostly over the ethnic Korean population.

However, the more the political and commercial hegemony of Japan increased over Korea, the more delicate the situation became for the Chinese minority in Korea. Their status was precarious and changed many times, ranging from enemies, free-riders, or scapegoats to the relatively privileged. The destiny of the Chinese minority in Korea was in danger, as Qing China still rivaled Japan. However, as long as the political relationship between China and Japan was good, the Chinese merchants and laborers were treated even better than the colonized Korean Japanese (Yang and Yi 2004: 41). During this time, the Japanese colonial administration protected the previous privileges enjoyed by Chinese merchants in the former Chosŏn dynasty. They received the same commercial advantages as Western foreign traders. The Chinese merchants were, then, individually engaged in their mercantile activities and made no efforts to establish particular organizations in Korea on behalf of their own interests. However, they gradually began to organize voluntary associations and benefited from mutual aid through familial and ethnic networks among themselves.

The ethnic Korean population regarded the relatively better treatment of the Chinese minority by the Japanese government as unfair. The Koreans even submitted a petition to the Japanese government to cut back on the employment of Chinese workers. Chinese residents were mocked as "swallows" – a migratory bird. This mockery implied that the Chinese merchants earned money in Korea, but spent it elsewhere, in China, for example, when they visited their hometowns during the Lunar New Year festival. Chinese merchants were regarded as parsimonious and unwilling to spend money in Korea. This situation refreshed and reinforced anti-Chinese sentiments that had existed since the first wave of Chinese immigration during the Chosŏn dynasty.

Aside from that, the status of the Chinese minority was still precarious, depending on international relations. Chinese residents were also often treated as potential enemies and suspected, for instance, of stirring up protests against the Japanese Empire. A considerable number of Korean dissidents immigrated to China and struggled in alliance with Chinese communist soldiers against Japan's colonial rule in East Asia. They founded a Korean exile government in Shanghai (1919) that undoubtedly annoyed the Japanese government. This might have been one of the reasons why the Japanese government took increasingly discriminatory measures against the economic activities of the Chinese minority in Korea beginning in the mid-1920s. For example, the monetary reform of 1931 considerably impeded

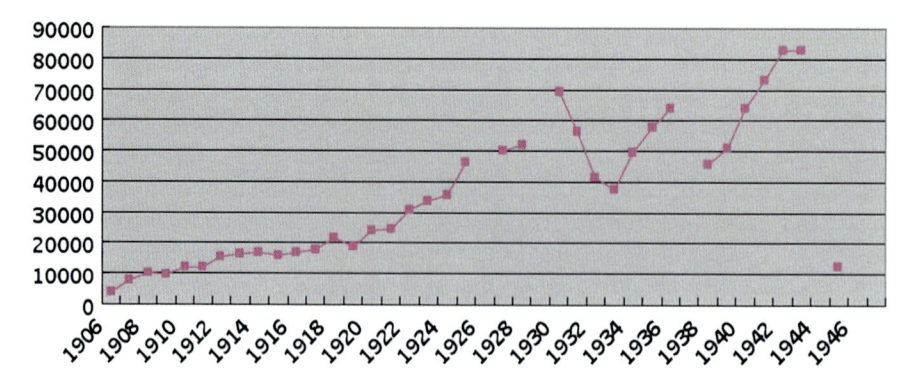

Fig. 9.1 The number of ethnic Chinese (until 1945) (Source: Park (1981: 31–32, 69). The number after 1945 is only from South Korea)

Chinese commercial activities. The Manchurian incident (1931) and the second Sino-Japanese War (1937–1945) endangered the existence of the Chinese minority in Korea even more.

Most Chinese residents in Korea refrained from taking collective action and coped with their situation individually. Some of them donated large sums of money to the Japanese colonial administration to guarantee their security. Other Chinese immigrated to other countries such as the United States. Figure 9.1 shows a sharp decline in the number of ethnic Chinese in Korea from 82,661 in 1942 to 12,648 in 1945. However, it also reveals that the number of ethnic Chinese in Korea has continually increased despite considerable ups and downs. This development illustrates the unstable and precarious living conditions of the Chinese minority in Korea. They were deeply entangled in the matrix of ethnicity and nationality between Japanese, Koreans, and Chinese.

As the colonial government and Japanese businesspeople retreated from the Korean peninsula in 1945, the ethnic Chinese enjoyed this economic boom and re-emerged as the most influential minority in Korea. Despite the unstable relationship between Japan and China over the previous decades, the Chinese merchants had been able to constantly manage businesses, establish social networks, and accumulate professional experience in Korea under the Japanese colonial government. Therefore, the Chinese merchants strongly benefited from a business boom by importing goods from China. On this basis, the Chinese merchants were actually able to control 86 % of the import trade nationwide in 1946 and 53 % in 1948. Moreover, many Chinese had moved to South Korea by the end of the 1940s in order to escape the Chinese civil war. From Incheon, they dominated the growing trade with Macao and Hong Kong. During the Korean War (1950–1953), they made a huge profit with their trade (weapons, textiles, etc.). However, this boom definitely ended with the consolidation of the nation-state in South Korea and the development of the Cold War order in East Asia.

9.2.2 Exclusion of the Ethnic Chinese Through Ethnic-Centered Nationality

From the beginning of the Cold War, the situation of the ethnic Chinese in Korea dramatically changed and deteriorated. First, the ethnic Chinese were cut off from their Chinese homeland and could not continue to benefit from transactions between both countries. Second, after becoming independent from Japan and the U.S. military government, the South Korean state considerably enhanced its institutional control over the population. The new government first clarified the conditions for membership and, by doing so, specified the boundaries of the Korean national state.

Considering the development of particular characteristics of citizenship status, South Korea, like almost all post-colonial states, has had to face two serious problems. First, they "share the imperative of national security, identity and welfare on equal terms with stable, post-industrial states, though their material and political conditions are vastly different" (Mitra 2008: 343–344). This first problem refers to the expectation of the whole population to simultaneously obtain full – civil, political, and social – citizenship (Marshall 1992: 8). In the case of South Korea, subsequent to the implementation of the nationality law, civil and political citizenship was to some extent ensured. However, the responsibility for "social" citizenship was assigned to the families. Under the influence of a traditionally strong Confucian orientation to family values, the South Korean government devoted itself exclusively to the promotion of economic growth. The families had to organize their social net by themselves. Chang (2007, 2010) describes this state as "developmental" citizenship.

Secondly, "in contrast with stable, industrial democracies of the West, these new (post-colonial) states need to transform *subjects and immigrants* – marginal social groups – into citizens entitled to enjoy all of the political and social rights" (Mitra 2008: 343–344). The second problem points to the universal nature of the modern concept of citizenship. Mitra indicates that "[n]ationality and citizenship may depend on each other but they are not necessarily congruent" (2008: 346–347). In the same vein, Ku stresses that "citizenship practices and public criticisms opened up a contested space for political resistance and meaning reconstruction" (Ku 2004a: 664; Ku 2004b).[4]

This "contested space" developed historically in South Korea after the end of Japanese colonial rule. With the formal establishment of South Korea as an independent nation-state, the conditions for citizenship became a hot issue. A major debate revolved round the redistribution of estate and capital that had previously been expropriated by the Japanese colonial government and returned to South Korea before the colonizers left the peninsula. It was taken for granted that these properties should only be given to former Chosŏn (ethnic) Koreans. In this way, the distribution of citizenship rights was inextricably linked with the distribution of interests and property, fortunes, and land. Korean nationality was considered to be the single and most basic condition for a person to be eligible for economic, political, and social benefits. Consequently, Korean nationality was given

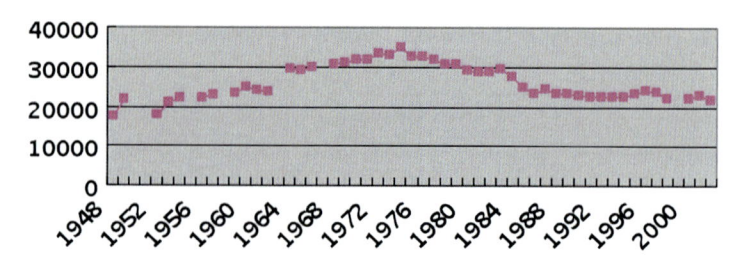

Fig. 9.2 The number of ethnic Chinese (since 1948) (Source: Park (1986): 118; Ministry of Justice, *Statistical Yearbook of Immigration Office* (1985–2005). All numbers are for ethnic Chinese in South Korea)

exclusively to ethnic Chosŏn Koreans. In the same vein, according to the nationality law of 1948, there was no question that Korean emigrants who had adopted the citizenship of other countries, such as China or the United States, could obtain Korean nationality upon their return.

Since the establishment of the South Korean nation-state, the residence status of the Chinese minority has been exclusively regulated by the nationality law. The members of the ethnic Chinese minority were categorized as foreigners without consideration for their long-term residence in the country and relatively high degree of social integration. Although they had lived for more than 50 years in Korea without offending Korean laws and contributed considerably to the economic development of Korean society, they were in no way considered to be eligible for Korean citizenship. On the contrary, the legal status of the Chinese minority became even worse than it had been in colonial times. Under these circumstances, many young Chinese left South Korea and immigrated, for example, to the United States because they were concerned about their future. This might be one reason why the number of ethnic Chinese stagnated for decades while the Korean population strongly increased (see Fig. 9.2)[5].

The Korean War (1950–1953) further deteriorated the situation of the ethnic Chinese because it peaked in a direct military confrontation between China (on the side of North Korea) and South Korea. Until 1992, diplomatic relations between capitalist South Korea and communist China were frozen. As a consequence, trade between the two countries – as the economic basis of the Chinese minority – almost completely broke down.

It was nothing new for the ethnic Chinese in South Korea to experience personal difficulties as a result of international political confrontations. In response to the changing political situation in Northeast Asia, most of them broke off all personal contact with PR China and adopted Taiwanese nationality so as to survive in South Korea. Since then, most ethnic Chinese living in South Korea have turned into Taiwanese nationals without changing their collective identity as ethnic Chinese.[6] Despite changing their nationality, they could not benefit much from normal diplomatic relations between Taiwan and South Korea. Due to the economic rivalry between the two countries, the trading activities of ethnic Chinese in South Korea remained at a constantly low level for decades. Furthermore, most of the ethnic

Chinese in Korea came from Shandong, an Eastern province of China, and they had no connection with Chinese residents in Southeast Asia or Japan that originated from the southern province of Gwandong on the Chinese mainland (Park and Park 2003). In other words, the Chinese in South Korea could rarely activate the so-called "bamboo network" to improve their economic situation. Meanwhile, Korean nationals began to expand their own business and trade network in Japan and the United States while turning their backs on China.

In this context, the South Korean government repeatedly made institutional efforts to limit the citizenship of the Chinese minority for the benefit of ethnic Korean nationals. Choe (2006) basically distinguishes two different citizenship and identity concepts: "Ethnic-centred national identity identifies nationhood with ethnicity and emphasizes the cultural homogeneity of a nation, while state-centred national identity allows for the coexistence of various ethnic groups under a state and emphasizes a common political goal shared by a nation" (Choe 2006: 89). According to Choe, South Korea represents a typical case of a post-colonial country that built its national identity on an ethnic-centered approach. This means that the "naturalization" of other ethic immigrants was almost impossible for decades (Lee 2004). Under these conditions, "fewer than 10 foreigners were naturalized every year in Korea from 1948 to 1985" (Ministry of Justice 2002). Naturalization through intermarriage was also constrained because the nationality law was based on the principle of patrilineality. Even the child of a Korean mother and a Chinese father was not eligible to apply for Korean citizenship (Nam 2010; Turner 2008).

The legal status of the Chinese residents suffered from the introduction of the personal resident registration system in 1968 in South Korea. Every Korean citizen received a personal number that remained unchanged for his or her entire life. Although it is called a personal *resident* registration number, Chinese residents were not registered in the same way, and therefore could not obtain such a number. For this reason, it was almost impossible for ethnic Chinese to live a normal life in South Korea. The personal resident registration number gives access to public life; without one, people have difficulty getting loans from banks, conducting online transactions, etc.

All of these political and administrative measures contributed to the systematic exclusion of the Chinese minority from active participation in economic, political, and social activities in South Korea. The South Korean government discriminated against ethnic Chinese depending on the international political situation and the public mood: "As soon as they are not needed anymore or their special success provokes envy among indigenous people, they are exposed to the attack of the natives without any protection" (Schwinn 2001: 214).

The exclusion of the ethnic Chinese began in the economic field. In 1951, an act was passed to restrict money exchange by foreigners. Subsequent to this, two monetary reforms followed in 1953 and 1962. Since Chinese residents in South Korea had kept most of their money in cash, the reforms resulted in an enormous loss for them. Under the Land Law of 1961, foreigners were also banned from owning real estate or getting loans. The monetary reforms were enacted to prevent money laundering by illicit moneylenders and weaken the influence of the Chinese networks that dominated the Asian economy. The message of the reforms in South Korea was unmistakable: when the Korean government reduced the value of the old currency, the capital assets of the Chinese residents was suddenly devalued to the point that their financial basis nearly collapsed.

In 1968, a new law prevented foreign households from owning or managing large real estate properties. For example, foreigners were not allowed to buy houses exceeding 660 m^2 or stores over 165 m^2. Foreigners were also not allowed to buy forests or fields. In the booming economy of the 1970s and 1980s, investments in real estate were one of the best ways to accumulate capital. Consequently, the Chinese minority was systematically prevented from getting a share of the double-digit growth rate of the South Korean national economy during this period.

The exclusion of the ethnic Chinese was not limited to the economic field but also extended to education. In postwar South Korea, education plays a central role in the realization of upward mobility and the social participation of the broad population in South Korea. In the Korean tradition, public and private organizations select their leading staff on the basis of formal educational qualifications. In this respect, particularly a person's university background is of great importance for his or her economic success. However, Chinese schools were neither integrated into the Korean school system nor accredited by the Korean government. Under these circumstances, the schools of the Chinese community (ironically) enjoyed great autonomy and played an important role in strengthening their solidarity in passing on the Chinese language and culture from one generation to the next. In doing so, they maintained the collective identity of the Chinese.

The denial of certification by Chinese schools strongly limited the upward mobility of the ethnic Chinese in South Korea. Graduates from Chinese schools could not attend higher educational institutions that required official certificates. As long as the economic activities of the Chinese minority were limited to small businesses and sectors with low professional qualifications such as Chinese restaurants and grocery stores, the children needed no higher education. Further-more, due to the decreasing numbers of Chinese residents in South Korea, many Chinese schools were closed. Their number decreased from 55 in 1974 to 34 in 1994, 26 in 1999, and, finally, 18 in 2006.

Surveillance of ethnic Chinese was performed by the police, the national tax office, immigration offices, and other district institutions belonging to the state. Protests in support of better treatment or enhanced participation were often too risky. Under the authoritarian regime (1961–1987), such activities could have resulted in deportation from South Korea. Likewise, they received very little assistance from Taiwan and China. Under these circumstances, instead of negotiating or resisting, the ethnic Chinese adopted a form of self-exclusion. The younger generations began to emigrate from South Korea to the U.S., Australia, Taiwan, and Japan, where living conditions seemed to be better, and they sought to connect with the Chinese diaspora. In particular, large-scale minority businesses moved to Taiwan, while only small-sized businesses remained in South Korea and tried to make a living.

9.2.3 Inclusion Under the Pressures of the Global Civil Society and Labor Migration

Since the transition to democracy in 1987, the legal situation of the ethnic Chinese in South Korea has slowly improved. The new democratic regimes provided a more responsive environment by strengthening human rights in general and minority rights in particular. The government deliberately set the improvement of the citizenship status of ethnic Chinese on the political agenda. Furthermore, after democratization, South Korea entered various international institutions such as the United Nations and the OECD. As a consequence, international legal regulations and governance structures increasingly affected the process of political decision-making. In this context, the economic activities of South Korean companies and civil society organizations also profoundly changed and were increasingly interlinked with "global" structures and processes. This new situation fundamentally challenged the social integrative capabilities of the South Korea nation-state (Schwinn 2001; Pohlmann 2006). The status of the ethnic Chinese who had lived for decades in South Korea emerged as a public issue that had to be discussed and solved in a legal way. According to Lee (2008a, b), in many cases the adjustment of nation-state-based concepts of citizenship has been inseparably linked with national interests and sometimes even nationalist aspirations. Thus, "citizenship . . . has once again emerged as a salient and complex problem in the age of globalization" (Mitra 2008: 363).

Since the 1990s, the South Korean public has become increasingly responsive to the concerns and claims of ethnic minorities in the political and economic sphere. Under these circumstances, Chinese residents who once kept silent about iniquities under the former authoritarian regime demanded serious improvements concerning their citizenship status in South Korean society. Choe (2006) argues that "the need for entrepreneurs, the pressure of (domestic and international) NGOs, and diplomatic relations" (Choe 2006: 86) have played an important role in reversing the strict citizenship policies of the South Korean government in the 1990s and 2000s.[7]

This process was further accelerated by the growing integration of the South Korean state into the international political community. For example, in 1990, South Korea joined the "International Covenant on Civil and Political Rights". In 1991, South Korea agreed to the principles of the "Convention on the Rights of the Child". This convention was the first legally binding international agreement that demanded a full guarantee of human rights – civil, cultural, economic, political, and social.

Keeping pace with governmental efforts to become a full member of the international political community, Korean civil society also became deeply involved in and interconnected with the global civil society (Ku 2002). Choe (2006) argues that "the modern idea of gender equality, combined with international covenants, and the growing power of NGOs led to the bilateral *jus sanguinis* revision of the nationality law" (Choe 2006: 106). This means that the rise of South Korean civil society in the 1990s contributed considerably to a process of cultural redefinition of Korean nationality and introduced a new concept of citizenship on the basis of universal rights and values. Consequently, the social status of ethnic Chinese in South Korea, which had previously only been regarded as a matter of diplomacy and international relations between South Korea and China, became a part of domestic discussions about human rights. In short, the ethnic Chinese are transforming from "them" to "us" in a broader sense.

Many ethnic Chinese organizations welcomed these changes and demanded the mitigation of repression, sanctions, and controls (Jang 2004). Civic activists established online groups and forums to encourage the exchange of information and opinions within the Chinese minority. The Human Rights Forum of Ethnic Chinese in Korea is an illustrative example: it is a kind of "Internet café" where over 200 ethnic Chinese in South Korea frequently meet to exchange information and opinions as registered members.[8] The members of this forum address a wide range of human rights issues in the ethnic Chinese community – not only in Korea but also worldwide. In addition, Korean lawmakers and civic groups, such as the MINBYUN Lawyers for a Democratic Society or a leading civic umbrella organization called the People's Solidarity for Participatory Democracy (PSPD) are paying increasing attention to the human rights situation of the Chinese minority in South Korea.

Just as the disruption of bilateral relations between China and South Korea afflicted the business activities of the ethnic Chinese in the past, the rehabilitation of diplomatic relations in 1992 provided new economic opportunities for them. After the overseas travel restrictions were lifted, young Chinese residents established, for example, tourist agencies to promote tourism from South Korea to Taiwan and China. They also remained engaged in small- and mid-sized businesses, such as Chinese restaurants, herbal medical clinics, pharmacies, grocery stores, etc. (Park and Park 2003). However, this time, the impact of international politics on the living situation of the ethnic Chinese in South Korea was rather indirect. Chinese immigration to South Korea has been reactivated. However, although the immigrants come from mainland China, their ethnic identity is mostly different from that of the Chinese residents in South Korea. The new immigrant group consists of ethnic Koreans whose parents and grandparents migrated to northern China during Japanese colonial rule. South Korean enterprises welcomed them as a cheap labor force. Their integration causes no problems because they were already familiar with the Korean language and culture. Despite having the same ethnic identity as the Korean population, the Korean government treated the Korean Chinese first as foreigners. During the intense debate about the legal status of the Korean Chinese, the attention of the Korean public also shifted to the situation of the ethnic Chinese residents, who demanded considerable improvements with respect to their legal status. The discussion about the legal status of ethnic Korean migrant workers from China that emerged in the 1990s was successfully linked with the issue of the citizenship of the ethnic Chinese in Korea.

In particular, after the Asian financial crisis (1997), the South Korean government and the mass media demanded the return of the economic capital of the Chinese diaspora from abroad to South Korea with the support of the ethnic Chinese trade network across many Asian countries and beyond. The Korean public re-evaluated the economic importance of the ethnic Chinese. The South Korean government quickly responded and attempted to attract, once again, the economic capital of the overseas Chinese to South Korea. In this process, legal restrictions against land ownership and real estate management by ethnic Chinese were abolished in June 1998. At around the same time, the nationality law was revised to improve the conditions for naturalization. According to the revised laws of 1997, a child could apply for Korean citizenship even if at least the mother was Korean. This means that the emphasis on the patrilineal line was replaced with the principle of bi-lineality. Apart from naturalization, the legal status of permanent Chinese residents was enhanced to *denizenship* if they had lived in South Korea for more than 5 years.[9] The denizens are not fully included as members of the Korean nation-state but endowed with certain citizenship rights, albeit to a limited degree. The unmarried children of ethnic Chinese residents who had legally resided in Korea for more than 5 years were also entitled to receive permanent resident status. Owing to revisions of the immigration control law in 2002, holders of a valid visa for denizenship were no longer required to go to the immigration office to extend their visas. In 2003, 8,000 permanent ethnic Chinese residents received South Korean citizenship.

In the following years, the social and political inclusion of the ethnic Chinese was enhanced considerably. In 2005, they obtained voting rights for the communal government. In addition, the government also gradually lifted the past regulations that had restricted their (economic) careers for many years. Thus, beginning in the 1990s, many young Chinese began to show an increased interest in attending universities to improve their upward mobility and become eligible for better career positions (Choi 2001). In 1999, under an ordinance from the Education Ministry, certificates from Chinese schools were accepted for admission at the universities if they met certain specific requirements. In 2003, the ordinance was changed and permitted children of Chinese permanent residents to attend Korean universities as long as one of their parents was a Korean citizen. The foreigners' special admission policy annually assigns 2% of new undergraduate places to foreign students without requiring an entrance examination. Taking this opportunity, young ethnic Chinese residents improved their educational qualifications to some degree. According to a survey of 300 large-sized trading businesses conducted by the Korea Chamber of Commerce and Industry (2008), the share of talented migrant workers from China hired in Korea ranks second in the world.[10] Among college graduates hired by large-sized businesses, the share of those from English-speaking countries is the largest (27.3 %), followed by Chinese (25.3 %).

Despite all these improvements, the inclusion of Chinese residents in South Korean society is still very limited. In 2008, Chinese residents were allowed to obtain foreigner personal registration numbers. However, since the numbering system for them is different from that of Koreans, their status as foreigners is still easily recognizable to everyone. Thus, Chinese residents are clearly identifiable as non-Korean residents. This could facilitate discrimination against non-Koreans. There are some indications that the rapid growth of Chinese businesses on a worldwide scale and the increase in the number of migrants and imported goods from China time and again revive old Korean stereotypes and prejudices against the ethnic Chinese. Negative slang terms for the ethnic Chinese – that appeared in colonial times for the first time – are still widespread. The nationalistic and racist undertones of these slang expressions often convey contempt for Chinese commercial transactions.

The next challenge is to improve social welfare services for the ethnic Chinese and, subsequently, the realization of social citizenship. During the early years of the twenty-first century, the Korean welfare system has expanded to a great extent. National Health Insurance and the National Basic Livelihood Security System were introduced in the aftermath of the Asian financial crisis. Although ethnic Chinese are required to pay the same amount for social insurance as Korean nationals, their access to the services and benefits of the social welfare system is considerably restricted (Park 2004, 2008: 163–174; Park et al. 2003). In other words, they are still more likely than Korean nationals to be treated unfairly and unequally in many areas of social life. In contrast to previous times, the ethnic Chinese are now eligible to publicly struggle for their civil rights in South Korea without offending against laws. In this regard, it is expected that they will continue with their efforts to increase their degree of inclusion in South Korean society.

9.3 Conclusions

After the first wave of immigration, the ethnic Chinese in Korea were mostly engaged in trade and business while living segregated in their local communities. For decades, their status strongly depended on the international relations among Korea, China, and Japan. When the political, cultural, and economic hegemony of China weakened, the ethnic Chinese had to deal with a gradual depreciation of their position. In this context, their coping strategies used to be individual, opportunistic, and self-exclusive.

After the end of the Japanese colonial regime, their status was formally regulated by the South Korean nationality law. The restriction of economic, political, and social rights was justified with a strong ethnic concept of national identity. Since Japanese politics regarded ethnic Koreans as second-class Japanese citizens, the colonial regime strengthened and stabilized the idea of an ethnically homogenous Korean nation (Shin 2006). Therefore, Chinese residents were considered foreigners although they had lived in South Korea for more than 50 years.

The ethnic Chinese were persistently excluded from participation in important social processes such as financial investment, capital accumulation, and real estate transactions. Furthermore, the Korean government refused to recognize certificates from ethnic Chinese middle and high schools, meaning that graduates from these Chinese schools in Chinese local communities were not admitted to South Korean universities. As a consequence, the career opportunities of ethnic Chinese were significantly restricted. Even the pro-democratic movement of the 1980s focused only on the political and social rights of Korean nationals while paying no attention to the suffering of the ethnic Chinese.

After the transition to democracy in 1987, the situation of the Chinese minority in Korea gradually improved. In the 1990s, the enhancement of citizenship rights emerged on the agenda of South Korean civic groups. The Korean democratic government joined the international political system and began to implement improvements for the ethnic Chinese, little by little, under the pressure of global governance institutions. At the same time, the ethnic-centred citizenship concept was revised and slowly replaced by a more universalist understanding (refer to Giulianotti and Robertson 2007).

However, there are still many restrictions. Having established a social welfare state, South Korea only provides social rights such as health services, national pensions, unemployment compensation, etc. to Korean nationals, while ethnic Chinese are not included. Although the ethnic Chinese have benefited considerably from recent changes, they cannot enjoy full citizenship. However, it appears that the ethnic Chinese are slowly on their way to becoming full members of Korean society in the future.

Currently, the status of foreigners appears to become more differentiated. In the current public discourse about the extension of single components of the citizenship concept, certain elements are undergoing discussion, such as an easier path toward naturalization, special advantages for permanent residents, approval of dual citizenship. At the moment, immigrants returning from English-speaking countries are, it seems, the main group that benefits from dual citizenship (Lee 2008a, 2008b). Another group of foreigners – migrant workers from Southeast Asian countries – are, more or less, excluded from these improvements. They remain ineligible for either dual citizenship or denizenship. Their present state indicates a trend toward increasing polarization among different groups of foreigners.

Endnotes

[1]*Hwagyo* in Korean.
[2]The genealogical document was licensed for a householder and included one's family tree following a patrilineal hierarchy, one's regional origin of ascent, and one's social status.
[3]The traditional four classes of Chosŏn society were the scholarly, agricultural, industrial, and mercantile classes. Within this social order, Confucian scholars from prominent families were the most highly respected and qualified to be high officials. Next were farmers, who were at the center of the production processes, followed by artisans. Finally, at the bottom of the social classes were tradesmen.
[4]Refer to "unequal differentiation" (Schimank 1996: 236) and "autonomy of social integrative dimension" (Schwinn 2001: 216) for further discussions.
[5]Refer to the database at http://www.laiis.go.kr (accessed 1 December 2010), "the 2009 official statistics of the Ministry of Public Administration and Security".

The number of Chinese nationals who have come to South Korea as migrant workers since the 1990s was excluded. In other words, the statistics indicate mostly the ethnic Han Chinese who immigrated over a 100 years ago and exclusively have Taiwanese nationality. Rhee (2009) calls the former "old hwagyo" and the latter "new hwagyo". The specific situation of the ethnic Koreans goes beyond the theme of the chapter. Refer to Seol and Skretny (2009) for details.

[6]They kept their Taiwanese citizenship even after the diplomatic break between South Korea and Taiwan at the same time, the diplomatic normalization (1992) with mainland China.

[7]Kern (2005) gives an overview of the democracy movement in South Korea.

[8]http://cafe.naver.com/koreanchinese, accessed 1 December 2010.

[9]The term *denizen* was used to describe a status approximately halfway between that of a citizen and a non-citizen, a status that can be obtained by a foreigner on the basis of his or her residence in the country.

[10]http://english.korcham.net/bbs/viewnotice.asp?code=reports&page=1&id=396&number=396&keyfield=comment&keyword=foreigner (accessed 28 January 2010).

References

Chang, K.-S. 2007. "The End of Developmental Citizenship? Restructuring and Social Displacement in Post-Crisis South Korea". *Economic & Political Weekly*, 15 December, 67–72.

Chang, K.-S. 2010. *South Korea under Compressed Modernity. Familial political economy in transition*. London and New York, Routledge.

Choe, H. 2006. "National identity and citizenship in the People's Republic of China and the Republic of Korea". *Journal of Historical Sociology* 19 (1), 84–118.

Choi, S. 2001. *Gender, ethnicity, market forces, and college choices: Observations of ethnic Chinese in Korea*. New York: Routledge.

Choi, S. 2008. "Politics, commerce, and construction of Chinese 'Otherness' in Korea: Open Port Period (1876–1910)". In *At home in the Chinese Diaspora: Memories, identities and belongings*, Eds. K. E. Kuah-Pearce and A. P. Davidson, 128–145. New York: Palgrave Macmillan.

Crowley, J. 1996. "European integration: sociological process or political project? *Innovation". The European Journal of Social Sciences* 9 (2), 149–160.

Crowley, J. 1998. "The national dimension of citizenship" in T. H. Marshall. *Citizenship Studies* 2 (2), 165–178.

Giulianotti, R., and R. Robertson. 2007. Forms of glocalization: Globalization and the migration strategies of Scottish football fans in North America. *Sociology* 41 (1), 133–152.

Hulbert, H. B. 1969. *The passing of Korea*. (Reprint of the 1906 edition, with a new foreword). Seoul: Yonsei University Press.

Jang, S.-H. 2004. "Han'guk hwagyo ŭi hyŏnsil gwa dochŏn" (Realities and challenges of Chinese Koreans). In *Han'guk ŭi sosucha, siltae wa chŏnmang* (Minorities in South Korea, conditions and perspectives), Eds. H. Choi, et al., 261–279. Seoul: Hanul.

Kern, T. 2005. *Südkoreas Pfad zur Demokratie: Modernisierung, Protest, Regimewechsel*. Frankfurt/M.: Campus.

Kim Haboush, J. H., and M. Deuchler (Eds.). 1999. *Culture and the state in late Chosŏn Korea*. Cambridge: Harvard University Asia Center.

Ku, A. S. 2002. "Beyond the paradoxical conception of 'Civil Society without Citizenship'". *International Sociology* 17 (4), 529–548.

Ku, A. S. 2004a. "Negotiating the space of civil autonomy in Hong Kong – Power, discourses, and dramaturgical representations". *The China Quarterly* 179, 647–664.

Ku, A. S. 2004b. "Negotiating law, rights, and civil autonomy. From the colonial to the post-colonial regimes". In *Remaking citizenship in Hong Kong: Community, nation and the global city*, Eds. A. S. Ku and N. Pun, 157–174. London and New York: RoutledgeCurzon.

Lee, C. 2008a. "Chugwŏn ŭi tal yŏngto hwa wa chae yŏngto hwa. Ichung kukchŏk ŭi norli" (The deterritorialization and reterritorialization of sovereignty. The logic of dual nationality). *Han'guk sahoe hak* 42 (1), 27–61.

Lee, C. 2008b. "Tal gukga chŏk simin gwŏn ŭn chonchae hanŭn ga?" (Does the postnational citizenship exist?). *Kyŏngche wa sahoe* 79, 62–87.

Lee, Y.-H. 2004. "Inchŏn kŏchu hwagyo ŭi ingwŏn siltae wa chŏngch'e sŏng" (Human rights situation and identity of hwagyo in Inchŏn). In *Han'guk ŭi sosucha, siltae wa chŏnmang* (Minorities in South Korea, conditions and perspectives), Eds. H. Choi et al., 296–317. Seoul: Hanul.

Mahoney J. 2001. "Path-dependent explanations of regime change: Central America in comparative perspective". *Studies in Comparative International Development* 36 (1), 111–141.

Marshall, T. H. 1992. "Citizenship and Social Class". In *Citizenship and Social Class*, Eds. T. H. Marshall and T. Bottomore, 1–51. London: Pluto Perspectives.

Ministry of Justice 2002. *Ch'urip guk kwalli tongge yonbo* (Statistical Yearbook of Immigration Office). Republic of Korea.

Mitra, S. K. 2008. "Level playing fields: The post-colonial state, democracy, courts and citizenship in India". *German Law Journal* 9 (3), 343–366.

Nam, S.-H. 2010. "The women's movement and the transformation of the family law in South Korea". *European Journal of East Asian Studies* 9 (1), 67–86.

Park, E.-K. 1981. "Hwagyo ŭi chŏngch'ak gwa idong: Han'guk ŭi kyŭngu" (Settlement and mobility of Chinese Koreans: The Korean case). Dissertation, Dep. of Sociology. Ehwa Woman's University, South Korea.

Park, E.-K. 1986. "Han'guk hwagyo ŭi chongchok sŏng" (The ethnicity of Korean Chinese). Seoul: Han'guk yŏguwŏn.

Park, H.-O. and J.-D. Park. 2003. "Han'guk hwagyo (Inchŏn hwagyo) ŭi gyŏngche hwaldong gwa sahoe chŏk chiwi e gwanhan yŏngu" (Study on economic activities and social status of Korean hwagyo (Inchŏn hwagyo). Report of Inchŏn Development Institute.

Park, K.-T. 2004. "Han'guk sahoe ŭi hwagyo dŭri nŭkki nŭn ch'abyŏl ŭi suchun" (Discrimination level felt by Chinese Koreans in Korean society). In *Han'guk ŭi sosucha, siltae wa chŏnmang* (Minorities in South Korea, conditions and perspectives) Eds. H. Choi et al., 280–295. Seoul: Hanul.

Park, K.-T. 2008. "Sosucha wa han'guk sahoe. Ichu nodong cha – hwagyo – honhyŏrin" (Minorities and Korean society. Migrant workers – Chinese Korean – multiracial). Seoul: Huminata.

Park, K.-T., et al. 2003. *Guknae gŏchu hwagyo ingwŏn siltae chosa* (Investigation on human rights situation of Chinese residents in South Korea). National Human Rights Commission of Korea.

Pohlmann, M. 2006. "Globalisierung und Modernisierung – Zentrale Annahmen der Globalisierungstheorien auf dem Prüfstand". In *Die Vielfalt und Einheit der Moderne: Kultur- und struktur-vergleichende Analysen*, Ed. T. Schwinn, 165–183. Wiesbaden: VS Verlag für Sozialwissenschaften.

Rhee, Y. J. 2009. "Diversity within Chinese diaspora: Old and new Huaqiao residents in South Korea". In *Diasporas: Critical and inter-disciplinary perspectives*, Ed. J. Fernandez, 111–126. Oxford: Inter-Disciplinary Press.

Schimank, U. 1996. *Theorien gesellschaftlicher Differenzierung*. Opladen: Leske + Budrich.

Schwinn, T. 2001. Staatliche Ordnung und Moderne Sozialintegration. *KZfSS* 53 (2), 211–232.

Seol, D.-H., and J. D. Skrentny 2009. "Ethnic return migration and hierarchical nationhood: Korean Chinese foreign workers in South Korea". *Ethnicities* 9 (2), 147–174.

Shin, G.-W. 2006. *Ethnic nationalism in Korea: Genealogy, politics, and legacy.* Stanford: Stanford University Press.

Turner, B. S. 2008. Citizenship, reproduction and the state; international marriage and human rights. *Citizenship Studies* 12 (1), 45–54.

Yang, P.-S., and J.-H. Yi. 2004. *Chinatown ŏm nŭn nara: Han'guk hwagyo gyŏngche ŭi ŏche wa onŭl* (A country without a Chinatown: Yesterday and today of the Overseas Chinese economy in Korea). Seoul: Samsŏng gyŏngche yŏngu so.

Chapter 10
Patterns of Citizenship and Political Action in Korea, Germany and the United States: An Analysis of the 2004 ISSP Data

Seokho Kim and Jonghoe Yang

Abstract Although there is enormous interest in cross-national differences in the patterns of citizenship and political action as globalization accelerates, we know little about how and why they vary among nations. This study attempts to compare institutional and attitudinal aspects of citizenship among Korea, Germany and the United States. By analyzing the 2004 International Social Survey program data, this study shows that the institutional and legal dimensions of citizenship in Korea and Germany are largely communitarian, in contrast to the individualistic-liberal pattern in the United States. It is also true that American citizens have the most liberal notion of citizenship, followed by German and Korean citizens. At the same time, however, American's idea of citizenship turns out to be the most republican among the three countries, with German's idea the least republican. The extent to which the behavioral aspect of citizenship is explained by the attitudinal one is the greatest in the United States, moderate in Germany, and the least in Korea, suggesting that American citizenship is more balanced and mature than other countries in the sense that its two aspects better interact with each other.

S. Kim
Department of Sociology, Sungkyunkwan University, 53 Myungryun-dong, Jongro-ku, Seoul 110-745, Korea

24-1305 Misung Apt, Apgoojungdong Kangnamgoo, Seoul 135-785, Korea

J. Yang (✉)
Department of Sociology, Sungkyunkwan University, 53 Myungryun-dong, Jongro-gu, Seoul 110-745, Korea

#1104 Lotte Castle Forest, Seocho-gu, Bangbae 4-dong, Seoul 137-836, Korea
e-mail: jhyang@skku.edu

M. Pohlmann et al. (eds.), *Citizenship and Migration in the Era of Globalization*,
Transcultural Research – Heidelberg Studies on Asia and Europe in a Global Context,
DOI 10.1007/978-3-642-19739-0_10, © Springer-Verlag Berlin Heidelberg 2013

10.1   Introduction

In the process of modern nation-building, each country has adopted its unique conception of citizenship, reflecting either cultural legacies or partisan interests or political history. As a consequence, there is a variety of models and meanings of citizenship. Scholars have made great efforts to identify and classify types of citizenship, and come up with several models of citizenship such as those of T. M. Marshall (1973), Bryan S. Turner (1986), D. Heater (1990) and others. Thus we may expect that the concept of citizenship varies among nations, which could be defined by one of these models. But this legal or institutional definition of citizenship, which is usually single and egalitarian, is not necessarily shared by ordinary citizens. They may experience citizenship differently- both from the official definition and among themselves – depending on their personal and contextual backgrounds.

And how they perceive citizenship, and what causes them to experience citizenship in particular ways, should be decided empirically.

It has also been noted by many that the status and quality of citizenship are not permanent and fixed, but contested and fluid, especially in times of change and conflict (Vandenberg 2000). Likewise people's experiences or perceptions of citizenship are likely to be variable in this age of accelerated globalization. Globalization implies greater exchanges of information, goods, and persons across national borders, due primarily to the advancement of communication and transportation technologies. Among the many effects of globalization are the erosion of national identities, the development of global-level norms, and the spread of cosmopolitanism. In a sense, globalization is promoting a global culture, a global consumer, and a global citizen. There are also counter arguments to this unifying and leveling-off effect of globalization, including theories of glocalization, regionalization and alternative globalization (Beck 1999; Held et al. 1999). Thus it is an empirical question whether globalization is indeed a force powerful enough to level-off the differences in citizenship among nations.

Citizenship is a "cluster concept", as Andrew Vandenberg describes (2000: 4), which includes diverse elements, aspects and dimensions. But it seems to be a common practice to distinguish between citizenship as a status and citizenship as a practice or behavior (Dalton 2008; Glenn 2000; Kim 2007; Miller-Idriss 2006). As a status, citizenship is regarded to be a set of legal and institutional rights and duties that a citizen possesses vis-à-vis the state, and to be fairly uniform among the citizens. On the other hand, citizenship as a practice emphasizes attitudinal and behavioral aspects, especially citizen's active participation in political process and public affairs. The concept of active citizenship has been advocated since the 1960s as essential to a satisfactory democracy (Almond and Verba 1965). Ideally these status and practice dimensions should be unified, which would contribute to social solidarity. But in an empirical setting, these status and practice dimensions do not necessarily coincide. In fact, we expect that patterns of relationship between these two dimensions differ across nation states.

The major purpose of this study is to investigate how people understand citizenship differently in different cultural, political and historical settings. Specifically, this study attempts to answer the following questions, by comparing institutional and attitudinal aspects of citizenship among Korea, Germany and the United States. First, do peoples' perceptions of citizenship differ among the nations with different historical, cultural and political backgrounds? Second, do the perceptions of citizenship differ from or coincide with the institutional aspects of citizenship in each nation? Third, are the behavioral dimensions of citizenship significantly affected by the institutional dimensions? Are the two dimensions unified in an empirical setting? What factors are responsible for active citizenship or political participation? In order to answer these questions, we shall analyze the 2004 International Social Survey Programme (ISSP) data for Korea, Germany and the United States. These three countries are expected to allow for good comparisons, because they are similar in that all are politically representative democracies, but differ in terms of cultural legacies and political histories. A more detailed description of cultural and political characteristics of these three nations will be given after the next section.

10.2 Definitions and Models of Citizenship

Due to its long history, the concept of citizenship carries with it many elements and dimensions. A review of the literature on citizenship suggests that there are at least four aspects or elements of the citizenship concept, which can be grouped into two dimensions, the legal-institutional dimension and the attitudinal-behavioral dimension. Some scholars name these two dimensions as status and practice (Miller 1999; Miller-Idriss 2006). The legal-institutional dimension has two aspects, which are status and membership. In the modern era of the nation-state, citizenship means, above all, membership of the nation-state to which one belongs. Here national identity and citizenship identity are fused into national citizenship, which has the dual feature of legal status and the feeling of belonging. The legal status, or nationality is usually conferred by the state, based either on the principle of *jus soli* or on the principle of *jus sanguinis*. The former principle literally means "right of the land" and states that one becomes a citizens by being born on a national territory. American citizenship is a prime example of this type of citizenship. On the other hand, the principle of *jus sanguinis* means "right of blood", that is, ascription of citizenship on the basis of descent (Kerber 1997). Until recently Germany closely followed this principle in its nationality policies.

As a legal status, citizenship involves a set of rights and duties of an individual in his or her relationship with the state. Citizenship rights may include free speech, religious freedom, free association, the vote, rights against self-incrimination and so on. Examples of duties or obligations are to pay tax, to obey the law, to do jury services, to serve in the military and etc. These elements of citizenship flow from a citizen's status and are usually defined by the constitution and/or other legal means. Citizenship rights have historically changed in the course of capitalistic modernization. T. H. Marshall offers a theory of citizenship that reflects historical changes of modern nation-states, specifically changes in the relationship between the state and

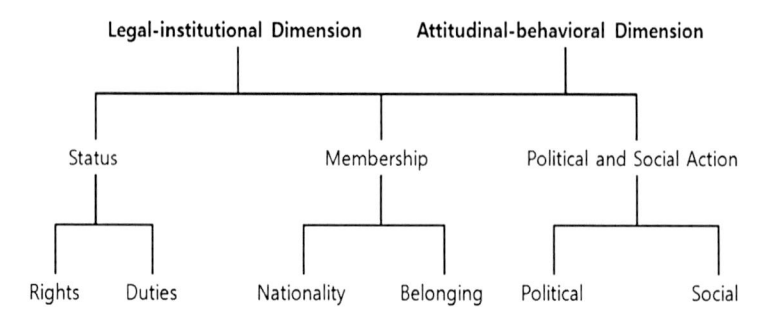

Fig. 10.1 Dimensions and elements of citizenship

the economy (Marshall 1973). His classification of citizen's rights into the civil, the political and the social refers to the successive increment of citizenship rights as the state intervenes more and more in the economy, evolving into a welfare state. In this theory, civil rights refer to such basic rights as free speech and religious freedom, whereas political rights denote the right to vote and to participate in politics. Social rights are welfare rights to receive education and social services to ensure an adequate standard of living. This theory has important implications for class differences and ideological orientations in the concept of citizenship.

Membership in a political community or national identity is defined not only objectively by nationality laws, but also by subjective feelings such as loyalty and fraternity. This aspect of citizenship often involves ethnic and cultural factors. The behavioral aspect of citizenship refers to political and social action, and is often described as active or engaged citizenship. For example, according to Dalton (2008: 81), "engaged citizenship includes the measure of solidarity, as well as two participation examples: being active in civil society groups and general political activity". Similarly, the active citizen is one who has "a sense of civic obligation, personal responsibility, self discipline and respect for others" and the "virtue of voluntary service in the local community" (Oliver and Heater 1994). These dimensions and elements of citizenship may be summarized as Fig. 10.1.

Other scholars add other elements to the above, such as knowledge, efficacy, and identity (Heater 1990; Porter 1993). But the above definition should be sufficient for our present purpose. There is a variety of classifications and models of citizenship depending on which elements or aspects are emphasized, and on different combinations of the elements. These models may be grouped into two types; one based on the status dimension and the other on the practice dimension.

The first type of models flows from the classical classification between the republican (or communitarian) and the liberal, which is based on two criteria, one emphasizing either rights or duties, and the other stressing either private individuals or members of communities. There are also variants of these two proto types. In many studies, communitarian citizenship is differentiated from the republican, in addition to the liberal model (Fraser and Gordon 1994: 91; Lister et al. 2003). Herman van Gunsteren (1994) divides the communitarian model into three, the communitarian, the republican and the neo-republican. Others identify three variants of the liberal citizenship, that is, the individualistic liberalism, the social-liberalism and the cultural pluralist model (Conover et al. 2004). But van Gunsteren's neo-republican model is simply a mixture of the three models, the communitarian, the republican and the liberal. Pamela Johnston Conover et al.'s cultural pluralist model is too close to the communitarian. Thus we have decided to adopt a four-type model which includes communitarian, republican, social liberal and individualistic liberal citizenship. We should like to give here a brief description of these four types of citizenship.

The communitarian model emphasizes a citizen's belonging and loyalty to a political community. He or she is supposed to identify himself or herself with, and integrate into, one's own ethnic and cultural community, resulting in an attachment to shared values and feelings of solidarity. In short, communitarian citizenship stresses membership of an ethnic or cultural community, thus conflating nationality with national identity (van Gunsteren 1994; Habermas 1994; Lister et al. 2003).

The republican model of citizenship is often regarded as a variant of communitarian citizenship (van Gunsteren 1994). It is the oldest one, dating back to the ancient Greek and Roman era. In old Greek city-states, the free citizens were supposed to actively participate in the political process, as evidenced in Aristotle's definition: "a citizen is one who rules and is ruled in turn" (Kerber 1997: 834). In the Roman Empire, politicians insisted on the quality of civic virtues that should be cultivated by the citizens, which means to perform military services and to devote oneself to one's duties and the law (Oliver and Heater 1994). This emphasis on civic duties and obligations, and active engagement in politics as well as in community matters has become a basic principle of republican citizenship (Lister et al. 2003).

The American and French revolutions in the eighteenth century liberated the subjects from the fetters of the monarchs and opened the age of modern democracy and national citizenship. Since then, there have been pressures for the liberation of civil and political systems and new liberal ideas of citizenship have set in (Oliver and Heater 1994). In the liberal tradition of citizenship, citizens are supposed to be treated equal regardless of their race, ethnic or cultural group membership. This type of citizenship is more concerned with the rights of a citizen than with his or her duties and obligations.

The individualistic version of liberal citizenship assumes that individuals are autonomous and free to pursue their interests, while remaining external to the state. This model focuses "mainly on individual rights and equal treatment, as well as on government performance which takes account of citizen's preferences" (Taylor 1994: 26). Political institutions have only an instrumental significance for utilitarian individuals to maximize their own benefits (van Gunsteren 1994). This model is "difference-blind" in terms of values and lifestyles, and has nothing to do with cultures, races, religions or genders.

The social liberalism, according to Conover et al. (2004), considers "the political community as an aggregate of interacting interdependent individuals" and emphasizes "the importance of civic duties and solidarity" (Conover et al. 2004: 1038). The state must contribute to the community as a whole, by promoting the citizen's social rights. This model is basically similar to T. H. Marshall's social citizenship which stresses the welfare state which provides an adequate standard of living for all citizens.

The second type of citizenship model is based on the citizen being active in political and social processes. In the ancient Greek-Roman concept of citizenship, a good citizen, as an ideal form of citizenship, is distinguished from an ordinary or passive citizen in terms of civic virtues and active participation in public affairs. In modern times, the concept of active citizenship has again been advocated as essential to democracy by such scholars as Gabriel Almond and Sidney Verba as early as 1960s. According to them, "(in democratic societies), the ordinary man is expected to take an active part in governmental affairs, to be aware of how decisions are made, and to make his own views known" (Almond and Verba 1991: 118). In a similar vein, Isin and Turner argue that "having an active, dynamic, and vital citizenry is an absolute precondition of democracy" (Isin and Turner 2007: 13).

In the simplest sense the concept of active citizenship refers to a citizen's active political participation, "playing an active role in determining his society's future" and "taking responsibilities for the collective decisions that are made" (Miller 1992: 96). In a broad sense, however, the concept includes contribution to social solidarity in addition to general political activity, in other words, being active both in civil social groups and in political processes (Dalton 2008). In the former sense, active citizenship means "active participation in churches, voluntary associations and clubs", which is characteristic of American democracy as observed by Alexis de Tocqueville (Isin and Turner 2007). Here, membership in social groups is an important indicator of active citizenship. Participation in various political activities, such as voting, participating in political meetings and movements, contacting government officials and politicians, and so on, is another aspect of active citizenship.

Theiss-Morse provides a useful model of political activities. She identifies four types of good citizenship based on four criteria of activities, namely, voting and being informed, conventional participation, contacting activities, and unconventional participation. The four types are the representative democracy type, the political enthusiast type, the pursued interests type, and the indifferent type. The representative democracy type strongly emphasizes a participatory activity in electoral politics, that is, voting and keeping oneself informed about politics, but is neutral to other political activities. It strongly rejects the idea of political alienation. The political enthusiast type accentuates diverse sorts of political participation, including protests and civil disobedience. This perspective believes that voting has less effect on government activities than other conventional or nonconventional political activities. The perspective of pursued interests argues that "a good citizen does not have to be interested or involved in politics" (Theiss-Morse 1993: 364). Instead, citizens should be involved in other group activities, partly because political elites are trustworthy. Finally the indifferent perspective has a view toward politics that is somewhat alienated, somewhat apathetic, and ambivalent about elites. This perspective does not reject voting but does not affirm other forms of participation. Theiss-Morse's study also reveals that there are some correlations between citizenship perspectives and such socio-economic variables as education, income, and age. This model provides a useful device to measure and classify the different degrees and types of political participation.

There is also an important issue regarding the relationship between the two aspects or dimensions of citizenship. In legal or institutional terms, the various elements or dimensions of citizenship are often regarded as unified and bound (Miller-Idriss 2006: 541). But in reality gaps appear between ideal and practical levels of citizenship and between institutional and behavioral dimensions (Miller-Idriss 2006; Wong and Wong 2004). In their empirical study on Chinese citizenship, for example, Wong and Wong revealed that citizen's perceptions of rights were not in line with those of responsibilities, resulting in a possible deficit in social solidarity. They also found that institutional factors had some effect on people's behavior with regard to social citizenship (Wong and Wong 2004). Similarly, whether the perception of status dimension coincides with, or has an effect on, political participation should have an important implication for social solidarity and democracy. Before analyzing empirical data on the perceptions of citizens in Korea, Germany and the United States, a brief review of legal and institutional aspects of citizenship in these countries is in order.

10.3 Legal and Institutional Aspects of Citizenship in Korea, Germany and the United States

10.3.1 Korea

Korea is one of the most homogeneous countries in terms of language, culture, ethnicity, and race. Korea has never had a feudal period in its history, but several absolute monarchies have ruled in its territory for a 1,000 years. In particular the last kingdom, Chosun, ruled the Korean peninsula with the Confucian ideology for about 500 years until the end of nineteenth century, when Japan forcefully colonized Korea. The first modern democratic government was established in 1948 in the southern half of the peninsula, after the 3 years of American military rule followed by the victory of the American-led allied forces over the Japanese army.

Modeled on the American and other advanced democratic constitutions, the first Korean (means as of here *South* Korean) Constitution in 1948 was very progressive at that time, and included not only civil and political rights but also social rights such as the rights to education, work, adequate living, family health, and equal access to national wealth (Choe 2006). At the same time, the Nationality Act was based on the *jus sanguinis* principle; "Korean nationality (citizenship) was accorded to a person whose father was a national of the Republic of Korea at the time when the person was born" (Lee 2008: 227).

However, more than three decades of dictatorial and military governments ensued since the inception of the modern nation-state, and curtailed some of the basic citizen's rights and democratic processes. Only in 1987, after a long period of popular struggles against the dictatorship, was democracy restored. The Constitution was also amended to expand and give a greater guarantee of citizenship rights, including the right to resist the government's unjust actions. It was, however, still the communitarian type of citizenship that the amended Constitution prescribed. The Confucian conception of the state, which regards the state as a "family-state", had been prevalent among the population (Kim 2007: 455). Most Koreans believed that Korea had a "single bloodline" and do not distinguish between nationality and citizenship (Lee 2008: 224).

But the communitarian conception of citizenship has recently been changing due to economic development and globalization. Especially the neo-liberal reform followed by the 1997 financial crisis has changed the whole society in a more liberal and cosmopolitan direction. At the same time foreigners residing in Korea have recently increased rapidly, and now number over a million or some 2 % of the population, due mainly to foreign workers and international marriages. As a consequence, the liberal type of citizenship and a flexible ideology are increasingly replacing communitarian citizenship and ethnic national identity (Kim 2007). Reflecting these changes, the National Assembly passed a law to grant Koreans residing permanently overseas the right to vote in national elections. The government is also considering allowing dual citizenship for certain qualified individuals. While retaining many of the communitarian elements, Korean citizenship is changing toward a more liberal and global type in response to the recent rapid pace of globalization and neo-liberal reform.

10.3.2 Germany

The first German nation-state was established in 1871. From the outset, the German nation was conceived as an ethnic and cultural community in which people shared a common language, religion, and history. Because a large number of the German population resided outside its borders, however, the nation was not congruent with the state. Thus citizenship was not defined in terms of territorial, civic and legal elements, but based on cultural, ethnic and linguistic ones (Anil 2005).

The first national citizenship law was enacted in 1913 and stipulated that citizenship was to be conferred on a person who is directly descended from a German parent, according to the *jus sanguinis* principle (van Krieken 2000: 131). This principle of birthright citizenship has become problematic since 1955 when Germany accepted immigration as part of its labor recruitment program. Immigrants from other countries including massive labor migration from Turkey have since been mounting, numbering about 7.3 million or forming 9 % of the population as of 2005 (Anil 2005: 453). But it was not until 1990 that the German government attempted to reform the existing citizenship policies to address the legal and other problems of long-term foreign residents in Germany. As a scholar observed, "Citizenship rights were still not generalized" and the second and third class citizens continued to be present until the 1960s (van Krieken 2000: 127).

The 1990 reform was the first step for the German government to develop national integration policies. In 1999, the German citizenship law underwent a major reform to allow qualified foreigners who meet certain criteria to apply for German citizenship. For example, children born in Germany of foreign parents who have resided in Germany for at least 8 years are eligible for German citizenship.

The law also has a provision for dual citizenship for those who were born of foreign parents. The new nationality policy may be said to have been supplemented by a *jus soli* policy while retaining the *jus sanguinis* component (Miller-Idriss 2006: 545).

Despite these recent reforms of citizenship policies, the German model of citizenship closely follows the communitarian one, revolving around an ethnic-cultural community of descent. The reforms may be interpreted as an effort "to define the border between citizenship rights and membership in the German national community by allocating a legal framework for citizenship practices while simultaneously reserving a cultural and ethnic framework for national membership" (Baban 2006: 190).

10.3.3 The United States

Unlike Korea and Germany, the United States was founded in the late eighteenth century by immigrants who came to this frontier land mostly from Europe for religious freedom and economic opportunities. Thus liberalism has been the dominant ideology in this heterogeneous, pluralistic and highly mobile society. Freedom, equality, individualism, autonomy, and competition are among the major values to which Americans have subscribed from the inception of the nation (Conover et al. 1991, 2004).

In the United States citizenship has been open to all free persons, regardless of religion, economic standing and culture. A legal provision to become an American citizen was laid first in the Naturalization Act of 1790. The law stipulated that three conditions, that is, "2 years of residency, a proof of good character and an oath to support the constitution of the United States", were required for citizenship. But this law is only for free white persons; African-Americans could only be naturalized after 1870, and were not given full privileges and immunities until 1965 (Kerber 1997: 842–843).

Today the majority of Americans become citizens by being born on its soil, according to the principle of *jus soli*. Citizenship is also conferred on those who are born to American parents in other countries (*jus sanguinis*). Naturalization is a third way of acquiring American citizenship (Kerber 1997). These principles became explicit in the Fourteenth Amendment, which was ratified in 1867 and states that "all persons born or naturalized in the United States and subject to the jurisdiction thereof, are citizens of the United States and of the State wherein they reside". The Fourteenth Amendment also established three important principles of citizenship: "the principle of national citizenship, the concept of the federal state as the protector and guarantor of national citizenship rights, and the principle of birthright citizenship" (Glenn 2000: 4).

But what citizenship means here is not sufficiently clear; the Constitution says only that "the citizens of each state shall be entitled to all privileges and immunities of citizens in the several states" (Kerber 1997: 834). It is assumed that everybody knows what the privileges and immunities or the rights and duties of a citizen are. The rights, as people generally understand them, include free speech, a right against self-incrimination, religious freedom, a jury trial and the vote. The main duties or obligations of a citizen are to pay taxes, to avoid vagrancy, to refrain from treason, to serve on juries and to do military service (Kerber 1997: 835).

The American citizenship rights and duties are basically liberal ideas, which are embodied in the Declaration of Independence. Citizens are regarded as independent and autonomous individuals who can make choices in the free market and pursue their own interests. Government is there only to help individual citizens to secure their rights and to pursue their own private and public happiness. Individual rights, autonomy and independence are so strongly emphasized that there is no such term as 'social citizenship' in the United States (Glenn 2000: 7–8). There are also some republican ideas in the United States that citizens should actively participate in political processes and in the community. But political participation as essential to citizenship is an issue of debate, not of general acceptance (Glenn 2000: 6).

The above characterizations of citizenship in these three countries are more or less the official versions, expressed in government policies and national laws. They also contrast clearly with the individualistic-liberal type of citizenship in the United States with the communitarian one in Korea and Germany, although some recent changes in the other direction are observed in all the three countries. However, citizenship policies and nationality laws do not necessarily reflect public opinions or people's experiences. Rather they are often decided by partisan interests or political considerations (Anil 2005). Many empirical researches show there are gaps and discrepancies, large and small, between the official definition of citizenship and that held by the general public, and between normative versions and experiential ones (Conover et al. 1991, 2004; Dalton 2008; Lister et al. 2003). In the following sections we will examine lived perceptions of ordinary people on various aspects of citizenship in the light of the existing theories and institutional aspects of citizenship.

10.4 Data and Methods

10.4.1 Data and Measures

The 2004 International Social Survey Programme (ISSP) data which contain the citizenship module will be analyzed so as to investigate the perception of citizenship in Korea, Germany, and the United States, and to identify an appropriate citizenship model(s) for each country. The 2004 ISSP citizenship module includes several questions which reveal various aspects of citizenship, such as duties and obligations of citizenship and democratic rights, and social and political participation. By analyzing the responses of ordinary citizens to those questions, this study attempts to determine which citizenship model best fits each of the three countries. At the same time, a lot of caution is required when directly comparing the patterns of citizenship perception among countries because the data to be analyzed is different from country to country – both as regard study design and data collection procedures. This is inevitable because languages differ, the training of interviewers differs, and the social and cultural characteristics of the interviewer-respondent interaction differ as well. Strictly speaking, differences or similarities in the scores for republicanism and liberalism between countries are always subject to the challenge that what seems different may not really be different (Verba et al. 1978: 32–36). For example, a higher score for republicanism in one country may simply reflect differences in the administration of the survey. Despite these potential problems, we shall compare the republican and liberal conceptions of citizenship among three countries.

The battery of duties and obligations of citizenship consists of 10 questions. Respondents were asked to give a score between 1 (Strongly Disagree) and 7 (Strongly Agree) for each item. The battery asks how important each of 10 items is to be a good citizen including "always vote in elections", "never try to evade taxes", "always to obey laws and regulations", "to keep watching on the actions of government", "to be active in social or political associations", "to try to understand the reasoning of people with other opinions", "to choose products for political, ethical or environmental reasons, even if they cost a bit more", "to help people in our country who are worse off than yourself", "to help people in the rest of the world who are worse off than yourself", and "to be willing to serve in the military at a time of need".

The battery of democratic rights is composed of six questions. Respondents were asked to give a score between 1 (Not at all important) and 7 (Very important) for all items. The battery asks how important each of the six items is in relation to people's rights in a democracy. It includes "that all citizens have an adequate standard of living", "that government authorities respect and protect the rights of minorities", "that government authorities treat everybody equally regardless of his or her position in society", "that politicians listen to citizens before making decisions", "that people be given more opportunities to participate in public decision-making", and "that citizens may engage in acts of civil disobedience when they oppose government actions".

The 2004 ISSP also includes the battery of political acts, asking whether the respondent has "signed a petition", "boycotted products for social or political reasons", "took part in a demonstration", "attended a political rally", "contacted officials or politicians to express one's opinion", "donated money", "contacted media", or been "involved in internet political forum" in the past.

10.4.2 Methods

The analyses of this study are divided into three parts.

First, in order to discover better citizenship models of attitudinal aspects for Korea, Germany, and the United States, this study examines mean scores on duties of citizenship and rights in democracy. Unfortunately, the 2004 ISSP does not include measures of national identity. The only communitarian element in the data is "understanding other opinions". By contrast, the data contains several measures of the civic republic perception of citizenship. This is denoted by seven items such as "never trying to evade taxes", "always obeying laws and regulations", "to keep watch on the actions of government", "to be active in social or political associations", "to help people in our country who are worse off than yourself", "to be willing to serve in the military at a time of need", and "that people be given more opportunities to participate in public decision-making process". Thus, due to the limitation of information on the communitarian element, this study does not differentiate between the communitarian and civic republican elements in the analysis. Instead, we shall combine one communitarian item and seven civic republican elements into the same group and call it republican perception of citizenship for the convenience of analysis.

On the other hand, the social liberal perception of citizenship is measured by "that all citizens have an adequate standard of living", and the individualistic liberal perception of citizenship is denoted by four items, including "always vote in elections", "that government authorities respect and protect the rights of minorities", "that government authorities treat everybody equally regardless of his or her position in society", "that politicians listen to citizens before making decisions". Thus, 5 out of 16 duties and rights items will be analyzed to estimate social-/individualistic-liberal perception of citizenship.

Second, in order to decide the best fitting citizenship model for behavioral aspects in Korea, Germany, and the United States, this study also investigates several items introduced by Theiss-Morse (1993). We shall try to determine whether Korea, Germany, and the United States are close to "representative democracy perspective", "political enthusiast perspective", "pursued interest perspective", or "indifferent perspective" based on the level of political activities such as voting, conventional participation, contacting, and unconventional participation. For example, if one country shows a higher level of conventional participation than another country, we regard the former as being less a case of a "pursued interests perspective" and "indifferent perspective" than the latter. Voting is measured by "voted in the last election", conventional participation by "signed a petition", "donated money", and "involved in internet political forum", contacting by "contacted officials or politicians to express one's opinion", and "contacted media", and unconventional activities by "boycotted products for social or political reasons", "took part in a demonstration", and "attended a political rally".

Lastly, the present study examines the complicated relationship between a republican perception of citizenship, a social-/individualistic-liberal perception of citizenship, and political activities by constructing a structural equation model. By doing so, we attempt to elucidate whether republican and liberal perceptions of citizenship are mutually interactive and whether political activities are positively or negatively affected by the two different kinds of perception. Before constructing a structural equation model, the confirmatory factor analysis of 13 items on republican and social-/individualistic-liberal citizenship perceptions is employed to see whether they can be grouped into the two dimensions (attitudinal – behavioral) as expected for Korea, Germany, and the United States, respectively.

10.5 Attitudinal Dimension of Citizenship: Communitarian, Republican, Social-Liberal, or Individualistic-Liberal in Korea, Germany, and the United States

Table 10.1 shows the mean scores on 13 items for republican and social-/individualistic-liberal perceptions of citizenship in Korea, Germany, and the United States. These items are divided into two groups of citizenship perception. The upper is the communitarian/civic republican aspect while the lower is the social/individual liberal aspect. The average points for republican and liberal values, respectively, are 5.63 and 5.98 in Korea, 5.24 and 6.11 in Germany, and 5.88 and 6.38 in the United States.

When compared to Koreans, Germans and Americans show more of a liberal tendency. However, Koreans also tend to highly value such liberal elements of citizenship as citizens' right to have adequate standards of living, voting in elections, equal treatment of all citizens, and accountability of politicians. The only difference is that in Korea the republican aspects of citizenship are also highly respected and just as much as the liberal ones, while they are less valued in Germany and in the United States. Especially in Korea, paying taxes, obeying laws, and citizens' right to intervene in decision-making process are the most appreciated republican values. Thus, considering the mixed tendency of republican and liberal conceptions, we think that the former type of citizenship is being replaced by the burgeoning latter type of citizenship in Korea. This speculation is consistent with our expectation that Korean citizenship is changing toward a more liberal type while retaining the communitarian and republican elements. In the previous section, we pointed out that although the communitarian conception of citizenship is dominant in Korea, there has been an emergence of liberal and cosmopolitan citizenship thanks to the recent economic development and globalization. This turned out to be partially true according to the results in Table 10.1.

Despite the biggest gap in the average score between republican and liberal conceptions being found in Germany, we do not define German citizenship as the strong liberal type but as the moderate liberal one. It is obvious that the liberal conception of citizenship is, on average, stronger than the republican one. However, the great gap between the two types of citizenship is mainly due to the abnormally low scores of being active in associations and serving in the military on the republican side. Furthermore, the average score for liberal conception in Germany is not as high as the one in the United States. In addition, social-liberal perception, as in "all citizens have an adequate standard of living" is, on average, stronger than individualistic-liberal one. Furthermore, among liberal elements, "voting in the elections" is rated lower than other liberal elements. Therefore, we conclude that the German model of citizenship is moderately social-liberal while containing a little bit of republican elements. The results are in line with our previous speculation that communitarian and liberal elements of citizenship coexist in Germany.

As expected, Table 10.1 clearly indicates that Americans tend to strongly emphasize liberal ideas of citizenship, especially individualistic-liberalism. Democratic rights such as citizens' right to have adequate standards of living, voting in elections,

Table 10.1 Mean scores on duties and obligation of citizenship and rights in Korea, Germany, and the United States

	Korea	Germany	USA
Republican			
Understand opinion of others	5.63	5.54	5.83
Never try to evade taxes	6.25	5.78	6.39
Always obey laws	6.19	5.97	6.47
Keep watch on government	5.52	5.24	6.13
Active in associations	4.52	3.71	4.63
Help less privileged-countries	5.40	5.51	6.04
Serve in the military	5.33	3.91	5.40
Citizen involved in public decision-making	6.20	6.30	6.16
Social-/individual-liberal			
All citizens have adequate standard of living	6.00	6.23	6.31
Always vote in elections	6.02	5.07	6.20
Government respect rights of minorities	5.55	6.24	6.23
Government treat everybody equally	6.09	6.50	6.63
Politicians take into account views of citizens	6.27	6.49	6.52
1: Not at all important ~7: Very important			

rights of minorities, an equal treatment of all citizens, and accountability of politicians are all highly respected in the United States. In short, the results imply that the social-/individualistic-liberal models may better explain the American citizenship. Specially, the individualistic-liberal perception of citizenship emphasizing freedom, equality, individualism, autonomy, and competition is predominant in the United States (Conover et al. 2004). Unlike our expectation that there are also some republican ideas regarding active participation in politics by citizens, however, Table 10.1 reveals that this element is placed at the bottom.

Figures 10.2 and 10.3 graphically illustrate the mean scores on 13 items for republican and social-/individualistic-liberal perception in Korea, Germany, and the United States. Figure 10.2 shows republican elements while Fig. 10.3 shows social-individualistic-liberal ones. Mapping the results of Table 10.1 on to the figures makes it possible to effectively examine the relative importance of citizenship elements within each country and to compare the level of citizenship among the three countries.

Interestingly enough, the rank order of republican elements is almost similar across all three countries. Figure 10.2 indicates that paying taxes, obeying laws, and citizens' right to intervene in decision-making processes are placed on the top whereas active involvement in political associations and service in the military are located at the bottom in Korea, Germany, and the United States. Other republican elements including understanding other opinions and keeping watch on the government are commonly placed in the middle. The conspicuous difference in service in the military among the three countries, however, is worth noting. The rank of this element is as high as that of other republican ones such as helping the less privileged

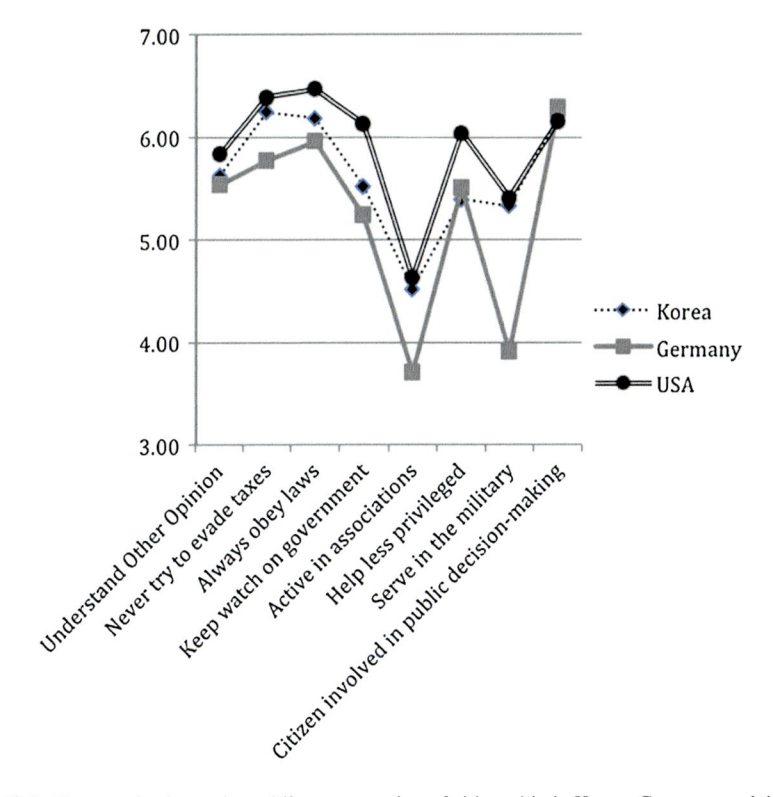

Fig. 10.2 Communitarian and republican perception of citizenship in Korea, Germany and the US

and keeping watch on the government in Korea, while it is definitely one of the lowest in Germany and the United States. It is also interesting to observe that being active in political associations as an important duty of citizens is the lowest in all three countries. This might be because active involvement in political associations is usually thought of as a right rather than a duty.

Figure 10.2 indicates that the United States leads in the republican conception of citizenship whereas Germany is placed at the lowest rank. Korea is in the middle. This rank order among three countries holds for all republican elements. By comparing the three countries, we observe that the United States comes first and Germany third in terms of republican perception of citizenship. In particular, the ascendancy of the United States over Korea and Germany is apparent for such elements as understanding other opinions, paying taxes, obeying laws, watching government, and helping the less privileged. In addition, Fig. 10.2 reveals that people in all three countries value the citizen's right to intervene in the decision-making process similarly. Both Koreans and Germans rate understanding other opinions and helping the less privileged as important duties of citizens. Figure 10.2 also shows that Koreans and Americans commonly emphasize being active in political associations and service in the military to the same extent.

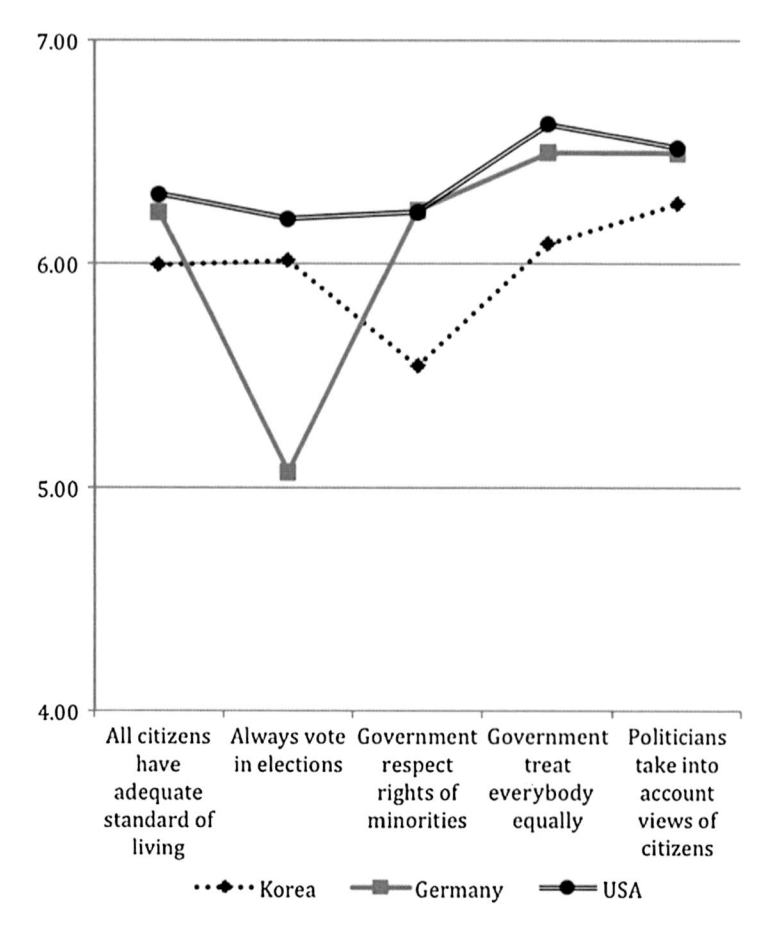

Fig. 10.3 Social and individual liberal perception of citizenship in Korea, Germany, and the US

Compared to the republican elements of citizenship, the social-/individual-liberal ones show a greater variety of patterns in their relative importance within the countries and their ranks among the countries. First, Fig. 10.3 shows that, among five social-/individualistic-liberal elements, citizens' right to have adequate standards of living and an equal treatment of all citizens are the highest, and accountability of politicians is in the middle in Korea, Germany, and the United States. Voting in elections is in the middle in Korea and the United States whereas it is in the lowest in Germany. The right of minorities is in the middle in Germany and the United States whereas it is the lowest item in Korea, reflecting the reality that Korean society is less culturally diverse than the other two countries. Second, Fig. 10.3 indicates that the United States leads in the social-/individualistic percep-tion of citizenship, Germany is almost at the same level as the United States, and Korea is at the lowest. Considering that liberalism has been the dominant ideology in heterogeneous and pluralistic American society, the overwhelmingly high scores for the liberal conception of citizenship seem to be apposite. While the scores on the liberal perception of citizenship in general are the highest in the United States, followed by Germany, and then Korea, there is one exception to this pattern. The average score of "voting in elections" is lowest in Germany while it is in the middle in Korea and in the highest in the United States.

The results show that the Korean perception of citizenship is, though not clear, characterized as a mixture of republican and social-liberal types, the German one as a moderate social-liberal type while containing republican elements, and the American one a strong individualistic-liberal type. Note that this classification can at most only reveal the relative position of each nation in terms of attitudinal aspects of citizenship. It is true that each country holds multiple characteristics of citizenship perception. Thus, the results and implications regarding the taxonomy introduced in this study should be understood in a relative sense.

10.6 Behavioral Dimension of Citizenship: The Representative Democracy Perspective, Political Enthusiast Perspective, Pursued Interests Perspective, and Indifferent Perspective

In the previous section, we compared the attitudinal dimension of citizenship among Korea, Germany, and the United States. In this section, we shall attempt to classify the three countries based on the behavioral dimension of citizenship, stressing the importance of actual participation by ordinary citizens. The behavioral dimension of citizenship is divided into four groups: "representative democracy perspective", "political enthusiast perspective", "pursued interests perspective", and "indifferent perspective". Voting is measured by "voted in the last election", conventional participation by "signed a petition", "donated money", and "involved in internet political forum", contacting activities by "contacted officials or politicians to express one's opinion", and "contacted media", and unconventional activities by "boycotted products for social or political reasons", "took part in a demonstration" and "attended a political rally".

In order to identify each country's relative closeness to or distance from each behavioral element, we utilize four types of political activities. According to the classification by Theiss-Morse (1993), each type of political activity corresponds to each behavioral model of citizenship. For example, the higher voting turnout stands for a higher degree of the "representative democracy perspective" and "pursued interests perspective", but for a lower level of "political enthusiast perspective" and "indifferent perspective". Conventional participation and contacting are negatively related to the "pursued interests perspective" and "indifferent perspective" whereas they have nothing to do with other behavioral dimensions. Unconventional participation is positively related to "political enthusiast", negatively associated with the "pursued interests perspective" and "indifferent perspective", and has nothing to do with "representative democracy".

Table 10.2 shows the proportion of respondents who voted in the recent general election or took part in political activities in the past in Korea, Germany, and the United States. It clearly reveals similarities and differences in the patterns and relative

Table 10.2 Percentage of political participation in the past in Korea, Germany, and the US

	Korea	Germany %	USA %
Signed a petition	49.1	55.7	66.6
Donated money or raise funds	27.1	67.5	50.1
Joined an internet forum	7.6	3.3	7.4
Contacted politician	10.4	20.3	43.2
Contacted media	5.0	13.2	14.5
Boycotted certain products	29.5	40.8	38.8
Took part in demonstration	18.6	31.9	18.7
Attended political meeting or rally	11.9	35.9	32.4

importance of political activities in the three countries. First, generally speaking, the level of political participation is higher in the United States and Germany than in Korea. Second, voting turnout is the most universal form of political participation although its rate is much lower in the United States than in Korea and Germany. The relatively high turnout rate in Korea and Germany confirms the above finding that these two countries have more republican characteristics than the United States. Third, besides voting, conventional participation including signing a petition and donating money is the most frequent political activity in all countries, and joining a political internet forum is the rarest one. It is interesting to see that signing a petition is the most enjoyed form of political activity in the United States whereas donating money is the most popular in Germany. In addition, conventional participation is not popular in Korea, implying that civil society composed of active involvement by ordinary citizens in their everyday lives is not as mature as in the other two countries.

Fourth, on average, contacting is the least common form of political participation in all countries although contacting politicians is relatively high in the United States. It seems that the Americans' propensity to actively contact politicians or public officials to express their political opinion reflects their individualistic liberal perception of citizenship. Fifth, unconventional participation is a more frequently used form of political activity than contacting in all countries. This tendency is more salient in Germany and Korea than in the United States. Regarding the higher level of boycotting products compared to other forms of unconventional participation, it is possible to interpret this as showing that the importance of new social movement such as women's movement, environmentalism, and consumerism is growing in the world. In brief, despite some variations in participation patterns between the countries, four types of political activities can be ranked as voting, conventional participation, unconventional participation, and contacting according to their popularity in each country.

Figure 10.4 allows us to compare the level of political participation among Korea, Germany, and the United States, thereby identifying each country's relative closeness to or distance from four types of behavioral dimension of citizenship, namely "representative democracy", "political enthusiast", "pursued interests", and "indifferent". First, voting turnout rate is highest in Germany, moderate in Korea, and lowest in the United States. Since this item is expected to predict high levels of the "representative democracy" and "pursued interests" perspectives and the low levels

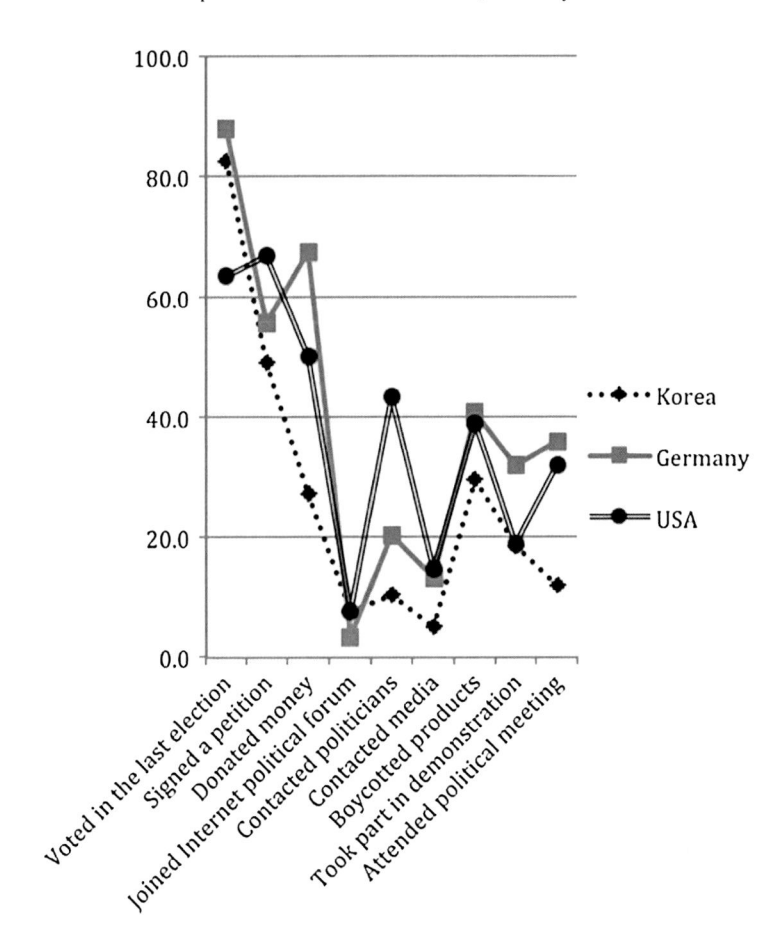

Fig. 10.4 Political activities in the past in Korea, Germany, and the US (behavioral aspect of citizenship)

of the "political enthusiast" and "indifferent " perspectives, it is reasonable to say that Germany and Korea are closer to the "representative democracy" and "pursued interests" perspectives and more distant from "political enthusiast" and "indifferent", compared to the United States. Second, conventional participation is much higher in Germany and the United States than in Korea, indicating that the former two countries are more distant from "pursued interests" and "indifferent" than the latter one. Third, contacting is highest in the United States, moderate in Germany, and lowest in Korea. According to Theiss-Morse's standard, Germany is the nation that least evinces the "pursued interests" and "indifferent" perspectives. The problem, however, is that the two measures of contacting – such as by contacting politicians and contacting media – differ in their nature, purpose, and opportunity. For instance, contacting politicians and public officials is more usual, easier and more accessible than contacting media. Thus, it is more persuasive to only rely on contacting politicians and public officials than contacting media in identifying the relationship between contacting and the behavioral aspect of citizenship. When using this standard, it seems to be acceptable to identify the United States as being most distant from the "pursued interest" and "indifferent" perspectives, which reflects American characteristics of individualistic-liberal perception of citizenship. This result supports conventional wisdom that the American political system is built around the pluralistic principle which emphasizes the influences of various political voices in the decision-making process. By contrast, Korean society is closest to the "pursued interests" and "indifferent" perspectives. Fourth, Fig. 10.4 shows that Germans are more likely to take part in an unconventional protest compared to citizens in the other two countries. The diverse sorts of unconventional politics are positively associated with "political enthusiast" perspective while they are negatively related to "pursued interests" and "indifferent". Therefore, it is possible to conjecture that German society is more strongly and positively associated with a political enthusiast perspective than the Korean and American counterparts, which suggests the dominance of a social-liberal perception of citizenship in this country. In addition, Germany is more distant from "pursued interests" and "indifferent" than the United States and Korea. In sum, the complicated results from the patterns of political activities make us infer that Korean society is closest to "pursued interests" and "indifferent" whereas the American society is most distant from "pursued interests" and "indifferent". The German society is close to "political enthusiast".

10.7   Relationship Between Attitudinal and Behavioral Dimensions of Citizenship: Influence of Citizenship Perception on Political Participation in Korea, Germany, and the United States

So far, this study has investigated the different ways people understand citizenship in Korea, Germany, and the United States. In particular, this study has attempted to understand the differences between three countries in terms of attitudinal and behavioral dimensions of citizenship. The analysis found that the republican model on the attitudinal dimension and the strong "pursued interests" and "indifferent" perspectives on the behavioral dimension generally characterize Korean society. German society is identified as having a moderate republican and strong social-liberal tradition on the attitudinal dimension and political enthusiast on the behavioral dimension. American society is characterized as having a strong individualistic-liberal tradition on the attitudinal dimension and less "pursued interest" and "indifferent" cultures on the behavioral dimension.

The results make us think that the attitudinal dimension of citizenship goes hand in hand with the behavioral one. The two citizenship dimensions are closely associated with each other. For example, the strong tendency of Germans to have a "political enthusiast" perspective can be explained by their prevailing culture of social liberalism. In this vein, it is meaningful to investigate the relationship between the two types of citizenship in each country. In order to elucidate the relationship between the attitudinal and behavioral dimensions of citizenship, this study adopts a structural equation model. Before moving on to constructing the model, the confirmatory factor analysis is employed to check whether the 13 items of attitudinal and behavioral aspects of citizenship can be grouped into the two dimensions of communitarian/civic republican and social-/individual-liberal perception of citizenship in Korea, Germany, and the United States, respectively.

Table 10.3 contains the results from the confirmatory factor analysis of citizenship perception for Korea, Germany, and the United States. All in all, the analyses show that the 13 items are categorized according to the attitudinal aspect of citizenship – such as communitarian/civic republican and social- and individualistic-liberal – with reasonably high reliability scores in Korea, Germany, and the United States. Each of the eight republican items and five social-/individualistic-liberal elements successfully forms its own factor. Thus, we have support here for the proposition that each factor represents an independent aspect of citizenship perception.

Simultaneously, the results also indicate not only that the demarcation between republican and social-/individualistic-liberal factors is clearest, but also that the factor loadings of all items are consistently stable in Korea. In Germany and the United States, although the levels of reliability for two factors are acceptable, the factor loading of the seventh item, service in the military, is too low to effectively contribute to the republican factor. If this item is deleted from the factor, its Cronbach's increases by almost 0.1. Thus, it is better to exclude this item from the structural equation models for Germany and the United States. On the other hand, the values of Cronbach's for political activities are consistently high, .825, and .830, and .815 in Korea, Germany, and the United States, respectively. Note that the voting turnout has been eliminated from the equation because of its different nature compared to other participation items.

Figures 10.5, 10.6, and 10.7 display the results of structural equation models estimating the relationship between republican perceptions of citizenship, the social-/individualistic-liberal one, and political activities in Korea, Germany and the United States. All coefficients are significant at .05 level and the model fits such that GFI and AGFI are acceptable. The results reveal similarities and differences among the three countries. First, the R-squares of the models are .46 for the United States, .24 for Germany, .05 for Korea. The extent to which the behavioral aspect of citizenship is explained by the attitudinal one is the greatest in the United States, moderate in Germany, and the least in Korea, suggests that American citizenship is more balanced and mature than in the other countries in the sense that its two aspects better interact with each other.

Second, in Korea, Fig. 10.5 indicates that the republican perception of citizenship, though weak, positively affects political participation while the social-/individualistic-liberal one does so negatively. Citizens who highly value the importance of civic duties and obligations are more likely to take part in politics while those who place emphasis on the instrumental significance of political rights are less likely to do so in Korea. These results confirm the previous finding that Korean society is aptly described by the republican model. Third, Fig. 10.6 shows that in Germany, the

Table 10.3 Confirmatory factor analysis of attitudinal aspects of citizenship

	Korea		Germany		USA	
	Factor loadings					
Variables	Republican	Liberal	Republican	Liberal	Republican	Liberal
Rep1	0.69		0.63		0.64	
Rep2	0.83		0.72		0.54	
Rep3	0.84		0.77		0.42	
Rep4	0.71		0.72		0.75	
Rep5	0.44		0.40		0.58	
Rep6	0.69		0.58		0.63	
Rep7	0.58		0.14		0.36	
Rep8	0.87		0.80		0.70	
Lib1		0.76		0.74		0.75
Lib2		0.70		0.55		0.64
Lib3		0.67		0.78		0.77
Lib4		0.77		0.89		0.89
Lib5		0.87		0.92		0.83
Cronbach's α	0.768	0.705	0.650	0.564	0.637	0.627
N	1,212		1,063		1,401	

*All loading are significant at $P < 0.01$

Rep1	Communitarian: Understand other opinion	Lib1	Social liberal: All adequate standard of living
Rep2	Republican: Never try to evade taxes	Lib2	Individualistic liberal: Always vote in elections
Rep3	Republican: Always obey laws	Lib3	Individualistic liberal: Government respect minorities
Rep4	Republican: Keep watch on government	Lib4	Individualistic liberal: Government's equal treatment
Rep5	Republican: Active in associations	Lib5	Individualistic liberal: Citizen oriented decision
Rep6	Republican: Help less privileged people		
Rep7	Republican: Serve in the military		
Rep8	Republican: Citizen involved decision-making process		

effects of republican and social-/individualistic-liberal perceptions on political participation are similar to those in Korea, but with a different intensity. Germans with a belief in the value of civic virtue are much more likely to get involved in politics whereas those cherishing the value of instrumental rights are less likely to be politically active. Considering that German citizenship is classified as being of the social-liberal type and typified by the "political enthusiast" perspective, the pivotal role of liberalism is justifiable.

Fourth, the American results are exactly the opposite of their German counterparts. Figure 10.7 reveals that the republican perception decreases the level of political activities while the liberal one increases it, reflecting the dominant culture of pluralism in the United States. Americans who are close to utilitarian values

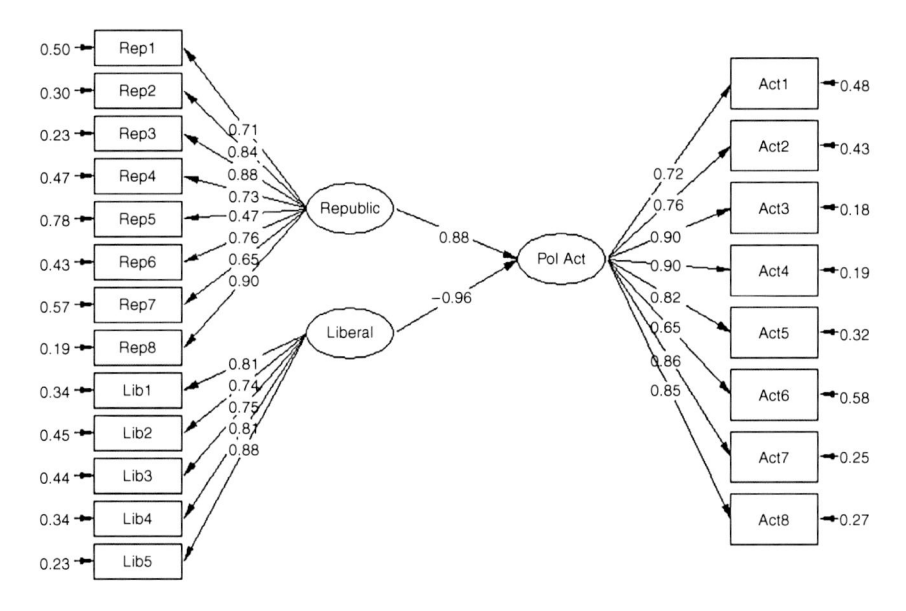

† Figures are obtained from the standardized solution in LISREL 8
‡ All coefficients are significiant at p<.05

				Variables	Political Behavior		
	N	1159					
	df	186			coeff.	s.e	t-value
	Chi-square	1073.67					
Model Fit	GFI	0.97	Structural Model	Republican	0.88	.43	2.05
	AGFI	0.96					
	NFI	0.87		Liberal	−0.96	.43	−2.23
	CFI	0.88					
	IFI	0.89					
	RMSEA	0.064		R-square			.05

Rep1	Communitarian: Understand other opinions	Act1	Political Behavior: Sign a petition
Rep2	Republican: Never try to evade taxes	Act2	Political Behavior: Boycott products
Rep3	Republican: Always obey laws	Act3	Political Behavior: Take part in demonstration
Rep4	Republican: Keep watch on government	Act4	Political Behavior: Attend pol meeting or rally
Rep5	Republican: Active in associations	Act5	Political Behavior: Contact a politician or official
Rep6	Republican: Help less privileged people	Act6	Political Behavior: Donate money or raise funds
Rep8	Republican: Citizen involved in decision-making	Act7	Political Behavior: Contact media
Lib1	Social Liberal: All adequate standard of living	Act8	Political Behavior: Join an Internet pol forum
Lib2	Individualistic Liberal: Always vote in elections		
Lib3	Individualistic Liberal: Government respect minorities		
Lib4	Individualistic Liberal: Government's equal treatment		
Lib5	Individualistic Liberal: Citizen oriented decision		

Fig. 10.5 Structural equation model of attitudinal and behavioral aspects of citizenship in Korea

are more likely to participate in politics as compared to those who think highly of civic duties and obligations. The results are consistent with the previous finding that American society is effectively explained by the individualistic-liberal model that

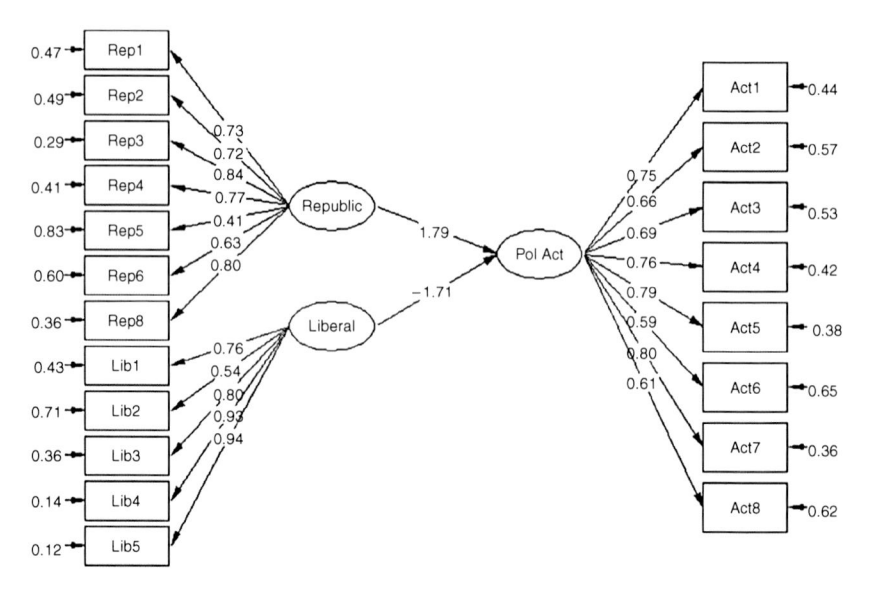

† Figures are obtained from the standardized solution in LISREL 8
‡ All coefficients are significiant at p<.05

Model Fit				Variables	Political Behavior		
	N	971			coeff.	s.e.	t-value
	df	167					
	Chi-square	1306.68					
	GFI	0.95	Structural Model	Republican	1.79	.57	3.16
	AGFI	0.94					
	NFI	0.80		Liberal	−1.71	.57	−3.00
	CFI	0.82					
	IFI	0.82					
	RMSEA	0.084		R-square			.24

Fig. 10.6 Structural equation model of attitudinal and behavioral aspects of citizenship in Germany

emphasizes the rights of citizens and equal treatment. By constructing the structural equation models for Korea, Germany, and the United States, this study has succeeded in ascertaining the relationship between the attitudinal and behavioral dimensions of citizenship. In sum, the results confirm that patterns of relationship between those two dimensions differ across the nation-states that have been examined.[1]

10.8 Conclusions

As is assumed from their political histories and cultural backgrounds, the institutional and legal dimensions of citizenship in Korea and Germany are largely communitarian, in contrast to the individualistic-liberal pattern in the United States. It is also true, from our analysis of the survey data, that American citizens have

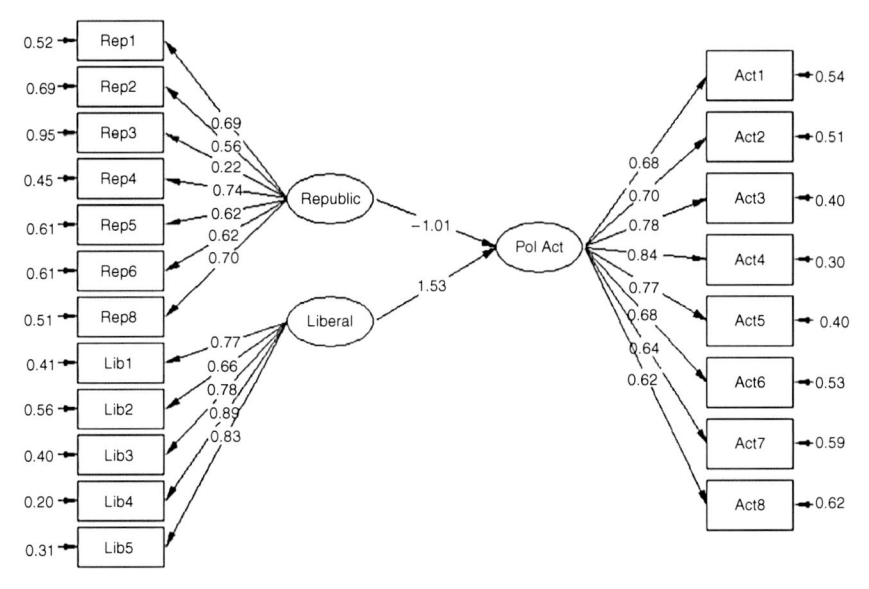

† Figures are obtained from the standardized solution in LISREL 8
‡ All coefficients are significiant at p<.05

Model Fit	N	1339		Variables	Political Behavior		
	df	167					
	Chi-square	1096.49			coeff.	s.e.	t-value
	GFI	0.97	Structural Model	Republican	−1.01	0.34	−2.94
	AGFI	0.96					
	NFI	0.82		Liberal	1.53	0.34	4.45
	CFI	0.84					
	IFI	0.84					
	RMSEA	0.064		R-square			0.46

Fig. 10.7 Structural equation model of attitudinal and behavioral aspects of citizenship in US

the most liberal notion of citizenship, followed by German and Korean citizens. At the same time, however, the American people's idea of citizenship turns out to be the most republican among the three countries, with Germany's idea being the least republican. These somewhat contradictory findings are due in part to measurement problems, but also reflect incongruities between the institutional and the attitudinal dimensions. Americans are known to be very individualistic, but also very keen on civic duties and obligations. On the other hand, Germans are less concerned about civic duties, but have a more social-liberal view of citizenship than Koreans. One possible explanation for this result is that the German nation has long been a welfare state, while Koreans have experienced harsh dictatorship and democratic struggles so that Koreans regard civic duties and rights as more important than Germans.

The structural equation models for the relationship between the attitudinal and behavioral dimensions of citizenship confirm that patterns of relationship between those two dimensions differ among the three nation states. The relationship is the strongest for Americans and the weakest for Koreans, implying that citizens' political attitudes are more readily translated into political behavior in the United States than is the case in the other two countries. The American citizens are also different from the German and Korean counterparts in that liberal attitudes towards civic rights have positive effects on political acts, while attitudes towards republican duties negatively affect political behavior in the United States, in contrast to the reverse effects found in Germany and Korea. In general, the republican type of citizenship is regarded to be closer to the model of an active citizen as seen in Germany and Korea. The American case is quite the opposite of what conventional wisdom tells us, probably because the American liberal is not a passive holder of civic rights, but an active defender of democratic ideals, as its history eloquently testifies.

These findings from the comparative analyses of the institutional and attitudinal aspects of citizenship and political behavior in Korea, Germany and the United States show that the concept of citizenship is not uniform across different nation-states with different political histories and cultural backgrounds. In other words, the concept is a socially- and culturally-embedded one and can be variable for different types of democracy. Likewise political behavior largely depends on people's actual interpretation of citizenship, rather than on its official or institutional definition.

Endnote

[1]One may question the validity of findings and their implications because the structural equation models introduced above do not simultaneously consider the effects of socio-economic factors on political participation. Hence, we conducted additional multivariate analyses controlling for sex, age, education, religion, and income, and confirmed that the direction and extent to which two types of citizenship perception affect political activities are the same as the results in Figs. 10.5, 10.6, and 10.7.

References

Almond, G., and S. Verba 1965. *The Civic Culture*. New York: Sage.
Anil, M. (2005). "No More Foreigners? The Remaking of German Naturalization and Citizenship Law, 1990–2000". *Dialectical Anthropology* 29, 453–470.
Baban, F. 2006. "From Gastarbeiter to" Ausländische Mitbürger: "Postnational Citizenship and In-Between Identities in Berlin". *Citizenship Studies* 10 (2), 185–201.
Beck, U. 1999. *What is Globalization?* Cambridge: Polity Press.
Choe, H. 2006. "South Korean Citizenship: The Institutional Changes since 1987 and their Effects on Citizens' Consciousness". (in Korean). *Democracy and Human Rights* 6 (1), 171–205.

Conover, P. J., M. C. Ivor, and D. D. Searling. 1991. "The Nature of Citizenship in the United States and Great Britain: Empirical Comments on Theoretical Themes". *Journal of Politics* 53 (3), 800–832.

Conover, P. J., D. D. Searling, and M. C. Ivor. 2004. "The Elusive ideal of Equal Citizenship: Theory and Political Psychology in the United States and Great Britain". *The Journal of Politics* 66 (4), 1036–1068.

Dalton, R. J. 2008. "Citizenship Norms and the Expansion of Political Participation". *Political Studies* 56, 76–98.

Fraser, N., and L. Gordon. 1994. "Civil Citizenship against Social Citizenship?" In *The Condition of Citizenship*, Ed. B. V. Steenbergen, 90–107. London: Sage.

Glenn, E. (2000). "Citizenship and Inequality: Historical and Global Perspectives". *Social Problems* 47 (1), 1–20.

Habermas, J. 1994. "Citizenship and National Identity". In *The Condition of Citizenship*, Ed. B. V. Steenbergen, 20–35. London: Sage.

Heater, D. 1990. *Citizenship: The Civic Ideal in World History, Politics and Education*. London: Longman.

Held, D., A. McGrew, D. Goldblatt, and J. Perraton. 1999. *Global Transformations: Politics, Economics and Culture*. Stanford: Stanford University Press.

Isin, E. F., and B. S. Turner. 2007. "Investigating Citizenship: an Agenda for Citizenship Studies". *Citizenship Studies* 11 (1), 5–17.

Kerber, L. K. 1997. "The Meaning of Citizenship". *The Journal of American History* 84 (3), 833–854.

Kim, S. 2007. "Liberal nationalism and Responsible Citizenship in South Korea". *Citizenship Studies* 11 (5), 449–463.

Lee, C. 2008. *Nation-Sate v. Nation-State: The Transformation of Citizenship and the State-Nation Nexus in South Korea. Paper presented in the Symposium on Globalization of South Korea: Its Impact and Opportunities*. 17-18 December, Seoul Korea.

Lister, R., N. Smith, S. Middleton, and L. Cox. 2003. "Young People Talk About Citizenship: Empirical Perspectives on Theoretical and Political Debates". *Citizenship Studies* 7 (2), 235–253.

Marshall, T. H. 1973. *Class, Citizenship and Social development*. Westport. Conn: Greenwood Press.

Miller, C. L. 1999. "Rethinking Citizenship Frameworks: Education for Citizenship Practice, Not Citizenship Status". *Education in Russia, the Independent States and Eastern Europe* 17, 19–31.

Miller, D. 1992. "Community and Citizenship". In *Communitarianism and Individualism*, Eds. S. Avineri and A. De-Salit. Oxford: Oxford University Press.

Miller-Idriss, C. 2006. "Everyday Understanding of Citizenship in Germany". *Citizenship Studies* 10 (5), 541–570.

Oliver, D., and D. Heater. 1994. *The Foundations of Citizenship*. New York: Harvester Wheatsheaf.

Porter, A. E. 1993. "Impoverished concepts of citizenship in the debate on the National Curriculum". In *Diversity, Citizenship and the National Curriculum Debate*, Eds. J. Gundara and A. Porter. London: Institute of Education.

Theiss-Morse, E. 1993. "Conceptualization of Good Citizenship and Political Participation". *Political behavior* 15 (4), 355–380.

Turner, B. S. 1986. *Citizenship and Capitalism: The Debate over Reformism*. London: Allen and Unwin.

Vandenberg, A. 2000. "Contesting Citizenship and Democracy in a Global Era". In *Citizenship and Democracy in a Global Era*, Ed. Andrew Vandenberg, 3–17. London: Macmillan.

Van Gunsteren, H. 1994. Four Conceptions of Citizenship. In *The Condition of Citizenship*, Ed. Bart van Steenbergen, 36–48. London: Sage.

Van Krieken, R. 2000. "Citizenship and Democracy in Germany: Implications for Understanding Globalization". In *Citizenship and Democracy in a Global Era*, Ed. Andrew Vandenberg, 123–137. London: Macmillan.

Verba, S., N. Nie, and J. O. Kim. 1978. *Participation and Political Equality: A Seven Nation Comparison*. New York: Cambridge University Press.

Wong, C. K., and K. Y. Wong. 2004. "Universal Ideals and Particular Constraints of Social Citizenship: The Chinese Experience of Unifying Rights and responsibilities". *International Journal of Social Welfare* 13, 103–111.

Part IV

Chapter 11
The Idea of Citizenship and its Institutionalization: Significance of India for the Korean case

Subrata Mitra

Abstract The chapters on the aspects of citizenship included in this book – both in terms of the narrative accounts from South Korea and the comparative aspects of citizenship – show the world-wide interest in this issue, which is one of the most salient problems of our times. However, the popularity of citizenship as a phenomenon comes with a necessary imprecision in its usage. Besides, the European origin of citizenship in its modern version tends to deflect attention from its universal significance, and identify its genealogy with an exclusively European provenance. This chapter seeks to balance this asymmetry of narrative and theory by bringing theory back in, illustrating the general conjectures emerging from this with illustrations from the case of citizenship in India, and to suggest some general inferences based on the cases of India and South Korea.

11.1 Citizenship: Ubiquitous and Conceptually Puzzling

Citizenship is a major political slogan in the world today. Under this label, one can find a disparate constituency of people in long established democracies, erstwhile subjects of colonial rule seeking equality with their former masters, immigrants, and disaffected people of all possible description, trying to assert their rights in the name of citizenship. Spread out across the globe, the presence of citizenship and citizen's rights on national and international agendas is a testimony to both the global reach of the discourse on citizenship as well as to the inner complexity of citizenship as an analytical category. However, the clarity of citizenship as a category is not at the same level as its ubiquity. Who is a citizen, who defines

S. Mitra (✉)
Department of Political Science, South Asia Institute, Heidelberg University,
Im Neuenheimer Feld 330, Heidelberg 69120, Germany

Friedrich-Ebert-Anlage 38, Heidelberg 69117, Germany
e-mail: js3@ix.urz.uni-heidelberg.de

M. Pohlmann et al. (eds.), *Citizenship and Migration in the Era of Globalization*,   211
Transcultural Research – Heidelberg Studies on Asia and Europe in a Global Context,
DOI 10.1007/978-3-642-19739-0_11, © Springer-Verlag Berlin Heidelberg 2013

who a citizen is, what distinguishes a citizen from one who is not, and which minimal rights and duties constitute citizenship are issues of great emotional appeal. Existing theory, as we have seen in the previous chapters, is not a satisfactory guide to clarity on these issues. As a matter of fact, depending on where one stands in the national and international nexus of power, the status of an individual in terms of his claim to citizenship can be both confirmed and contested, depending on which strand of liberal theory of citizenship one draws on.[1]

The analysis below considers the conceptual basis of citizenship through an inquiry into its philosophical and social construction, and sets the stage for the construction of a flow diagram that seeks to capture the dynamic process of citizen-making in terms of its underlying parameters, some of which go beyond the realm of everyday politics. Towards this objective, I undertake a brief survey of the social constructions of citizenship, the evolution of the formal category of citizens from antiquity to present day, the inner differential of liberal theory of citizenship to cater to its complex empirical nuances and finally, to unite the various strands of citizen-making in the form of a tool kit.

11.2   Citizenship, Migration and Cultural Flow

Citizenship has been a key feature in the development of the state from classical antiquity to the present day. In an apparently seamless 'flow', the core concepts of the Greek city-state and the Roman Empire, representing, respectively, the salience of descent and law, became the foundation stones of the European idea of citizenship as it evolved from Greece and Rome through the turbulent centuries of medieval Europe, passing through the early modern state and finally, acquiring the institutional status of the citizen of liberal democratic Europe. One of the most significant results to emerge from the symposium where the chapters of this book were first presented, was an overview of the flow of citizenship in the European context, connecting the Greek *polis* and the modern democratic state.[2] This grand narrative treats the modern nation-state as the main site for the location of the citizen and does not take into account those who have dropped out of history during the evolution of modern state. The 'losers' in the story of the making of the modern European citizen have not, of course, vanished into complete oblivion. Their memories have been locked away into the myth of their nationhood and memories of lost battles. Such people, located at the margins of modern nation-states – the Scots and the Chechens for example – are the subjects of trans-cultural history, which is engaged in putting together these lost pieces of global history in order to re-constitute narratives that have gone out of focus, but which for that reason are not irretrievably lost.

Those engaged in the comparative analysis of citizenship in Europe would perhaps note that the European narrative of citizenship does not take into account discontinuities, war and breakdowns in established orders. However, those who lost the battle for supremacy did not necessarily disappear. As we learn from the losers' strategies – nationalist myths that are written into memory as the history of lost glory – and the re-use of sacred sites (the Acropolis – the Athenian birth-place of modern citizenship – has been successively a Greek temple, Christian church, Ottoman mosque) tell the story of the loss and recovery of European nationalisms.[3] The Greco-Roman tradition did not disappear with the onset of the European medieval period that introduced the concept of trans-European citizenship to the conceptual pool. The original Republican tradition was revived by the early modern states, as the Jacobins set off to liberate their own people and others in the name of restoring republican values. The modern democratic state and citizenship, as one finds in Marshall (1950), strove to extend citizenship rights to the whole population, riding on the buoyant welfare state.

Political action and academic research on citizenship exhibit a rich diversity of approaches to the current condition of citizenship, both as concept and political phenomenon. They express varying perspectives on how the institution of nationality can accommodate itself to contemporary levels of migration.[4] The problematic nature of citizenship today is in part linked to the demise of the concept of the state in the twentieth century, the very time when the powers of the empirical state were growing inordinately. That demise was related to a sequence of factors that are of great consequence for citizenship. In the first place, within the ethos of the twenty-first century, both the state and the nation stand not as exclusive repositories of exclusive sovereignty. Instead, the individual as citizen is the ultimate arbitrator. "State was further stigmatized by linkage with a superannuated idealism of the nation's corporate will, which now either passed into the equally mystical notion of society", sometimes an idealized world order – or was dispelled by empirical analysis and the decompositional method. Marxist theory, increasingly influential, tended to reduce the state to an epiphenomenon of economic domination and class struggle. Liberal theory, which had traditionally preached a minimal and consensual state with formal-legal anchorage, tended more and more to identify the state with the coercive power of regimes and to confuse it with the realm of "unfreedom". In the United States, whose new modes of political power would achieve hegemony by midcentury, the national experience had stressed a diffused notion of political community overweighed by the activity of voluntary associations and private profit-making corporations. Abandoning institutional analysis for behavioral analysis in the presumed interest of greater realism and empirical specificity, political science strove to eliminate the notion of state altogether. Substituting the state with concepts such as "group, political system", and "political process", political science sought to align its manner of analysis with parallel developments in psychology and sociology. That same political science also tended to see the functions and jurisdictions of the state (or whatever other term was used) as the arena of countervailing social and economic forces – at most, as a regulator of pluralism without independent majesty; at the minimum, as a "black box"where they resolved their periodically shifting claims.[5]

11.3   Liberalism and the Challenge of Multi-cultural Citizenship

It is not surprising that there should be increasing calls for a 'theory of citizenship' that focuses on the identity and conduct of individual citizens, including their responsibilities, loyalties and roles. There are, however, at least two general hazards in this quest. First, the scope of a 'theory of citizenship' is potentially limitless – almost every problem in political philosophy involves relations among citizens or between citizens and the state.[6] In their survey, Kymlicka and Norman try to avoid this danger by concentrating on two general issues that citizenship theorists claim have been neglected due to the overemphasis in recent political philosophy on structures and institutions – namely, civic virtues and citizenship identity. The second danger for a theory of citizenship arises because there are two different concepts which are sometimes conflated in these discussions: citizenship-as-legal-status, that is, as full membership of a particular political community; and citizen-ship-as-desirable-activity, where the extent and quality of one's citizenship is a function of one's participation in that community. We should, however, expect a theory of the good citizen to be relatively independent of the legal question of what it is to be a citizen, just as a theory of the good person is distinct from the metaphysical (or legal) question of what it is to be a person. While most theorists respect this distinction when developing their own theories, we shall discuss a fairly widespread tendency to ignore it when criticizing others' theories of citizenship – as for example by contrasting their own 'thick' conception of citizenship-as-activity with an opponent's 'thin' conception of citizenship-as-status. In addition, the question asks how we can construct a common identity in countries where people not only belong to separate political communities, but also belong in different ways – that is, some are incorporated as individuals and others through membership to a group. The great variance in historical, cultural, and political situations in multination-states suggests that any generalized answer to the question of citizen-ship will be overstated. It might therefore be a mistake to suppose that one could develop a general theory of the role of either a common citizenship identity or a differentiated citizenship identity in promoting or hindering national unity. Here, as with the other issues we shall examine in this survey, it seems unclear what we can expect from a,theory of citizenship'.

11.4   Citizenship: Concept, Model, Measurement and Institution

Citizenship is a liminal category – with a political edge and a moral stretch. The political cutting edge entitles the citizen – as opposed to the alien and the subject – to certain rights, to be shared in common with others; the moral depth binds him in empathy and solidarity to others like himself. Citizenship has to be understood as *both* signifier and signified of cultural flow. It is both product and process, a window

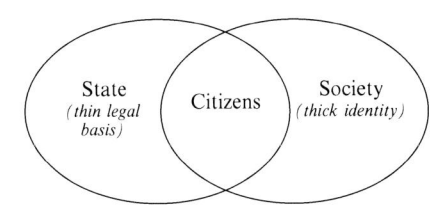

Fig. 11.1 The Modern 'Post-colonial' State, Traditional Society and Citizenship: Overlapping Legal and Moral Categories

that provides a glimpse on the global flow of ideas, *and* is itself a product of the same conceptual flow. (Figure 11.1)

In the contemporary world, globalization, which was meant to make citizenship and national boundaries ever less salient, has in fact revived their importance. The agenda of contemporary international politics is crowded with competing claims of the state and supra-stage agencies on the loyalty of individuals and ethnic groups. In the absence of a global political order with binding character, nation-states, acting in their capacity as the collective voice of their citizens, remain the most important agents of accountability and enforcement. The complex process through which subjects and immigrants become citizens, thus pitches territoriality and ethnicity as competing norms for the entitlement to citizenship. Caught in this double bind, citizenship has become a contested category and a political problem of global importance.

11.5   India: Turning Subjects into Citizens

The Indian case, seen in comparative and cross-national perspective, opens up the analytical space for the comparative and general dimensions of the problem of citizenship.[7] One learns from the Indian case that when it comes to citizen-making in a post-colonial context, not only the constitution and law matter, but also politics, and most of all, history (path dependency) matters enormously. India's relative success at turning subjects into citizens, more successfully at least than neighbouring Pakistan or Sri Lanka, is a function of India's political structure, process and memory, woven together in an institutional arrangement that draws its inspiration both from the modern state and traditional society.[8]

Drawing on my previous work on governance,[9] I would maintain that India's relative success on the issue of citizenship can be attributed to the fact that these tools of citizen-making are used with unusual vigor and imagination by the political decision-makers in India. The typical strategy launches a three-prong attack on the conflict issuing from the hiatus between the general legal norms of the state and the assertion of political identity contesting the state. India makes stakeholders out of rebels by adroitly combining reform, repression and the selective recruitment of rebels into the privileged circle of the new elites (see Fig. 11.2 Below).

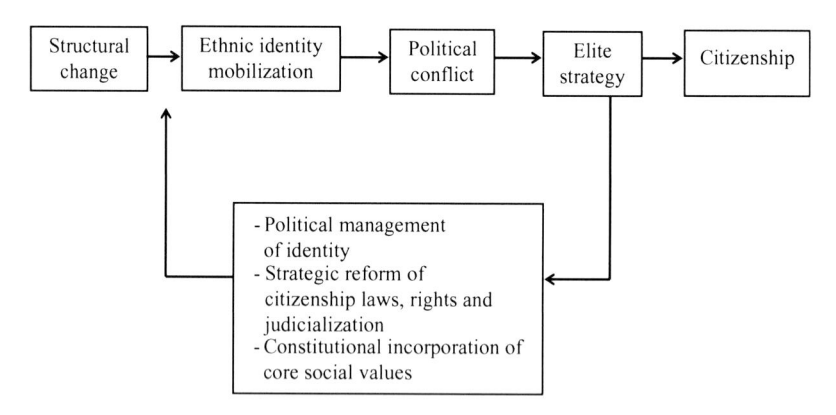

Fig. 11.2 A rational choice, dynamic neo-institutional model

The model weaves together several insights that we gain from the Indian attempt at turning subjects into citizens in a form that can be used as the basis of comparison across countries.

The first and foremost of these is the fact that in Indian discourses and public policies, citizenship is conceptualized as both a 'product' and a 'process' – which is tantamount to saying that citizen-making is a primary objective of the constitution, modern institutions and public state policy. These three processes are reinforced, on the other hand, by the momentum generated from below, as people assert their citizens' rights and articulate them through a complex repertoire that effectively combines political participation with strategic protest. Both the state and the *janata* – India's generic category for politically conscious and articulate participants in every-day politics – draw on categories that are indigenous as well as imported, and the process stretches out into memories of self-hood and rights, of empowerment through a chain of associations that links people in one part of the country to another.[10] One consequence is the emergence of the hybrid citizen – a liminal category that joins the protester and the participant, stretching the accommodating capacity of the political system and blunting the edges of anti-system behavior. The model of 'citizen making' given above highlights the role of elites and strategies of reform. It also explains India's attempts to generate differentiated and multi-level citizenship – new conceptual tools with relevance for policy-making – as categories germane to her politics. That makes citizenship an excellent case study of 'conceptual flow where practices, notions, institutions of citizenship have been transferred, imported, emulated and adapted to successfully, and in some cases unsuccessfully, to meet local needs and constraints.'

The constitution of India, and the network of institutions and political practices that it has spawned, have deeply affected the evolution of citizenship in India. The direct contributions of the constitution are to be seen in the conflation of the republican, liberal and communitarian traditions of citizenship in the Preamble,[11] the articulation of rights and duties of citizenship in key sections of the constitution, in the interplay of individual and group rights, and finally, in the specification of cultural and ethnic arenas within which citizenship is expected to flourish. (Figure 11.2)

The Constituent Assembly of India, indirectly elected by legislators who were themselves elected under restricted franchise, took over two years to produce the Indian Constitution: it is the world's longest written document of its kind and has been amended 97 times (as of 2012) since its inception. However, its core still carries the original stamp of its creators. The debate on the floor of the constituent assembly, particularly on the contentious issue of citizenship, anticipated the conflict between the principles of territoriality and ethnicity as the identification of the citizen. This debate, parts of which can be found in the box above, conveys the passions and political cross-currents that went into producing the fundamental rules that govern citizenship in India.

Independent India, which emerged from within the British Empire, was schooled in the British tradition of territorial citizenship. But the British, and subsequently the Muslim League, had regarded primordial identity – caste, religion, kin, tribe, family and the all-encompassing term of ethnicity – as the basis of identity in India. The Congress Party had, however, aspired to the same norms of territoriality as the basis of the state and citizenship, rather in the tradition of the modern European liberal democracies where these rules are governed by the Treaty of Westphalia (1648). Just as the Muslim League, claiming to represent all the Muslims of South Asia, had campaigned for the Partition of India and to carve out a territory as a homeland for Muslims, the Congress Party resisted this on the grounds that India was one nation and should remain united. Independence, from this point of view, came as a pyrrhic victory for Congress, because West and East Pakistan were carved out of British India and were made into the state of Pakistan. This historical outcome was already in the offing, and the Constituent Assembly Debates reflect the agonizing issue of how to devise a formula of citizenship that would do justice to both the moral will to be a citizen of India, regardless of where one was born, and to territoriality, where the decision of those speaking in the name of a territory – state, province or native kingdom – would be binding for all those who live on it.

The Indian Constitution that resulted from these deliberations, adopted a fuzzy solution to the contentious issue of citizenship. Like most constitutions in the world of liberal democracies, it avoids the terminology of nation and nationality. Citizenship is the constitutional key word for dividing the world between 'us and them'.[12] Expressed in terms of rights, the Constitution includes citizens'rights which aim to protect the individual against arbitrary interference by state authority. However, almost all none of these rights are restricted to the states' own nationals. What is constitutive of an Indian citizen's status are positive rights (especially social rights) and political rights (primarily the right to vote and to stand for election). In historical comparison and in political theory they constitute the criterion of exclusion which distinguishes the fully effective status of a citizen from other forms of membership, especially from that of mere subjects.

The status of a citizen also includes social rights (e.g. the directive principles of state policy and now the entire jurisprudence that evolved with the judicial activism of the Indian Supreme Court judges). In this context, social class also plays an important role in the citizenship debates. The view that citizenship can be understood as a status that gives one the rights to a certain bundle of entitlements, benefits and obligations, derives from T. H. Marshall (1950). Marshall's catalogue of civil, political, and social rights is based on the cumulative logic of struggles for expanding democracy in the nineteenth and early twentieth century. Civil rights arise with the birth of the absolutist state, and in their earliest and most basic form they entail the rights to the protection of life, liberty, and property; the right to freedom of conscience; and certain associational rights, like those of contract and marriage. Political rights in the narrow sense refer to the rights of self – determination, to hold and run for office, to enjoy freedom of speech and opinion, and to establish political and non-political associations, including a free press and free institutions of science and culture. Social rights are last in Marshall's catalogue, because they have been achieved historically through the struggles of workers', women's, and other social movements of the last two centuries. Social rights involve the right to form trade unions as well as other professional and trade associations; health care rights; unemployment compensation; old age pensions; and child care, housing, and educational subsidies. These social rights vary widely across countries and depend on the social class composition prevalent in any given welfare state.[13]

Citizenship may have had its origin in political struggles and political philosophy, but the way the constitution treats it, it is essentially a legal concept. The Indian Constitution employs it in Part II. While drafting this section, the Constituent Assembly sought to figure out who, as of 1950, would have a right to Indian nationality and citizenship. The absence of racial distinctiveness as a necessary condition for citizenship was explained by a crucial exchange in the Constituent Assembly Debates (CAD).[14] Citizenship proved to be amongst the most disputed issues, debated for almost 2 years and with more than 120 amendments moved during the sittings of the Constituent Assembly. This trend continued both in further policy initiatives and in their interpretation. However, the ongoing contestation of Indian statehood and citizenship in Kashmir and the North-Eastern regions of the country show that the problem of citizenship in India is still an open frontier for the theorist, just as it is for the policy maker.

11.6   Rebels into Stakeholders: The Room to Maneuver Within the Post-colonial State

The Indian record of successfully turning subjects into citizens has cross-national significance because, rather than being a unique attribute of Indian culture, it is based on an institutional arrangement containing several important parameters. First of these are the legal sources of citizenship as formulated in the Indian Constitution (articles 5–11), the Constituent Assembly Debates (which provide insights into the controversy surrounding specific articles), and legislation undertaken by the national parliament to enable and amend, depending on the case, the original provisions of the constitution. 'Judicialisation' of citizenship is yet another means of synchronizing the provisions of the law and the new demands emerging from society.[15] The assertion of identity and linkage to India has emerged as a supplementary basis of Indian citizenship, in addition to birth and residence. Property and citizenship have constantly been interwoven.. In the case of Kashmir, the laws have always had a slightly different tinge due to the special agreement that the Indian Acts would not normally be applicable in Kashmir.[16] In the last decade, case law has tended towards a more flexible and all-encompassing understanding of Indian stipulations with relation to property, while naturally the onset of economic liberalization has given wing to an even greater judicial liberalization of these concepts. Similarly, recent laws allowing Non-Resident Indians to own property have already been registered in case law.

11.7 Entangled and Trans-national Citizenship: Towards a Post-liberal Theory of Citizenship

The liberal response to these problems can be seen in terms of a mutation of the ideas of T. H. Marshall. Written during the period of post-war reconstruction in Britain, Marshall's work on citizenship has to be seen in context of the wider debate on the welfare state and the arguments that were being promulgated at the time for an extension of state provisions in the area of national welfare. Marshall's core contribution was to argue that the extension of citizenship could act as a political instrument of integration to counter-balance the divisive forces of class inequalities. To justify his position, Marshall constructed a theory of citizenship based on the central claim that citizenship had grown incrementally and was expressed progressively, in three different dimensions, namely the civil, the political and the social. The eighteenth century, according to his schema, had witnessed the development of civil rights, targeting mainly the legal status and civil rights of the individual – rights which were to be defended in a law court. Core rights in this case referred to freedom of speech, the right to a fair trial and equal access to the legal system. Moving on to the nineteenth century, Marshall noted the extension of political rights, as an outcome of the working-class struggle for political equality, through greater access to the parliamentary process. Improvements under this rubric related to electoral rights, the invention of the secret ballot box, the creation of new political parties, and the expansion of suffrage. Finally, the twentieth century, according to Marshall, engendered 'social rights', which included claims to welfare, entitlements to social security, unemployment benefits, etc. In addition to this stage-by-stage account of citizenship, Marshall observed the emergence of a 'hyphenated society', a social system where there was perpetual tension between the need for economic profitability, the taxation requirements of the modern state, and the rights of citizens to welfare provisions.

An influential figure in the sociology of citizenship, Marshall has spawned a number of critics. Anthony Giddens (1982) for instance has criticised Marshall for developing an evolutionary perspective on the historical emergence of citizenship which begins to seem teleological. Giddens also pointed out that citizenship rights are not a unified, homogenous set of social arrangements and that these themselves can become the basis of conflict and contestation. It may further be added that the Marshallian explanation fails to take into account the case of post-colonial states and societies, where political and civil rights came *before* social rights.

The putative universality of the liberal view of citizenship masks a particular historical and cultural context. As the theorist Rajeev Bhargava asserts:

Well, the universalist outlook was not universalist in the first place. It was very particular-istic. Once you sort out the community issue, and settle the issue of belonging, then the basis of that citizenship becomes irrelevant. Just to take an example: if I have a school where I will only admit Catholics, then the Catholics will go to that Chapel but then it will lose its religious appeal after a while since everybody shares and believes in the same thing. And then, in this context, you can say that religion doesn't really matter since everybody has the same faith (. . .).[17]

Considerations of citizenship of whatever kind demand an idea of citizenship. There cannot be an idea of citizenship without an account of the subject of citizenship. Yeatman argues that the subject of citizenship is "the individual" – considered as an integrated unit of organic and subjective life. It is this idea of the individual that is the referent for the idea of self-preservation in early modern civil philosophy. It is difficult to appreciate the significance of self-preservation"without using the vantage point of post-Freudian accounts of the self to open it up. Citizenship concerns the status of the human being considered as a person (a self).[18]

Contemporary social movements of the oppressed have weakened the link between citizenship for everyone, on the one hand, and the two other senses of citizenship–having a common life with and being treated in the same way as the other citizens – on the other. They assert a positivity and pride in group specificity that counters ideals of assimilation. They have also questioned whether justice always means that law and policy should enforce equal treatment for all groups. Embryonic in these challenges is a concept of differentiated citizenship as the best way to realize the inclusion and participation of everyone in full citizenship.

Looking at this point, Young argues that far from implying one another, the universality of citizenship – in the sense of the inclusion and participation of everyone – conflicts with the other two meanings of universality embedded in modern political ideas: universality as generality, and universality as equal treat-ment.[19] First, the ideal that the activities of citizenship express or create a general will that transcends the specific differences of group affiliation, situation, and interest, has in practice excluded groups judged incapable of adopting that general point of view; the idea of citizenship as expressing a general will has tended to enforce homogeneity among citizens. To the extent that contemporary proponents of a revitalized citizenship retain that idea of a general will and communal life, they implicitly support the same exclusions and homogeneity. Thus I argue that the inclusion and participation of everyone in public discussion and decision-making requires mechanisms for group representation. Second, although differences exist between groups as regard their capacities, culture, values, and behavioral styles, some of these groups are privileged and strict adherence to a principle of equal treatment tends to perpetuate oppression or disadvantage. Thus the inclusion and participation of everyone in social and political institutions sometimes requires the articulation of special rights that attend to group differences in order to undermine oppression and disadvantage.

11.8 Conclusion

I have argued in this epilogue that progress in the field of citizenship is contingent on a rigorous exegesis of its empirical content, on the process of its transmission and its complex genealogy, which connects the imported with the indigenous.[20] The conceptual boundary of a specific phenomenon is of great interest for the research on citizenship. Is citizenship a logically bound entity that is defined by a simple set of features in which all instances possessing the crucial attributes have a full and equal degree of membership?[21] In response to this question, I have formulated citizenship as an interface between the state and society – a third space – whose inhabitants unite the rights germane to their membership of the political community and the sense of identity, identification and obligation that membership of the society entails. As such, while we achieve some form of conceptual clarity with regard to the category of the citizen, its empirical references remain bound to the context. The first approximation of the category thus opens the issue to the larger vista of the 'flow' of citizenship, which is a complex theoretical problem in its own right. The commonsensical, everyday reference to the flow of objects suggests a movement from one place to another in a steady unbroken stream, and a 'continuous mass', in a manner that would be interpersonally visible, rather as one would think about the flow of blood in veins and arteries, of water flowing downstream or electricity moving across a conductive medium. Can one attribute these characteristics to the flow of citizenship from one context to the other?

Citizen-making is a prime function of the modern state and a sensible strategy for governance and administration in any society. Tracking the core concept of citizenship as it traveled from Europe to Asia, this epilogue explores the phenomenology of citizenship and the trans-lingual and trans-cultural facets of its evolution. By trans-lingual we mean phenomena that exist but have not yet been transposed into any specific language system. Similarly, trans-cultural refers to phenomena that exist in the existential world but have yet to be acknowledged by high culture as part of an everyday spectrum of manners, customs, and rituals. So, we are looking at citizenship within a very broad spectrum of concepts that can be formally a part of the culture, linguistically articulate, and exist in the inner world of the actor, but have not yet been articulated in terms of science, language, society, culture or theory. This book as a whole explores the institutions, political processes and symbols used to profile a model citizen. The complex process of acculturation, by which the imported becomes indigenized and hybridized, involves agency and strategy that innovatively produces an asymmetry that reflects the uneven nature of such flows, the cultural context, and the balance of power.

The critical evaluations of Marshall's foundational writings present an important lesson in the contemporary analysis of citizenship. Too 'English' and too closely tied to the specific context of an expanding post-war economy, a stable cultural foundation, and the solid framework of the welfare state, Marshall had held up the elimination of social ostracism as a worthy and feasible goal of social policy. The quantitative implications of Marshall's liberal citizenship had set for a goal the attainment of full citizenship coverage where everybody will achieve his civic, political and social rights. Even in England, as Marshall's critics point out, the emergence of gender, race, immigration and region as salient cleavages questioned the simple cultural premises of his basic assumptions.[22] The decline of the welfare state made the rights-driven citizenship idea even more contested. As we move from Marshall's post-war England to the contemporary scene, the new frontiers of research on citizenship shows wide vistas of interesting empirical and theoretical problems that are in urgent need of attention.

This book and others of its genre have set the stage for a comprehensive discussion of citizenship in its trans-national and comparative context. The analytic and narrative accounts of citizenship undertaken here explore the meaning of citizenship in the inner world of the actor and the observer on the basis of conversations with experts and actors, identifies the gap in the conceptual landscape of citizenship that the book seeks to meet. Together, the Indian and the South Korean cases show the consequences of conceptual flow and hybridization, the dynamic of citizenship, its anomalies such as the case of immigrants in Korea, and most importantly, the national narrative as a discourse in its own right, influenced by but autonomous of globalization. By showing that different origins might still lead to similar ends, citizenship in South Korea and India help 'provincialise' Marshall, and question the hegemony of western modernity for a fixed point for the analysis of modern society and politics in general.[23]

Endnotes

[1]Contrast, for example, the status of the Kashmiri or Chechen insurgents from the multi-cultural and liberal approach of Marshall. Is the act of rebellion an assertion of one's identity, evidence of empowerment, or an infringement of one's loyalty to the state? Neither multi-culturalism nor liberal democratic theory can easily accommodate these contradictory aspects of the rebel's persona and political obligation.
[2]A recent symposium on "the Development of Citizenship in a Transcultural Context", which brought together the doctoral fellows and research groups which constituted Area A (Governance and Administration) of the Excellence Cluster, generated very helpful insights for the work of the group. The symposium held in Athens, 7–11 December 2009, was organised by Project A11 of the cluster.

[3]The architectural technique of leaving empty spaces in the memorial building, proudly displaying fragments of Athenian antiquity, anticipating the return of the, Elgin' marbles is an attempt to draw attention to what I have described as discontinuity above.

[4]Neumann, Gerard L. (2002). "Citizenship Today: Global Perspectives and Practices by T. Alexander Aleinikoff and Douglas Klusmeyer". *The American Journal of International Law* 96 (2), 514–517 (review article).

[5]Kelly, George Armstrong (1979). "Who needs a Theory of Citizenship?" *Journal of the American Academy of Arts and Sciences* 108 (4). Also, the need to rethink the state in its normative proportions is endorsed and views about how we might start are given.

[6]Kymlicka, Will, and Wayne Norman (1994). "Return of the Citizen: A Survey of Recent Work on Citizenship Theory". *Ethics* 104 (2), 352–381.

[7]See Subrata Mitra, ed. Citizenship as Cultural Flow: Structure, Agency and Power (Springer, 2013).

[8]A detailed discussion of the contextual features specific to India that also play an important role – such as the uncertain nature of divinity in Hinduism – are beyond the remit of this concluding piece, but need to be taken into account for a deeper inquiry into the role of religion, culture and context in providing space for citizenship in 'divided' societies – and new states. See Subrata K. Mitra, "Kashipur Revisited: Social Ritual, Electoral Politics and the State of India", in *Jaganath Revisited: Studying Society, Religion and the State in Orissa* (Hermann Kulke and Burkhard Schnepel Eds., 2001) for an analysis of the cult of Jagannath that gives an example of inter-community accommodation and its role on extending a sense of dignity to those previously excluded from the mainstream, from the South-Eastern State of Orissa

[9]See Subrata K. Mitra (2005). *The Puzzle of India's Governance: Culture, Context and Comparative Theory*. London: Routledge.

[10]The links between terms of discourse in everyday politics and trans-linguality and trans-culturality are yet to be investigated in greater depth.

[11]The Preamble to the Constitution of India announces this intention with boldness and clarity.

WE, THE PEOPLE OF INDIA, having solemnly resolved to constitute India into a SOVEREIGN SOCIALIST SECULAR DEMOCRATIC REPUBLIC and to secure to all its citizens:

JUSTICE, social, economic and political;

LIBERTY of thought, expression, belief, faith and worship;

EQUALITY of status and of opportunity;

and to promote among them all

FRATERNITY assuring the dignity of the individual and the unity and integrity of the Nation;

IN OUR CONSTITUENT ASSEMBLY this 26th day of November, 1949, do HEREBY ADOPT, ENACT AND GIVE TO OURSELVES THIS CONSTITUTION.

[12]"The question of citizenship became particularly important at the time of the making of our Constitution because the Constitution sought to confer certain rights and privileges upon those who were entitled to Indian citizenship while they were to be denied to 'aliens'. The latter were even placed under certain disabilities." DURGA DAS BASU, INTRODUCTION TO THE CONSTITUTION OF INDIA 74 (2001).

[13]SEYLA BENHABIB, POLITICAL THEORY AND POLITICAL MEMBERSHIP IN A CHANGING WORLD 410–11 (2002).

[14]"[T]his article on the question of citizenship has been the most ill-fated article in the whole Constitution. This is the third time we are debating it. The first time it was you, Sir, who held the view which was upheld by the House that the definition was very unsatisfactory. It was then referred to a group of lawyers and I am sorry to say that they produced a definition by which all those persons who are in existence at the present time could not be included as Citizens of India. That had therefore to go back again and we have now a fresh definition which I may say at the very outset, is as unsatisfactory as the one which the House rejected ..." (Dr. P. S. Deshmukh, Constituent Assembly Debates).

[15]Izhar Ahmad Khan v. Union of India (UOI), AIR 1962, SC 1052. The case dealt in detail with the following questions: the rights to and of citizenship; the issues of partition-related citizenship; the value of a passport in determining citizenship; and the question of domicile versus citizenship. The issue in this case was the constitutional validity of Section 9(2) of the Citizenship Act, 1955, which dealt with the termination of citizenship. This case exemplified the policies which discouraged multiple or even dual citizenships, and held that upon acquiring in any manner the citizenship of another country, an Indian citizen automatically loses Indian citizenship.

[16]See Bachan Lal Kalgotra v. State of Jammu and Kashmir, AIR 1987, SC 1169.

[17]Interview with Rajeev Bhargava, Delhi CSDS 20 December 2008.

[18]Yeatman, Anna (2007). "The Subject of Citizenship". *Citizenship Studies* 11 (1), 105–115.

[19]Young, Iris Marion (1989). "Polity and Group Difference: A Critique of the Ideal of Universal Citizenship". *Ethics* 99 (2), 250–274.

[20]Those who are in pursuit of a trans-disciplinary 'theory' of citizenship will do well to heed the advice of the Indian sociologist T. K. Oommen. "Creation of clear concepts is a pre-requisite for theory building. And if concepts and theories are rooted in and isomorphic to the life-world of the people, their potentiality to avoid human misery will also be substantial. I consider this combination as the real task and promise of social science" Oommen (1997: 49–50).

[21]See Eleanor Rosch and Carolyn Mervis (1975). "Family Resemblances: Studies in the Internal Structure of Categories". *Cognitive Psychology* 7, 573. The counterargument against an over-tight boundary comes from the apprehension that without clear boundaries a concept will be susceptible to 'stretching' as, in that case, "there will be no limit to a concept's extension". Hanne Andersen (2000). "Kuhn's account of family resemblances: A solution to the problem of wide-open textures". *Erkenntnis* 52, 313.

[22]"Marshall's 'Englishness' had its time and place, but that has passed." Martin Bulmer and Anthony Rees (1996). "Citizenship in the twentieth century". In Martin Bulmer and Anthony Rees (eds.), *Citizenship today: the contemporary relevance of T. H. Marshall*, 279. London: UCL Press. Based on Mann's contribution to the volume, they argue that a comparative analysis of citizenship, even within the relatively homogeneous European cultural context, requires the reformulation of Marshall's concept.

[23]See Dipesh Chakrabarty (2000). *Provincializing Europe: Postcolonial Thought and Historical Difference*. Princeton: Princeton University Press. For a comparative reference to the case of South Korea, see Seungsook Moon, "The Idea and Practice of Citizenship in South Korea". In this volume, chapter two.

References

Bachan Lal Kalgotra v. State of Jammu and Kashmir, AIR 1987, SC 1169.

Basu, Durga Das. 1998. Introduction to the Constitution of India. Prentice Hall; 18th edition.

Benhabib, Seyla. 2002. "Political Theory and Political Membership in a Changing World" In Political Science: The State of the Discipline, edited by Ira Katznelson and Helen V. Milner. New York: W.W. Norton & Company.

Chakrabarty, Dipesh. 2000. Provincializing Europe: Postcolonial Thought and Historical Difference. Princeton: Princeton University Press.

Dahrendorf, Ralf. 1994. "The Changing Quality of Citizenship" In The condition of citizenship edited Bart van Steenbergen. London: SAGE.

Dr. Deshmukh, P. S., Constituent Assembly Debates, Thursday, the 11th August 1949, Constituen Assembly of India- Volume IX. Online available: http://parliamentofindia.nic.in/ls/debates/vol9p10a.htm (last visit, 17.01.2013)

Eleanor Rosch and Carolyn Mervis. 1975. "Family Resemblances: Studies in the Internal Structure of Categories". *Cognitive Psychology* 7, 573–605.

Hanne, Andersen. 2000. "Kuhn's account of family resemblances: A solution to the problem of wide-open textures". *Erkenntnis* (52) 3, 313–337.

Interview with Rajeev Bhargava, Delhi CSDS 20 December 2008.

Izhar Ahmad Khan v. Union of India (UOI), AIR 1962, SC 1052.

Kelly, George Armstrong. 1979. "Who needs a Theory of Citizenship?". Dædalus - Journal of the American Academy of Arts and Sciences 108 (4). 21–36.

Kymlicka, Will, and Wayne Norman. 1994. "Return of the Citizen: A Survey of Recent Work on Citizenship Theory". *Ethics* 104 (2), 352–381.

Martin Bulmer and Anthony Rees. 1996. "Citizenship in the twentieth century" In Citizenship today: the contemporary relevance of T. H. Marshall, edited by Martin Bulmer and Anthony Rees, London: UCL Press.

Marshall, Thomas H. and Bottomore, Tom. 1950. Citizenship and Social Class (Cambridge: Cambridge University Press)

Mitra, Subrata K.. 2001. "Kashipur Revisited: Social Ritual, Electoral Politics and the State of India" In Jagannath Revisited: Studying Society, Religion and the State in Orissa, edited by Hermann Kulke and Burkhard Schnepel. New Delhi: Manohar.

Mitra, Subrata K.. 2005. The Puzzle of India's Governance: Culture, Context and Comparative Theory. London: Routledge.

Mitra, Subrata K. ed. 2013 Citizenship as Cultural Flow: Structure, Agency and Power (Springer).

Neumann, Gerard L. 2002. "Citizenship Today: Global Perspectives and Practices by T. Alexander Aleinikoff and Douglas Klusmeyer". *The American Journal of International Law* 96 (2), 514–517 (review article).

Oommen, T.K.,ed. 1997. Citizenship and National Identity: From Colonialism to Globalism. New Delhi: Sage.

Yeatman, Anna. 2007. "The Subject of Citizenship". *Citizenship Studies* 11 (1), 105–115.

Young, Iris Marion. 1989. "Polity and Group Difference: A Critique of the Ideal of Universal Citizenship". *Ethics* 99 (2), 250–274.